D1602719

PIECES OF LIGHT

Pieces
OF
Light

A YEAR ON COLORADO'S FRONT RANGE

by

Susan J. Tweit

Drawings by Ann W. Douden
Foreword by J. David Love

ROBERTS RINEHART, INC. PUBLISHERS

1990

Copyright © 1990 by Susan J. Tweit
Published by Roberts Rinehart, Inc.
Publishers
Post Office Box 666, Niwot, Colorado
80544-0666
International Standard Book Number 0-911797-72-6
Library of Congress Catalog Card Number 90-60330
Printed in the United States of America

Designed by Clifford Burke

Grateful acknowledgement is made for permission to reprint an except from Arctic Dreams, by Barry Lopez. —Copyright © 1986 Barry Holstun Lopez. Reprinted with permission of Charles Scribners' Sons, an imprint of Macmillan Publishing Company.

Also to A.B. Guthrie, Jr. for permission to use his phrase "West is another word for magic."

West is another word for magic.
—A.B. Guthrie, Jr.

For Richard and Molly, who walked with me;
Bob and Joan and Bill, who taught me how to see;
David, who believed in me;
and Rick, who made this book real.

Contents

Acknowledgements

I am lucky in having an abundance of friends and colleagues who contributed to this project: to those who generously answered questions or critiqued my opinions and theories; who listened when I needed support, or reassured me when my faith flagged; and those who simply left my morning writing hours undisturbed—thank you all.

Special thanks to my family: to my husband, Richard, whose supply of hugs and encouragement is endless; my step-daughter, Molly, whose enthusiasm for exploring rarely flags; my father, Bob, and my mother, Joan, who unstintingly shared their sense of wonder with their children; to my brother, Bill, who inspired me to keep learning; to my nieces, Heather and Sienna, who love me anyway; and to my grandad Olav.

Thanks also those friends who constituted a writers-group-at-a-distance: Gail Adams, Laura Arnow, Judy Hetland, J. David Love, Suzanne MacAulay, Anne Model, Blanche Sobottke, Terry Winfield.

My daily walks brought me many acquaintances, some whose names I do not know but whose faces and greetings grew familiar—thanks for piercing a writer's loneliness. Others became friends. In particular, Mary Lynda Frommer provided much more than a good cup of tea.

And thanks to those who made the whole of this book more than the sum of its parts: Rick Rinehart for making it possible, Clifford Burke for the elegant design, Ann W. Douden for 'seeing' with her illustrations, Carrie Jenkins for careful editing and enthusiastic promotion, J. David Love for writing the introduction and correcting my geology, and Joan and Bob Tweit for thoroughly checking the natural history and editing the rough draft. Any errors or omissions are, of course, my own responsibility.

Susan J. Tweit
February, 1990

Foreword

As I read Susan Tweit's elegant and exciting manuscript, I was reminded of other gifted writers from the past, such as Thoreau and John Muir, and some of the moderns such as John McPhee, Annie Dillard, Gretel Ehrlich, and Gwen Frostic. Each has incorporated his or her own style and distinctive personality into magnificent messages that are easily understood by the public. I had already been considerably influenced by these writers when, several years ago, I guided a Life magazine photographer around the mountains of northwestern Wyoming for several weeks. I tried to show him that mountains are not just lumps of rock but, instead, that each has its own different, exciting, and complex history (as people do), and that all life on and adjacent to these mountains is dependent to some extent on the rock composing them. He, in turn, showed me the beauty of his world as seen through the eyes of a photographer. Afterward, he sent me a copy of Gwen Frostic's little book To Those Who See and inscribed it "for one who sees." Frostic had written, in part:

> To those who see with wonder in their hearts and know—
> what glories there can be for those who see...

Susan Tweit is one who sees farther, more clearly, and with a broader perspective than most of us. She has the gift of appreciative observation and curiosity that is translated into a distinctive and eloquent kind of writing. She has, in clear and jargonless prose, "intertwingled" the art of nature with natural science and also with the cold hard facts of environmental abuses. Her specific theme is the Colorado Front Range and its inhabitants. In addition, however, she also explores the philosophy of the way humans deal (and should deal) with urban and rural environments not only here but elsewhere in the world.

Several years after my experience with the Life reporter, it was my privilege to meet Susan while she worked as a vegetation ecologist for the U.S. Forest Service in northwestern Wyoming. We shared many interests and I was especially impressed with the way she related plants and animals to bedrock geology. Even more impressive to me was that she, even though still in her twenties, had an almost encyclopedic knowledge of a wide variety of related and very important disciplines that were only marginally familiar to me. Thus began a friendship that, during the last ten years and more, has not only greatly enriched my own life but has also helped me to understand the importance of the part of her life that has now become this book.

Susan had undergraduate and graduate training in geology, ecology, and botany and developed a scientist's disciplined mind. She has worked as a field scientist, a photographer, a journalist, an administrator; receiving awards for excellence along the way. She has written weekly natural history columns for several Wyoming newspapers, as well as a two-volume Writers Handbook. These talents and diverse interests, combined with an extraordinarily sensitive perspective and appreciation of the earth and its inhabitants, have all been brought into focus in *Pieces of Light*.

Susan's book is an honest, direct, and refreshingly unique account of a year spent with her husband and daughter in and near Boulder, Colorado. Her attitude toward life and death during and prior to this interval was sharpened poignantly by having to come to grips with the onset of a rare and apparently progressive and debilitating nerve deterioration. She has faced this with courage, inner strength, and wisdom, and has surmounted bouts of self-pity. Despite the ever-present shadow of time running out, there is nothing morbid in her book. It is upbeat, winsome, funny in part, and contains many lyrically beautiful passages that read like the most sensitive kind of poetry. In contrast, when she writes about urban development, destruction of stream environments, and water misuse, her descriptions and recommendations are direct, hardhitting, pungent, clearly defined, persuasive, and are substantiated with solid scientific data.

Facts and anecdotes from many disciplines add spice to and are interwoven with day-by-day living during a full year with all of its changing seasons, changing faunas and floras, changing weather, and very perceptive and rather startling observations on the effects of these changes on people in the area. I have read and reread with awe, respect, and great enjoyment these many little but important and unfamiliar tidbits of data. I am sure that other readers, not only those along the Front Range, but elsewhere in the world will be astonished and intrigued as Susan calls attention to the myriads of the earth's wonders that they have missed or have not appreciated, even in their own familiar areas.

Readers will also be impressed by the charming descriptions of the harmonious family threesome, Susan, husband Richard, and stepdaughter Molly, who, wherever they might be, and despite the traumas of their "graduate school grind," deliberately took advantage of precious moments together to enjoy and learn more about the good and bad things in their environment. Their example of how to use their inner resources to create a wonderful way of living is eloquently presented and should be a model "to those who see," as well as to those who want to see.

J. David Love
Laramie, Wyoming
January 11, 1990

September

Monday, 7 September ⁊• This has been a journey of the heart. We have come home.

Home is the arid basins, valleys, and plains that lap at the foot of the Rocky Mountains. I have lived in many places in my life, but only the dry, open country of the Rockies tugs at my heartstrings. We had been living away for what seemed long years, these last three near Puget Sound in Washington State. When my husband Richard decided this spring that he wanted to return to the Rockies in order to finish his doctorate in economics, I didn't hesitate a moment. I could hardly contain my excitement. We both resigned from our jobs; we put our house and woods up for sale; Richard found a consulting job in Boulder, Colorado, and off we went. I'd never lived in Boulder before, never lived in any city before, but neither mattered. The region was right. It had the magic of arid landscapes: sweeping winds, clear light, and overhead the all-encompassing sky.

We left our house in the woods near Olympia, Washington, Saturday; today we are home—although we have not yet found a place to live—in Boulder, Colorado. The journey, in a one-ton rented truck, towing our venerable Volvo station wagon, took two and a half days and spanned nearly half a continent. We have changed worlds, trading the claustrophobic, moist verdance of the red cedar and hemlock forests that crowd the ocean's edge in western Washington for the vast, brilliantly lit open spaces of the plains at the eastern edge of the Rocky Mountains. The long days spent at the wheel of the big truck, traveling slowly up and down across the inner spaces of the West, blur into one long seamless image, a film with no frames.

Saturday morning we rose in the darkness, groggy and slightly disoriented by our now-bare house. (Just the day before the bed had stood where our sleeping bags now lay crumpled.) Richard gathered the last few things and went out the back door into the damp predawn chill to start the truck. I stood drinking a cup of tea at the sink in the silent, empty kitchen, looking out, as the darkness receded slightly, at the faintly visible silhouettes of drooping cedars, spire-like hemlocks, and stiff Douglas firs piercing the mist over the pasture. I remembered how the wet grass matted down where the deer slept after grazing on the apple drops; how on rainy grey winter days the world shrank as both the clouds and the cedar trees sagged low over the house; how the trilliums bloomed in spring like white flames in the dark woods; how the great blue herons, long legs dragging, flew slowly over the house towards their rookery on Eld Inlet… I jumped, startled, as the truck engine roared to life and Richard turned on the headlights. Time to go.

I looked around at the empty rooms once more, left my house keys on the kitchen counter and went out through the dark utility room to the back door. I opened the door quietly and walked through. Outside, in the clammy, cold near-dark, the air smelled of cedar and the seaweedy odor of low tide. I pulled the door closed, took a deep breath, and gathered my memories, leaving the place ready for other lives. It was someone else's house now. I walked past the woodshed and out the gate, clicking the latch tight behind me.

This morning, just a little more than forty-eight hours and a little less than 1,600 miles later, we drove south out of Laramie, Wyoming. The truck coughed and sputtered in the thin air 7,000 feet higher than our driveway near sea level by Puget Sound. Our journey neared its end. One more pass to climb, one more state highway map to unfold, one more mountain range to cross.

From Laramie to Boulder we followed old tracks, completing a circle in our wanderings. Four years and one month ago, Richard and I and my step-daughter Molly took this road when we moved away from Laramie. That August evening we

stopped at the top of the hill at Pumpkin Vine Buttes just as
the sun was setting. We looked back at the view over the
Laramie Basin, picked a nosegay of fragrant, feathery sage
leaves to tuck in the visor of our car, and said good-bye to
Wyoming and the Rockies—forever, we thought then.

This morning, the sun slid over the gentle swell of the
Laramie Range as Richard and I drove south across the level
green of the Laramie Basin grasslands towards Colorado. Our
spirits rose as our bones warmed. We passed familiar landmarks: red, rutted twin wheel tracks leading across the grasslands to the small cluster of cottonwoods that marks one of
the few springs of the basin; the university field station standing alone under its gnarled cottonwoods; mushroom-shaped
vermillion sandstone buttes rising from velvet-green wet
meadows where a haze of fragrant purple wild irises bloom in
late June.

As the truck slowly chugged up the last long grade above
the post office/store/bar that marks Tie Siding, I looked back
at Wyoming. A hundred miles north on the skyline, at the
upwarped end of the basin, the triangular shape of Laramie
Peak stuck up like a grey fang. Far past it, hidden by the curving rim of the earth, lay the rumpled topography of the
Bighorn Basin and the grotesquely eroded shapes of the
Absaroka Mountains, my home before I met Richard.

I turned again to look forward, just as we topped the long
rise of the last pass. The "pass" is really a high, rolling plateau-
like expanse of dry grassland. Like a web of golden-brown
skin, it joins two mountainous fingers—the Laramie Range
and the Medicine Bow Mountains—in the Front Range uplift.
Around us pink, rounded, bare hillocks ruptured the thin
grassy cover, monoliths eroded from the granite that pushed
up these mountains. South and west rose high, rocky peaks:
fifty miles south, the snow-spotted peaks of the Mummy
Range in Rocky Mountain National Park punctured the morning sky; farther still, off to the southwest, the white, serrate

3

wall of the Park Range marked the west edge of North Park. Nearer, below the grassy divide we drove across, lay the hummocky, forest-clad landscape of the Red Feather Lakes Basin, lumpy as a well-worn mattress. The view danced, the normally clear air shimmering with a diaphanous haze of wind-borne smoke from distant forest fires.

On across the miles of high grasslands, we slowed for a curve in the highway. State Line, Colorado, and the big "Welcome to Colorful Colorado" sign flashed past in less time than it took me to unfold the Colorado state highway map. We drove downhill through scattered ponderosa pines and granite monoliths, past the white clapboard church at Virginia Dale. The truck was moving fast now, whipping its Volvo tail around the curves, swooping down steep hills in the grasslands, down, down, down, towards the plains.

Farther downhill, the highway sliced through massive layers of tilted sandstone, and ran arrow straight down a valley shaped by the thick slanting layers. A red valley, the colors of the rock ranging from soft salmon to brilliant rusty orange red. West of the road the valley was bounded by hogbacks of 300-million-year-old Fountain sandstone, hard pink- and salmon-colored rock layers formed of sands and gravels when erosion recycled the rocks of an earlier generation of Rocky Mountains. East of the road were tall cliffs of vermillion rock: Chugwater sandstone, one of a series of similar-age redbeds that edge the Rockies along their eastern flank from Montana to New Mexico, irony sands deposited at the edge of the sea that drowned the mid-continent during the Triassic, 240 million years ago, and rusted in that oxidizing environment.

Past the end of a linear valley, we joined the Cache la Poudre River in its tumbling race out of the Front Range. We wound alongside its fringe of tall cottonwoods through the uptilted, spiky hogbacks of the outer foothills. Suddenly we emerged, bursting onto the immense openness of the Great Plains. The hot sun beat down on us, the morning frost in

Laramie already far away. We turned south; on our right, the abrupt wall of towering mountain ridges that are the Front Range; on our left, hundreds of miles of plains extending east past the curve of the earth. We drove along that edge between mountains and plains in the clear light, past miles of alternating green lawn/shade tree subdivisions and rectangular fields to the valley where Boulder Creek plunges through the last foothills to meander across the plains.

Home.

Wednesday, 9 September ❧ So soon after our arrival, I am leaving, going to California to speak at a conference. Strapped in this seat on a jet, dressed in a silk suit, I feel as if I am backtracking, returning to my old life. For a panicky moment I imagine unbuckling my seatbelt, grabbing briefcase and carry-on bag and rushing off the plane before the door slams shut. I should be at home.

Tears prick my closed eyelids as I think of Richard, pouring his orange juice and grinding his fragrant coffee beans in the small kitchen of the apartment we found on the west side of town. It is at the edge of Mapleton Hill, within walking distance of both Richard's office and the base of the rocky hogbacks that are the first waves of the Front Range. Quiet neighborhoods of tree-lined streets and huge turn-of-the-century houses promise peaceful walks. Our south-facing kitchen and living room windows frame the neighboring rooftops, the dancing green foliage of urban shade trees, the wild, undulate ridgeline of Boulder Mountain, and the intensely blue sky. I want to be settling in, wandering the neighborhood, looking for the first vivid autumn colors spotting the maple leaves, listening for coyotes singing from the ridges above town, watching the dark night sky for Orion and the other fall constellations.

I hear the jet door slam shut; the engines whine. I swallow hard, trying to rid my throat of the lump there. Already I miss the sight of the round golden globe of the sun setting behind the ridges above our apartment; the smell of the dry, resinous mountain air flowing downhill at night; the wide arch of crystalline clear morning sky above at sunrise.

We are airborne. Denver spreads out over the dusty plains beneath the climbing jet. Quickly we turn and head southwest, over wave after wave of foothills, towards South Park and the grey, snow-spotted peaks of the Continental Divide.

Early this morning, Richard walked me downtown to catch the airport bus. The streets were quiet still, the air cool, tangy, and dry. Overhead, the leaves on the spreading silver maples, cottonwoods, and green ashes rustled in the fresh breeze. Three magpies fluttered out of a silver maple in front of us, flashing bright black and white wings, trailing absurd long iridescent tails.

The open oval of South Park pushes back the cluttered peaks below us. As we continue west, puffy cumulus clouds congeal over the landscape like cream rising to the top of unskimmed milk. Soon the mountains and valleys are gone, blotted out. With no landmarks, I am cut off. I cannot see where I am going, so I close my eyes and sleep as the jet rushes through the air.

Monday, 14 *September* ❧ We had thunderstorms tonight, the first thunderstorms I've seen in nearly three years. I've missed the drama of thunderstorms, their wild winds, flickering lightning, and sonorous rolls of thunder—such powerful evidence of the workings of this world. I was so excited that I went outside and stood still, head upturned to watch the lightning jump through the clouds. Gusts of wind whipped around me, driving big splatters of cold rain. I paid them no heed, lost in the wild beauty of the storm.

Now the air is chilly and wet, pleasant after the day's heat. It smells of lightning (actually, the sharp, pungent odor is the ozone produced when the electrical charge that is lightning superheats the air) and of renewed activity by the denizens of the now-wet soil.

Thunderstorms are produced by the towering castellated clouds that we traditionally call "thunderheads." These giants, their turreted heights extending three or four miles up into the atmosphere, are of the cloud genus cumulonimbus, from the Latin roots for "heap" (*cumulo*) and "rain" (*nimbus*).

Before the towering thunderclouds, first comes a skyful of bumptious, fleecy cumulus. As a traditional Navajo saying describes the process: "Many sheep must grow before the rains come." Cumulus build when the air at the ground is unstable enough to allow sun-warmed, moist air to rise through the cooler air aloft, disturbing the normally stable horizontal air layers. The warm, moist air cools some as it rises, but, as it cools, its moisture condenses. Water condensing releases energy (heat) and warms the air around it, causing it to rise (like air bubbles rising in a pan of boiling water). Hence, as the warm air rises higher into cooler air, its moisture in turn condenses, giving off heat to the air around it, which rises, and so on, forming a lively, but invisible, convection column. With fresh moist air drawn in at the base of this convection column, a fast growing cumulus cloud soon forms, bumpy like a cauliflower above, usually smooth below (the level lower surface indicates the height at which the air is cool enough for moisture to begin to condense and form the cloud).

But to mature into a thunderstorm with the wild turbulence that I so love, two conditions must coincide: strong updrafts and plenty of moisture—either already in the air or evaporating from the ground. Together, updrafts and moisture act synchronously to belly the cloud upwards past the point where water vapor becomes ice. Then it becomes a cumulonimbus, a storm factory, with complex up- and downdrafts and potential for lightning, thunder, and torrential rain or hail.

Thunderstorms grow in the sky like giant organisms, the whales of the atmosphere. In fact, they are dynamic, growing systems. Lyall Watson, in *Heaven's Breath: A Natural History of the Wind*, eloquently describes a thunderstorm

> stand[ing] on a foot of cool hard rain, with a heel of drizzle and a toe of rolling squall, feeling its way forward step by step. Drafts of warm air rise about its body, flaring out at the head into an anvil of ice and hail. The anatomy is characteristic and well-defined. Morphologically, it is divided into what can almost be called functional body parts. Behaviorally it is unique in the non-living world, defying the tendency of most inorganic systems to slide into inertia. Thunderstorms go on doing something, moving, exhanging material and information with their environment. They even reproduce themselves by giving rise to daughter storm cells near the edges as the mother clouds move past maturity into senility and decay.

Thunderstorms are usually quite local: the area under one cumulonimbus cloud may receive several inches of rain, while the surrounding air, kept clear and dry by cool downdrafts from the thunderstorm, receives none. They are often intense. In the Big Thompson flood in July of 1976, for instance, one cumulonimbus cloud stalled over the Big Thompson drainage (an area in the Front Range east of Estes Park, Colorado) produced between eight and fifteen inches of rain.

Updrafts in thunderstorms develop into dangerous, gale-force winds. Watson tells of a squadron of eight fully laden bombers in World War II, flying north from Australia. All eight planes flew into a massed line of cumulonimbus clouds. Only two flew out.

Thunderstorms are much more frequent over the Rockies than anywhere else in the nation because of the unstable air produced by the sharply undulating topography. Though Boulder is not the thunderstorm capital of the United States (that honor goes to the Sangre de Cristo Mountain Range, west of Raton, New Mexico, according to Richard Keen, in *Skywatch, A Western Weather Guide*) it is an excellent location for thunderstorm activity. Some fifty rattle-and-bangers per year electrify the air over Boulder between May and October. Boulder's location at the foot of the mountains means that conditions are right for the necessary turbulence. The surrounding plains provide abundant sources of moisture and sun-warmed air.

Rocky Mountain weather, like the fierce, ephemeral intensity of this evening's thunderstorm, is invigorating. Tangy air, booming clangor, vivid skies metamorphosing from bumptious sheep to towering lightning-hurlers—the weather here is anything but moderate.

Tuesday, 15 September ⚬ This evening Richard took me to a place that he discovered on his way to work. We walked up Maxwell Avenue in the cooling air of evening, and across Mapleton Hill on Sixth Street towards Boulder Canyon. Where Sixth Street ends is a tiny park, perched at the edge of the hill overlooking Boulder Creek. What once was a short, steep stretch of street is now a bit of open space bridging the irrigation ditch and spilling over the hill. It is just big enough to have a streetside flower bed, a seating area at the brow of the hill and a pedestrian path leading downhill. We stopped there, perched together on a bench at the edge of Mapleton Hill, and watched the afterglow of the sunset in the sky above the swelling wave of the foothills.

Soon, the leaves on the big cottonwood down the slope began to rustle, heralding the first tongue of cold air flowing down Boulder Canyon. Then came another soft current of air, cooler still and smelling of pine needles. It was the mountains exhaling: the thin air around the high ridges and peaks cools quickly at the end of the day and pours downhill like water—in channels or streams with currents, waves, ripples, and eddies. In the morning, the flow is reversed when the sun touches the peaks and ridges, warming the thin dry air and slowly pulling new air up from below. As the heavy cool air streams downwards in the evening along creek bottoms, it flows under warmer air, creating cold spots—frost pock-ets—in low places.

We climbed several steps to the upper edge of the park, just a few yards from the bench, and crossed a startling thermal boundary. Uphill, the air remained hot and dusty from the day, laden with auto exhaust and the wastes of urban life. We walked back down to the bench and sat down, crossing again the invisible, but tactile, discontinuity. We were bathed again in the cool flow. I shivered, turned up the collar of my denim jacket, and leaned on Richard's warm shoulder.

Luminous gold rays fanned in the western sky. Dark shapes of deer moved among the scattered junipers and ponderosa pine on the lower flanks of Flagstaff Mountain. Around us, sumac leaves glowed crimson, then deepened to blood red as the light faded. The cottonwood leaves continued to rustle, and the cool breath of the mountains flowed on, washing the evening clean.

Thursday, 17 *September* ❧ Today the weather is unexpectedly soft, drizzly and dark, as if the ancient conti-nental sea has returned to cover the Great Plains, bringing us a damp oceanic climate. Stratus clouds (from the Latin "spread" or "layer") trail a low, pearly grey blanket over town. The air is wet and chill—classic western Washington weather.

This morning's grey light and penetrating dampness made me melancholy. Finally, lonely for heat and warmth and the sound of other human voices, I left the quiet apartment and walked over the hill to a half–coffee house, half–used book-store. It occupies a beautiful old building with gold lettering on tall, arched front windows, a spacious interior with bare, polished wood floors and high, tin ceilings. And, most impor-tantly for me, it offers good tea. (Steaming hot water from the espresso machine, loose tea, a prewarmed pot, and real cream—the works.)

I stood patiently in line at the front counter, waiting for my turn, looking around at the people crowding the tables in the front room. If I were writing a novel, this would be one of my regular field trips to collect characters. At the table next to me, a man in unobtrusively elegant clothing, tailored as if his body had been made to fit the clothes, rather than the reverse, talked on a cellular phone while he fiddled with the keyboard of his portable computer. (His dark suit jacket was draped neatly over the back of an unused chair, the sleeves of his immaculately pressed white shirt were rolled up to suit the informal atmosphere.) Two tables away lounged a group of kids dressed in smooth black leather and shiny studs, their hair—matte black streaked with blaze orange, purple, kelly green, ruby red—out-shouting the brightest flock of parrots. Voices of many tones and accents spiraled overhead with the curls of smoke from dozens of cigarettes. A wealth of detail filled the room, and I drank it in hungrily as an antidote to my usual solitude. But after my a few minutes of standing in line, the babble of sound and shifting kaleidoscope of humans overwhelmed me. I paid for my pot of black currant tea with relief and escaped to the relative quiet of the back porch, past the crowded tables and the woodstove. I pushed open the screen door with one elbow, balancing tea pot, cup, saucer, and cream pitcher carefully, and went outside to a small round table tucked under the deep roof overhang at the back of the building.

Much better. Only one of the other tables was occupied. The foggy, chill air drifted in and out under the porch roof like a tattered grey veil. The clouds blew by above, sometimes trailing so low that they obscured even the buildings across the alley, sometimes raising to reveal the luscious green carpet of the grasslands covering the base of the foothills at Chautauqua Park, above town.

For a moment, looking down at fingers tinged blue by the chill, and mist drifting past in grey wisps, I was disoriented, back in Olympia on the porch of another coffee house. Then the screen door slammed behind a parrot-blue-coiffed young woman, jerking me abruptly back to Boulder, slightly dizzy. Moving does that to me.

Boulder sits on the western North American continent, in geologic terms, on the margin between the unstable mountain region and the craton, the stable center part of the continent. In geographic terms, Boulder is located at the foot of the Front Range of the Southern Rocky Mountains, at the western margin of the hundreds of miles of level, mostly treeless Great Plains. Boulder lies in the north part of the South Platte River drainage, where Boulder Creek tumbles out through a slot in the hogbacks that edge the Front Range. The original town of Boulder was laid out on the floodplain of the creek—most of the downtown, including the municipal offices and the Pearl Street Mall are on the floodplain. As it grew it sprawled up and out over the adjacent mesas to the north and south of the floodplain, as well as east onto the farmland of the piedmont, the valley between high plains and mountains.

Yesterday, I climbed the steep trail up Mount Sanitas, the second and higher hogback that rears up above Mapleton Hill. I perched on a knobby, upended bit of Fountain sandstone at the apex of the ridge and surveyed the landscape. I traced the contours of the mountains behind me; followed the hills down to the flat line of the mesas, the mesas out to the eastern horizon of the distant edge of the plains; untangled the lines of creeks and irrigation ditches; mapped the regular pattern of the streets below me. The geology and landforms and vegetation, at first jumbled, gradually sorted themselves into meaningful patterns. I sat on an edge—not the discontinuity between the world of salt water and the world of land that we left behind in western Washington—a mountain and plains edge, an abrupt vertical dislocation. Over the hundreds of miles of plains stretching eastward from my seat, the flora and fauna change very little. But in the first thirty miles west of the discontinuity, the change is similar to traveling hundreds of miles north. The flora of the high Rockies is dominated by plants from the Arctic and from other island (geographically isolated) mountain ranges around the world, resulting in an ecosystem that is more like that of Barrow, Alaska, or the Altai Mountains, high above the Mongolian Plateau, than the ecosystem of Dacono, Colorado, twenty miles east on the plains.

Mount Sanitas—a hogback of rough, orange-red Fountain sandstone—gives a splendid view of the discontinuity. My rough sandstone perch was once horizontal, buried beneath thousands of feet of sediment, themselves deposited under an ancient shallow sea that spread over the level center of the continent. Then the expanding Pacific crustal plate collided with and began shoving itself under our continental plate, wrinkling the surface of the continent like a bedspread pushed from west to east. The Front Range thrust itself up, slowly bending the laminated layers of horizontal sediments to near-vertical as the mountains rose above the still-level plains. The sediments thrust up by the bulging core of the mountains were displaced four vertical miles relative to the same sediments on the plains, but erosion as the mountains grew kept the range to its current mile-and-a-half superiority. Mount Sanitas and the hogback to the east mark the bend where the layers of sediments emerge from beneath the plains and fly upwards, reaching for the sky.

Below, Mapleton Hill dips at a gentler angle, cutting across the uptilted formations east of this ridge. Stripped of its Victorian houses, tidy rectangular yards, and streets lined with overarching silver maples, Mapleton Hill reveals itself as an alluvial terrace cut by an ancient stream that poured out from the mountains, dropping sediments onto an older, higher surface of the Great Plains. The flat-bottomed valley of Boulder Creek truncates Mapleton Hill on the south side; across the valley is University Hill, a similar alluvial surface.

The margin where plains become mountains is blurred by local topographic, soil and climatic conditions. Geologically, the eastern part of town is on the relatively flat plains and the extreme western edge (like Mapleton Hill) spreads up into the foothills of the Rockies. But there is no sharp boundary with "Southern Rockies" green on one side and "Great Plains" golden yellow on the other like a road atlas. The flora and fauna of the plains mix with those of the mountains, smudging the edge into a zone several miles wide.

What a marvelous edge it is—the endless grasslands of the Great Plains, the cool mountain forests, and even the Arctic all within reach. And this morning, as the grey stratus veil drifted under the porch of the cafe, loosing its damp chill, it felt as if the ancient ocean had returned too.

Friday, 18 *September* ❧ Today is my birthday. My present was a trip to Saratoga, Wyoming, to soak in Hobo Hot Springs, a favorite place from our Laramie years.

After three days of western Washington-like rain, this morning dawned gloriously clear, though cool. A pile-into-the-Volvo-and-drive-somewhere-with-the-windows-rolled-down sort of day. We drove north out of Boulder and along the base of the Front Range. For the first fifteen miles or so, the highway flirts with both mountains and plains, part of neither: it traces their undulating margin, now climbing up over the base of a hogback rimmed with stunted ponderosa pines, now dipping down into a draw dotted with straw-colored clumps of wild rye and shivering with the waxy leaves of plains cottonwoods.

Somewhere east of Loveland we missed a turn and lost our usual Boulder-to-Laramie shortcut. We wandered north on small farm roads, slowing to cross irrigation ditches lined with the furrowed bone trunks of cottonwoods and tangled golden switches of willows. At one point, the road swooped down a small hill, dropping out of the brilliant green and glowing umber patchwork of irrigated corn and dry wheat fields, into a shaley draw sparsely dotted with scraggly clumps of grease- wood and saltgrass. Swoosh around the bend at the bottom of the draw, along below a high earthen dam and up the hill on the other side. Glancing back over our shoulders out of habit to see if the dam actually held water, we caught a glimpse of acres of cracked mud, a small puddle of wind-whipped water in the middle, and at the edge, a group of brilliant white birds. Big birds, with awkward flattopped heads and huge, un- gainly beaks. "Pelicans!" Richard and I shouted in unison, grin- ning at each other as the Volvo topped the hill and we lost the reservoir from view. White Pelicans, either a breeding colony or a group migrating south, camped out on this tiny reservoir hemmed by corn- and wheatfields, the suburbs of Loveland marching closer every year.

Intent on hot springs, we drove on through the farmland (cottonwood leaves shimmering and rustling overhead as we sped by) and through the western edge of Fort Collins, blocks and blocks of it, each street corner a precise right angle, each block exactly as long as the block before and after. Tidiness like that makes me weary. I closed my eyes for a moment and saw again that small group of huge white birds sprinkled like grains of salt on the edge of the reservoir under the immense sapphire blue dome of the fall sky.

Past Fort Collins, we drove back into a cool shady tunnel of crooked old cottonwoods. Old cottonwoods. Suddenly I real- ized that all along the drive from Boulder, I'd seen no young cottonwoods. I replayed the drive in my memory, past the miles of farms and fields and suburban development, the irri- gation ditches and streams lined with riparian forests. All the cottonwoods I had seen were old, twisted, gappy, missing limbs, leaning crookedly, dying. And no new little ones grow- ing up to replace these gnarled old giants. Why? What is hap- pening that the cottonwoods are not reproducing?

Many of the remaining cottonwood riparian forests furnish

year-round pasture for domestic stock, either cattle or horses. The grassy understories looked like they had been closely mowed—the grass cropped so short that it was smooth enough for a golf green (with tall skeletons of thistles like flags marking the holes). Long-term heavy grazing can have drastic impacts on cottonwood riparian communities. Continued overuse equals slow removal of the palatable plants, eventually reducing the shrubs, forbs, and grasses to those eaten only as a last resort, like wild roses and thistles. Worse still, overuse compacts the fragile soil, so that more water runs off the now-hard surface than sinks in, pouring into the streams, carrying along soil and debris. The streams, higher and carrying more sediment, begin to cut downward, eventually stranding the roots of the riparian vegetation above the resultant lower water table. The old cottonwoods finally die, crooked and rotten inside, leaving hard-packed streambanks baking further in hot sun without their shade. New cottonwoods may germinate, but they cannot survive long in these streamside deserts. To keep the now-bare ditches and streambanks from eroding, we don't plant new riparian vegetation; instead we pave the banks with a thin coating of cement. It is easier, cheaper. And so the runoff increases and the streams flow faster along the hard banks and erode more deeply.

Development has also contributed to the lopsided age structure of the cottonwood community. As the suburbs spread ever outward, farms are sold and so are their water rights. Irrigation ditches that once supported lush threads of cottonwood forest are diverted to municipal pipes—to water lawns, wash cars, carry sewage. Where once were ribbons of riparian forest, now twisted old cottonwoods thread thin lines across subdivisions, tracing the nonexistent flow of dewatered irrigation ditches or streams. These cottonwoods eke out a meager existence on lawn watering, but without a flowing stream or ditch, the diverse understory of shrubs and grasses that once formed a narrow band of riparian vegetation cannot survive. The old cottonwood trunks stand alone now, furrowed bark splitting and peeling, pale dying skeletons of a once-lush riparian forest.

What will happen when the cottonwoods are gone? Imagine the roads without their patches of cool shade, imagine fall without their blaze of golden leaves and incessant rustling. But beyond the pleasure that they give to us humans, cottonwoods are integral to the structure of riparian forests: their tangled roots help hold in place the dark organic soil that in turn nurtures other plants and animals. The rich soil also acts as a "water bank," absorbing rain and snowmelt water and releasing it slowly over the season, smoothing the peaks and valleys in streamflow. When the cottonwoods go, without their shade, so go the willows and the shrubby understory of wild plum, chokecherry, hawthorn, wild rose, snowberry, and currant, and the grasses and forbs. Without the grass, shrubs, and trees, where will the white-tailed deer, who need the cover and cool shelter of the riparian areas, go to breed and rest and feed? What about the striking black-and-orange northern orioles who hang their pendulous nests from the tall cottonwood branches? And the great blue herons, who also depend on big cottonwood or other riparian forest trees with sturdy, spreading branches to support the ungainly platform nests of their rookeries? Or the red-headed woodpeckers, drumming for insects on cottonwood and peach-leaved willow limbs? Or tiny yellow common yellowthroat warblers, singing loudly from the willow thickets shaded by the cottonwoods? Or opossums, or foxes, or raccoons? Where will the plains leopard frogs live, their guttural chorus part of spring and summer nights? Or the barred tiger salamanders, spending their days in cool, moist tunnels in the soil? And bullheads and channel catfish? What about the dragonflies, hawking on their sparkling, tissue-thin wings for smaller insects?

The lush, productive cottonwood riparian communities are diminishing on all fronts. On the edges of our growing towns and urban areas, we are replacing the fields and cottonwood-lined irrigation ditches with acres of sterile, asphalt-paved shopping centers or suburban ranchettes, each with their neatly trimmed water-hungry lawn, asphalt driveway, and bowling-green-overgrazed-two-acre pasture. We have begun to plant cottonwoods in our urban/suburban forests, recognizing their value as fast-growing shade trees. But just planting cottonwoods will not replace the complex tapestry of riparian forests. Each of the wide variety of other species contributes its special bit of form, texture, color or function to the whole intricate pattern. Without the rest of the threads, it isn't the same tapestry. To me and the deer and the orioles and the bullheads and the mice and the leopard frogs and the warblers and the dragonflies and the host of other life that need the cottonwood riparian communities, it just isn't the same.

Tuesday, 22 *September* ❧ Yesterday afternoon the small crooked clump of box elder trees that grow in the untended ground between our gravel parking lot and the condominiums next door suddenly exploded with chattering. A noisy flock of big yellow birds descended all at once and began crawling up and over the branches, eating the clusters of winged seeds hanging down from the branch tips. They sounded at first like starlings. But their bodies were gaudy yellow and plump, with flashing black-and-white wings. Not starlings at all. It was their beaks though—huge, yellow, and cone-shaped, like theatrical false noses—that gave away their identity. Only finches, the primary seed eaters of the bird world, have such disproportionately large bills, designed to crack open seed husks. The bills, huge even for finches, cried out these birds' name: grosbeaks, evening grosbeaks.

There must have been a dozen of them, clambering ungracefully over the spindly box elder branches, eating the clumps of seeds, chattering constantly, just like parrots. Their boisterous behavior even scared away the fat grey squirrels who usually defend the little clump of trees with vigorous scolding and chattering.

Flocks of evening grosbeaks are common in towns in the autumn, temporarily colonizing maples and box elder trees while they devour their seeds. In summer, evening grosbeaks breed in the montaine or boreal conifer forests. But this time of year they are on the move to wintering sites. In urban areas, they often winter in groups near feeders, especially feeders with sunflower seeds. Sans human handouts, these big finches spend their winters nibbling on spruce, fir, or maple seeds and buds. Boulder, with the abundance of silver maples, box elders, and bird feeders, is probably an evening grosbeak paradise.

Box elders (a kind of maple, hence the other common name, "ash-leaved maple") are considered a trash tree in Boulder, a weedy species that most people don't want growing in their yards. They are native to the deciduous forests of the Midwest and thread their way across the Great Plains as part of the riparian forest community. Box elders are not particularly prepossessing trees: they grow fast like cottonwoods, but because their wood is brittle they rarely attain such a stately size or form. Like most maples, their flowers are tiny and easily overlooked; unlike most maples, their leaves are unsymmetrically three-parted and do not blaze with fiery color in the fall. Further, female box elder trees are host to box elder bugs, striking black-and-orange insects that appear by the thousands in late summer and early fall. Box elders, in short, are not a landscaper's dream.

This particular clump of three trees, none taller than twenty feet, is a volunteer. In this respect, I am thankful for the landlord's careless maintenance: with tidier care, the little clump of weedy trees would have been removed long ago. Box elders produce a tremendous quantity of winged seeds that, because they persist long after most maple seeds have twirled away, provide a natural food bank. Thus, the spindly clump of box elders guarantees a steady stream of seed eaters—birds, squirrels, and insects—to our autumn yard.

The flock of bright yellow evening grosbeaks stayed all afternoon, flashing their gaudy colors, shaking the box elder branches with their clumsy feeding, and chattering. When they finally departed, the whole flock gone in a rush, the yard seemed unnaturally silent, as if they'd taken a bit of life with them. Even the usually noisy squirrels crept about quietly all evening.

Wednesday, 23 September ᐧᐧ Today is the first day of fall—last night was the autumnal equinox. The nights and days are now about equal length, but soon the days will be shorter. The year is winding towards the long cold nights of winter. Autumn is a season of transition, between summer, the season of abundant and exuberant life, and winter, the quiet season when much of life is dormant, waiting for the earth to move closer to the sun again and the days to lengthen. Hormones direct the rituals of change: leaves on maples, cottonwoods, oaks, and other deciduous trees turn brilliant, gradually lose their color, and finally drop; birds from hawks to hummingbirds, some animals, and even fragile monarch butterflies migrate to wintering areas; raccoons, skunks, mice, and other animals and insects prepare to hole up for the winter; the pace of human lives slows too, we succumb to melancholia more frequently, we sleep longer hours.... Even fall weather is in transition: gusty, strong winds; days running the gamut from summer's heat to winter's snapping cold; precipitation from rain to sleet to snow. Rarely is the weather forecast the same for two successive fall days.

The equinoxes and the solstices are the turning points for the seasons, markers in the sun's yearly cycle. Historically, human cultures revolved around the changing seasons. The solstices and equinoxes signaled the times to plant or harvest, or the end of deepening winter. Rituals, feasts, and celebrations marked these crucial celestial events. Our modern culture, though, largely ignores the changing seasons. We pass our lives in climate-controlled buildings, detached from the rhythms of life outside our homes, offices, schools, and cars.

The study of astronomy began with the need to chart the cycles of the sun and moon in order to predict the times of the equinoxes and solstices. It has only been in the rational era of modern science, with its emphasis on logic instead of emotion, that we have lost interest in celebrating the solar rhythm. Perhaps that will change. If the earth really is a giant self-regulating organism as some theories now suggest, then the solar cycle regulates the beat of its life. Today, after the autumnal equinox, the beat is beginning to slow in preparation for winter.

Tonight, Richard walked with me to my class on the university campus. On the way he showed me another walk that he discovered. He is really the explorer of the two of us. I explore only until I find a path or walking route that suits me and then I walk that route every day, learning its details— colors, textures, patterns; smells and sounds—until it becomes familiar. Richard is always pushing at the boundaries of his territory, scouting a new route, a different alley, walking several blocks out of his way to check out a park or a place with a view. We walked over the hill and through downtown to the greenbelt along Boulder Creek, and followed the path downstream.

The greenbelt is a linear park, only several hundred yards wide, but nearly five miles long, a verdant ribbon winding along Boulder Creek from the mouth of Boulder Canyon east right through downtown and out onto the plains. A hard-surfaced path follows the creek for the whole length of the park. Along the way are benches and picnic tables in eight pocket parks—wide places in the greenbelt—and in two larger parks. It is a wonderful place. Despite being bridged by numerous busy city streets, hemmed in by houses, yards, commercial districts, and even a football field, and losing part of its flow to diversion dams, the creek and its green ribbon of vegetation host trout and raccoons, dippers and other wild lives. The strip of rushing mountain stream, shadowed by enormous cottonwoods and peach-leaved willows, stitches the foothills to the plains.

It is a popular park, and last night was no exception—we were passed by joggers and cyclists, roller skaters, people in wheelchairs, and a skateboarder. Warm days year-round bring hordes of people out of downtown offices and shops to sit in the shade of the big trees along the creek, or run and cycle the path. On weekends, the path is choked with people young and old, large and small, of every variety and description, walking, running, skateboarding, bicycling, or just sitting. People float the creek's cool waters with inner tubes. Late spring and early summer high water lures kayakers to dance the creek's obstacle course of low bridges and diversion dams. Fly-fishing season brings out numerous anglers to try their skill on its trout. In winter, skiers use the path when sufficient snow falls on Boulder. The cool shade and wild tangle of vegetation also attracts a small population of homeless people, both residents and passers-through, who find the greenbelt attractive warm-weather camping and panhandling space.

I'd walked parts of the path before, upstream from downtown to Richard's office near the mouth of the canyon, downstream past the Arapahoe Avenue bridge, but never wandered downstream as far as we walked tonight. The creek muttered and gurgled as it flowed along its rocky bed, a cool downstream breeze rustled the jungle of leaves all around us, golden evening sunlight pierced the shady canopy in dust-flecked rays. The rumble of traffic and other city noises receded, washed away by soft sounds. The air was filled with the pungent sweetness of peeling cottonwood bark. A belted kingfisher gave its rattling cry as it flew downstream. We stopped to watch for trout in the clear water but didn't see any. It didn't matter. We forgot about the surrounding city, strolling in another time, free of the march of seconds, minutes, hours.

Overhead was a nearly continuous, dancing green canopy: the waxy deltoid leaves of big cottonwood trees; shiny, long, lance-shaped leaves dangling from multi-trunked peach-leaved willows; bleached green, three-parted box elder leaves already fading to the pale yellow of fall. At eye level was a mosaic of shrubs and small trees: cottonwoods and willows, chokecherry and wild rose, box elder and green ash trees, wild plums, all stitched to the overstory by the strong ropes of wild grape and clematis vines.

It is hard to imagine Boulder without the greenbelt and creek path. It seems such a logical part of the city. But the idea of preserving Boulder Creek as a strip of natural park running through urban Boulder has been a long time germinating. Eighty years ago, in 1910, Frederick Law Olmsted, Jr., son of the designer of New York's Central Park, created a master plan that recommended protecting Boulder Creek as a free-flowing, wild creek. The idea, and the creek's riparian vegetation and trout population, languished for decades. In the meantime, gravel was dredged from the creek bed and parts of the creek were channelized for flood control. Construction encroached on the downtown section of the creek bed, and overgrazing broke the banks on the east end. Cottonwoods were removed or died as water was drawn down for irrigation and lawn watering. Where the cottonwood overstory was breached, the balance failed and the remaining riparian vegetation wasted away, no longer able either to filter runoff or to shade the creek bottom from the summer's hot sun. Populations of trout and other riparian and aquatic creatures dwindled. Finally, in 1983, the city brought alive Olmsted's grand vision with the Boulder Creek Project, including protection of the greenbelt, construction of the Boulder Creek Path, and extensive stream rehabilitation to make Boulder Creek not only pleasant for people, but liveable for wildlife also. That meant reconstruction of the actual creek channel to provide good habitat for trout and other aquatic life—adding boulders and other structures so the stream would regain pools and riffles; revegetation of denuded bank sections to provide shelter, food, and cover; and negotiations between the city and major water users to ensure a sufficient year-round streamflow to keep trout populations alive. It worked: the trout are back in the upper sections, belted kingfishers patrol the creek, at least one pair of great horned owls nests in the cottonwoods, great blue herons fish the pools, dragonflies hawk sunny spots above the water— and we humans crowd the path in hordes.

The greenbelt is a good example of the problems of competing land uses along the Front Range, and in any arid area. Riparian areas like this—because of the available water, dense and verdant vegetation, cover and shade, and resultant diversity—are critical to the survival of more mammal, bird, fish, reptile, amphibian, and insect populations than any other habitats. Even the species that do not actually live in riparian habitats depend on them as travel corridors, feeding areas, migration rest stops—the list goes on and on. Yet riparian ecosystems are the tropical rain forests of North American arid areas: the most likely ecosystems to be thoughtlessly abused for short-term gains. We dam the streams to store water, creating widely fluctuating reservoirs that eventually silt up; we cut down the cottonwoods and replace them with "more desirable" trees; we divert the flows, de-watering the streams to maintain our green lawns; we straighten out the kinks and line their banks with concrete for flood control. And so the riparian jungles disappear. When we do preserve a relatively free-flowing stream and its green ribbon of cottonwood forest, we put a path along it, displacing the wildlife with joggers, walkers, cyclists—a monoculture of humans.

I love walking this path, but is my pleasure worth the cost

of displacing the myriad species of wildlife from one of the precious few remaining riparian areas? Given the choice between developing a path through Boulder along this creek or putting the path somewhere else and keeping the creek wild to accommodate the white-tailed deer, great horned owls, northern orioles, dippers, ducks, leopard frogs, salamanders, and other wildlife, what should we chose? The trade-offs are not clear. Some of the wildlife live here anyway, deer certainly continue to travel the creek corridor at night, and raccoons and other urban wildlife use the creek, but without the enormous numbers of humans using the slender riparian zone, there would be more space for other lives. On the other hand, the creek path does much good in terms of education, by exposing people to the beauty and wonder of the natural world. The question involves rights: do we humans have the right to preempt other beings' habitat? I don't think so. We are acting like greedy children, grabbing the whole plate of cookies, asserting that they belong to us, and refusing to share. Still, there is no simple solution, along Boulder Creek, or anywhere.

We crossed the creek on a creaky suspended footbridge and climbed a switchbacking path onto the university campus. Below, the steep hillside was shaded by the box elders and cottonwoods of the riparian forest, the ground festooned with thick brown stems of wild grape vines. At the top of the hill, above the green canopy, we turned and stood under the spreading branches of a ponderosa pine, looking north along the cresting wave of the foothills where the plains suddenly bend upwards into mountains. Below us wandered the green line of the creek, cutting through the regular pattern of the city streets; past town, the wide sweep of ochre plains stretched to the horizon. The sun slanted low, coloring the world with dusty golden light.

After my class I walked back across the university campus to meet Richard in the student center. It is a big campus, cluttered with buildings and twisting walkways. I became absorbed in watching the stars in the obsidian-black sky and forgot to pay attention to where I was. I missed the student center and had to backtrack between a group of old buildings, through enchanting archways leading to dark courtyards full of trees and in one case, a pond. All mysterious and obscure, inviting exploration.

Monday, 28 *September* ᴥ This morning Richard and I got up at about six o'clock to climb the Mount Sanitas trail—it goes up a ridge above town just six blocks from our house, at the mouth of Sunshine Canyon—and watch the sun rise. When we left the apartment, the street lights were still on, but the night was already wearing off. We walked quickly uphill on Mapleton Avenue in the chill air, past quiet old houses, the only noise the rustling of silver maple leaves overhead. Rusty black crows chased each other silently through the air between spreading maple branches.

Past the hospital we turned up the trail into the grassland at the base of Mount Sanitas. The sky was already light enough to outline Sanitas's dark ridgeline where it rises and falls like a stegosaurus's backbone, but the sun wasn't up yet. Eager to be on the ridge before sunrise, we took the steep trail that climbs up the breeched end of the ridge. As the predawn greyness slipped away, we hurried upwards. Finally we scrambled, nearly out of breath, onto the spine of the ridge. We walked along until we came to a gap in the backbone with a view east over Boulder and across the plains. There we found perches on the cold rocks, backs resting against the rough sandstone slabs, and settled in to watch the show.

Pale, pearly light washed across the entire sky, brightest in the east and grading almost imperceptibly to twilight behind us in the west. Clouds rimmed the eastern horizon, flat grey above but already blushing faintly pink where the sun came closest to the edge. Finally a vertical fiery streak flared up the

26

clouds straight east of where we perched, and, as if switched on, an intense orange spotlight pierced a hole in the cloud band. With that burst of light, the day began. A small flock of finches flew chattering overhead, mourning doves cooed from the shrubs along the creek below us, a wren trilled in the canyon, chickadees began calling in the box elder trees below. And the first slice of the orange orb that was the morning sun peeked over the clouds.

It happens every day: the sun bursts over the rim of the plains, birds begin to sing; flower blossoms open; lizards stir as the first rays of sun warm the rocks; breezes flow uphill, laden with sounds, smells, heat, and moisture. Far below, we watched the steady stream of taillights pour out onto the plains on the Denver-Boulder turnpike—early commuters on their daily trip to Denver. Off they drive, mechanically pursuing their routine, locked in their cars, unable to hear, smell, feel the beginning of the day. Do they even notice the sun rise? Does this gift of a new day lift their spirits, or is it simply an annoyance causing them to squint and reach for sunglasses to shade eyes dulled by the monotonous grey ribbon of road? Fortunately, the sunrise, all color and sound and cool smells of life stirring, does not depend on our awareness or appreciation. Noticed or not, the gift of life occurs each day.

We sat mesmerized by the changing light as the sun rose past the clouds. What a magnificent way to begin the day! I felt as if our silent watch was inadequate to express our appreciation. Surely there is some ceremony to greet the sun. We merely bowed, then rose stiffly and clambered off our cold, lichen-encrusted seats to begin the silent trek downhill.

Halfway down the steep ridge, hunger pulled our thoughts to more pedestrian considerations. We hurried back down the quiet streets to breakfast as the sun rose higher in the sky and the world continued its daily journey.

October

Friday, 2 *October* ❧ I am trying an experiment, auditing a class called "Contemplative Natural History" given by the Naropa Institute. The professor, a paleoecologist from the University of Colorado, is attempting to teach the class to experience their relationship with the natural world. She wants us to wordlessly feel the world, to absorb it through our senses, rather than to use our intellect to learn plant and animal names, geologic formations, and other factual knowledge. Her philosophy is that once we give a thing a name, we focus on the name, losing touch with other equally important, but less tangible, aspects. I agree with her idea, and I think that she is right in asserting that science in general has gone too far in rejecting emotional and/or intuitive knowledge, but I suspect that she is overreacting in turn, like a pendulum swinging to the opposite extreme. I'm not sure that you can develop a meaningful connection with a landscape without knowing some of the facts about it. Part of a relationship is based on feelings and intuitions, nonquantifiable knowledge; part on facts and intellectual inferences, quantifiable knowledge. How can you begin to know a place without knowing something about it besides your emotional reaction? I have an advantage over most of the class—I know many of the facts about this landscape, its structure, the processes that work on it and make its inhabitants tick, who the inhabitants are and their relationships. I'm allowed to attend the class as the resident skeptic and plant ecologist.

Our project for the quarter is to pick a place, an aspect of a place, or a particular view and develop a relationship, writing regularly about our emotional experience. This sunny, warm afternoon was our practice session. We all piled into the teacher's mini-pickup (six of us crammed into the bed, the rear bumper nearly dragging) and drove up to Bald Mountain Park, just west of Boulder up Sunshine Canyon. We began by meditating, seated in a circle in the dry grass under a fragrant cluster of ponderosa pines.

The sun was like a warm blanket on my back and the hot, dry air sweet with pine scent. I sat quietly for a while, said my prayers of thanks for the day, then got up and wandered up the hill towards the ridge of Bald Mountain. I like to be up high, where the wind blows and the world spreads out below from horizon to horizon. The dry bunchgrasses crunched underfoot as I climbed.

At last, slightly out of breath, I came out on the narrow, wind-scoured ridgetop. At the peak of the hill, five college-age young men were hanging out drinking beer and enjoying making noise. I gathered my silence around me and veered off down a sharp-spined shoulder. About fifty yards away, just far enough that the beer-drinkers' noise faded, a solitary stunted ponderosa pine grew at the crest of the ridge. My spot. I sat down underneath it, facing north to take in the splendid view: on my left, the jagged grey line of 13,000-foot-high peaks that form the Continental Divide; on my right, the distant expanse of the plains under a fine brown smudge of smog. I leaned my back against the warm, rough bark of the ponderosa, dug a smooth spot for my tailbone in the gravelly soil, took off my glasses, and sat quietly, at home.

The ponderosa pine I leaned against was short, no more than twelve feet tall, but with the well-developed limbs and branches of a mature tree. I estimated its age to be at least 100 years, and probably older. (Oh, for an increment borer to remove a thin, round core and count the rings!) Much to my surprise, it was heavily colonized by dwarf-mistletoe plants. Dwarf-mistletoe are odd, highly specialized plants that parasitize conifers, unable to survive without a host tree. They actually grow on and in the tree, their roots penetrating the branches to obtain food from the tree's vascular system, their leafless yellow-green angular stems protruding from the bark like miniature shrubs. Dwarf-mistletoe flowers are quite inconspicuous, but the sticky seeds they produce disseminate in a spectacular way: when mature, the seeds are shot out of the fruit like bullets, hurled up to forty-five feet. If they hit a conifer needle, the seeds stick until the next rain and then slide down the wet needles to a branch, where they germinate and root, beginning the cycle on a new tree. Tiny neon-bright mistletoe branchlets poked out near the ends of each ponderosa branch. The tree looked as if it was possessed, its gnarled grey body inhabited by a spiky green spirit.

The top of the ridge was dry, nearly bare of vegetation. Soil formation on an exposed ridge like this is incredibly slow, the parent rock yielding only grudgingly to the prying force of ice expanding and contracting or of plant roots growing; and to the chemical erosion of fungi hyphae in lichens dissolving their way between the crystals. The resulting gravelly soil is ever so slowly enriched by the decomposition of small amounts of organic matter from the sparse above-ground plant and animal communities, and by the burrowing actions of the soil flora and fauna. The soil on this particular ridgetop is almost pure rock; a thin, light-colored sandy layer of barely deteriorated granite called grus. It forms a rough surface of knobby, angular pebbles and sand. Under my magnifying glass, the grains of sand resolve themselves into individual crystals of quartz and whitish feldspar and a few darker grains from some ferric minerals. The larger pebbles are coated with a mineral stain like the whitish caliche salts that coat rocks on the surface of arid soils in the grasslands 4,000 feet below, except that this stain is rusty-colored from oxidized iron.

I closed my eyes and felt around me blindly with my fingers. Everything I touched was dry, most of it rough or actually sharp: crystalline edges of the gravelly soil, hard angular stems of mistletoe, rough and brittle desiccated remains of blanketflower leaves and stems, needle-like spiny leaves of prickly gilia, sticky, rough stems and involucral bracts of gumweed, scratchy crustose lichens.

With my eyes closed, it was easier to listen. The wind dominated the sounds, rushing by in pulses, rattling the dry grass and whooshing through the stiff ponderosa needles. Far away to the west, a raven croaked hoarsely, then flying closer, croaked again. I became absorbed by dropping the dry, almost weightless blanketflower leaves on the rocks around me to hear the pottery-like tinkle they made. A sound like porcelain bells, each leaf shattering when it hit.

After a while, I opened my eyes to look at the colors of the lichens. Different colors of lichens grow on different kinds of rocks, reflecting variations on the mineral content of the rocks. The lichens growing on this granitic rock, high in quartz and feldspar, were various shades of green—from cool, icy blue-green to bright acid green. Absent were the chromatic orange and yellow lichens that grow on the volcanic rocks of the Absaroka Mountains in northwest Wyoming or the Cascades and Olympic Mountains of Washington State.

A Mountain Bluebird flew overhead, cerulean blue as the bright sky, calling softly as it passed. Next a blue-black Steller's jay flew down the spine of the ridge, gliding on the updrafts between slow flaps of its dark wings. It swooped down the side of the ridge in graceful shallow arcs.

After an hour, I grew restless, my tailbone beginning to ache from its hard seat. I looked at my watch, wishing that I could write. But my assignment was just to sit and watch and feel. So I sat.

I looked around at the sparse, dry vegetation. The ridge crest was fringed with clumps of needle-and-thread grass, a bunchgrass of arid sites. The slender golden stems bent perpetually west, bowing gracefully before the upslope wind. Each clump of narrow, almost wiry basal leaves is overtopped by a long stem bearing loose panicles of scaly grass flowers. The resultant seeds, a single one from each flower, have one absurdly long, tail-like awn (the "thread" of the needle-and-thread) and a sharp, pointed needle-like end (the "needle"). Molly, my step-daughter, learned to identify needle-and-thread when she was just four years old—she and her dad used to have play fights with the seeds. They are sharp enough to stick in skin and so make very effective darts.

Closer by were the small, perfectly round halves of bladder-pod mustard seed pods. The flower stalk is at least two inches tall, dwarfing the rest of the plant. The even ranks of round seed pod halves give it the look of a miniature microwave tower with its ranks of round dishes.

I sat still for so long that a short-horned grasshopper, as long as my little finger, its chitinous body dusty blue-grey with brilliant crimson hind legs, jumped up onto my jeans. It crawled around sampling the worn denim with its strong jaws, searching for an edible part. When the wind stilled, I could hear the rasping sound of its jaws trying vainly to chew the thick fabric. Short-horned grasshoppers, also called locusts, are the abundant grasshoppers of grasslands and fields. A walk on a hot late-summer afternoon is empty without the dry snapping sound of short-horned grasshopper wings flying from underfoot. I watched it for a long time, until it crawled up inside my pants and I gently shooed it out. The grasshopper leaped suddenly off my leg in a high arc, landing about three feet away.

The sun's warmth made me drowsy, but the cool wind, the sharp pebbles in the gravelly soil under my rump, and the hard ridges in the ponderosa bark against my back kept me awake.

Finally the two and a half hours were up. I got up stiffly and took one last look at the magnificent view before walking slowly down the hill.

Despite my skepticism, I found the quiet sitting and patient watching meaningful. I left with a better connection to that particular ridge—the place took me in. But would I have that connection without the base of factual knowledge of what I saw, heard, smelled and felt around me? I don't know. I have the knowledge and so cannot experience what learnings would have taken place, what relationship developed, without it. I do know that my ties to this landscape are strong, and not entirely intellectual. Those luminous threads are spun from days and weeks and months of time spent outside, getting the feel of the land. Perhaps not so consciously absorbing it as today, but similar experiences. The connection comes, I think, from knowing the place intellectually *and* emotionally.

Tuesday, 6 *October* ✹ Boulder is sometimes derisively nicknamed "Oz" for its unusual variety of alternative spiritual, political, and cultural opportunities. The Oz label also applies in a positive, wonderful sense, to the extraordinary plants clothing the foothills and mesas around Boulder, including some of the strangest and most unexpected species found anywhere in the Rocky Mountains. Scattered through the mesas and lower foothills are prairie and eastern deciduous woodland species, remnants of a once-extensive flora now common only on the eastern edge of the Great Plains. In the foothills and the mountains are an even stranger group of species, remnants of an older flora that spread across the continent in a more temperate climate before the great ice ages—at least 3 million years ago. Now, many of these species' nearest relatives grow no closer than the Appalachians, or equally distant locations. All persist as relicts of a different climate, as odd and out of place as if a few dinosaurs roamed the foothills, survivors of the great age of extinction.

I stumbled on the Oz side of the local flora accidentally. Not long after we moved here Richard and I went for a walk in the foothills above the National Center for Atmospheric Research on Table Mesa. As we walked, I paid attention to the patterns of vegetation on the land, speculating about why this species was growing here and that there, trying to sort out the mosaic formed by the interaction of climate, topography, and soil type. Most of the plants were Rocky Mountain species, except for the clumps of a wine-red grass, taller and less bunchy than most of the other grasses. The height, color, and habit of growth reminded me of little bluestem, familiar from the tallgrass prairies nearly a thousand miles east in southern Illinois. Little bluestem is a distinctive part of both the tall- and midgrass prairies. It grows as far west as central Kansas and Nebraska. But not, I thought, here in the arid country west of the hundredth meridian.

I pulled William A. Weber's *Rocky Mountain Flora* out of my knapsack and identified a clump. It was indeed little bluestem, the "wine-colored grass" of Willa Cather's midwestern prairies. According to Weber it peters out as the grasslands extend west, reappearing only in isolated spots along the Front Range and in the Black Hills of South Dakota, another refugium of the once-extensive midwestern flora. What happened?

At the time of the last glacial age, the climate of the Rockies was cooler and wetter than it is now. The now-tree-less Great Plains were then covered by mixed woods and mid- or tallgrass prairies. Paper birch, wild sarsaparilla, and hazel-nut grew in the woods, along with wood lily, lobelia, and pale lousewort; little bluestem and other tallgrass prairie species grew on the drier sites. As the glaciers receded, the climate gradually grew warmer and drier. The deciduous woods and tallgrass prairie couldn't survive the climate shift. The change probably didn't happen suddenly—not in human' life-times—rather over hundreds of thousands of years. (The post-glacial climate shift is a natural crisis comparable to the growing pollution-caused crisis of global warming, except that the current crisis is apparently unfolding much more quickly.) As the years grew warmer and drier, the forest and tallgrass grasslands died out very slowly, persisting longest in pockets of cooler, more moist microclimates, like stream bottoms, north-facing slopes, and ravines in the foothills. Elsewhere, the forest and tallgrass prairie shrank eastward towards the wetter climates of eastern Iowa, Missouri, southern Minnesota, Illinois, southern Wisconsin and Michigan, and Indiana. Left behind along the Front Range, relics of a long-ago climate, the pockets of little bluestem, paper birch, hazelnut, and the others somehow survived.

The older, Tertiary-era, relicts are most visibly represented by Boulder raspberry, a low, white-flowered shrub found in cool, shady locations in the foothills. Boulder raspberry produces raspberry-like fruits, but, contrary to its scientific name, *Rubus deliciosus*, its berries are dry and hard, not delicious at all. Like the remnants of the tallgrass prairie/deciduous woods flora, these once-widespread species survived gradual but drastic climate changes, persisting only in cooler, more moist pockets. Jamesia, another Tertiary relict, is a shrub with leathery, creased leaves and lovely clusters of fragrant, mock-orange-like flowers. Now found only in Front Range canyons and one site near Wolf Creek Pass, Jamesia is more widespread as fossil leaves than as live plants: impressions of its leaves etch shale layers deposited 26–38 million years ago in western Colorado.

We tend to see the world in terms of how it looks to us today, forgetting that what we look at is by no means static or unchanging. The Ozian flora around Boulder is a reminder that the world is not fixed, but rather a complex system, continually adapting and responding to change. Climates come and go, floras come and go, dinosaurs come and go…. What hubris is it that gives us the idea that we will remain forever?

Tonight's moon will be full. The harvest moon, the huge round moon that signals the end of the growing season, the time to begin preparing for winter. I'm looking forward to my first real winter in four years.

Friday, 9 October ➴ Last night, three raccoons ran up the stairs outside our living room window, their nails clacking loudly on the wooden stair treads. The large grey mother led, the two smaller young of the year followed hard behind. It was quite startling to look out the window and see raccoons there. I suspect that they come for cat food; one of the apart-ments upstairs is home to a large ginger cat whose owner keeps a dish of cat food outside the door. This must be a regu-lar dining stop for the raccoons because they seemed to know where they were going—after they passed the window, the steady rhythm of their nails told me that they headed purposefully along the balcony with no pausing to sniff and cast about.

Boulder's urban wild mammal population is large and sur-prisingly diverse, partly because of the lush habitat created by thousands of planted trees and acres of landscaping. Raccoons are one of the three most commonly sighted wild animals in Boulder, along with deer and skunks. Other members of our urban fauna include bats, shrews, mice, weasels, ground squir-rels, cottontail rabbits, and muskrats. All are opportunistic species, able to adapt to human activity and common in town wherever pockets of usable habitat exist. Therein lies a prob-lem: what seems like usable habitat to a raccoon may be hotly contested by the humans who live there. At this time of year, the problem is exacerbated by the approach of denning sea-son. Wildlife from bats to raccoons are on the prowl for win-ter homes and will take up residence in whatever suitable space they find, including attics, chimneys, crawl spaces, porches, garages, woodpiles.

Our relationship with wild animals is a bit schizophrenic: how we behave depends partly on whether we think of the animal as a "good" animal or not; basically, whether they com-pete with us in any way. If a numerous and opportunistic species prefers the habitat we humans prefer, we see the species as "bad" animals, and we generally resolve the con-flict by transplanting or killing them. It doesn't take much soul-searching to decide to transplant a group of skunks that have invaded your crawl space for the winter—you can be pretty sure that they will find another shelter and survive. But what about other species, for instance, grizzly bears, whose habitat is now scarce and also, because much of it is "pristine" and beautiful wilderness, increasingly pressured by human use? When conflicts arise with the big bears, it is not nearly as easy to transplant them since so little usable habitat remains for grizzlies. How do we resolve conflicts with species, like the grizzlies, with which we don't seem to be able to coexist? Would we ever think of closing a wilderness area to human use in order to allow grizzlies to have an undisturbed home?

Later last night I heard the raccoons hissing and squealing right outside our bedroom window under the apple trees. They come in the evening to eat the apples and often get into fights with the feral cats that consider that tangle of trees and shrubs their turf. My sympathies are entirely with the raccoons, although I might prefer a backyard with shortgrass prairie, burrowing owls, prairie dogs, and rattlesnakes, at least the raccoons are wild. But even those sympathies carry a value judgement. Are raccoons really "wilder" than feral cats? I fell asleep to the unearthly symphony of squealing and hissing, still wondering.

Monday, 12 October ❧ I've begun to settle in. I've

chosen a favorite walking route over Mapleton Hill to downtown, and the splendid view of the spiny Front Range is familiar enough that I'm beginning to look around and notice details. This afternoon as I walked back up and over the hill from town, I examined the sidewalks underfoot. In this turn-of-the-century neighborhood, they are beautiful, made of fine-grained red flagstones, not cement. Each rectangle of stone is different: some are dark rusty red with a blackish stain on the surface, some pale reddish-pink, the color of salmon flesh; some are nearly flat, some have a wavy surface like ripple marks in the sand of a stream bottom. All are gently worn by half a century or more of foot traffic. The flags are Lyons sandstone, the same rusty-red sandstone used to face many buildings in town and almost all of the buildings on the university campus.

These slabs of rock I walk on each day represent a period in Colorado's history that we can only imagine, long before the ridges of this Front Range towered above Boulder. They are Permian, deposited between 240 and 280 million years ago, as sand dunes, probably near the shores of the great continental sea that covered the Midwest and Great Plains for millions of years. The sand that built the dunes eroded from the easternmost range of the ancestral Rockies, the mountains that were pushed up and eroded away long before these Rockies. After thousands of years of accreting sand and shifting about as dunes do, being shaped and reshaped by the wind, the dunes were eventually stilled, buried beneath other debris as climates and sea shorelines changed. Then they slowly cemented into the lovely salmon-colored layers of rock that we call Lyons sandstone.

Life was very different when the dunes were forming. Although mountains lined the western horizon and the climate was generally arid, the world was populated by insects, fish and reptiles—no dinosaurs yet—and the vegetation was dominated by tree ferns, other fern-like plants, and the first coniferous plants. The Rockies that we know wouldn't be thrust up for nearly 200 million years. The first mammals were at least 50 million years away; flowering plants would not appear for another hundred million years or so. Humans first showed up in Africa about 237 million years after the dunes blew into rippled hills—and we appeared in North America only about 20,000 years ago, just an eyelash-blink of time in the rock's life.

The flagstones were quarried near Lyons, Colorado, the type locality, that is, where the formation was first described. This particular sandstone formation is sought after because, besides its lovely color, it breaks easily along the parallel cross-bedding planes, making good flags and building stone.

The bedding planes are actually the successive wind-deposited slanting surface layers of the ancient dunes—not the surface parallel to the Permian ground. Sometimes the surfaces of the flagstones are beautifully rippled, like the ripples left by waves receding down a sandy beach, except these ripples were drawn by the Permian wind, between 240 and 280 million years ago; sometimes the surfaces show footprints of four-footed animals that walked the dunes.

As I walk through town, I look at the flags under my feet, noting how the ripples lie, searching for footprints. When the wind blows across the surface of the flags now, no grains of sand move. The ripples are still, frozen in time, the ocean long gone, the sand no longer free to drift like smoke across the surface of the dunes.

Friday, 16 *October* ✒ This afternoon was another Contemplative Natural History class—this one focusing on Boulder-area geology. It was a beautifully sunny and cool day, the sky a penetrating shade of blue. Yellow cottonwood leaves glinted in the sun. We piled into three vehicles and drove south on Broadway, then along the range towards Golden. Our first stop, a pullout by the side of the highway going up onto a mesa at the edge of the plains, offered a splendid view of the mouth of Eldorado Canyon.

We sat silently in the grass by the pullout for about five minutes to get the feel of the place before the professor began talking about geology. I settled myself in the tan dried grass facing the range, a pink, glacier-smoothed sandstone rock my backrest. The dry grass under me was prickly, each stiff stalk bending only grudgingly under my weight. The sun warmed my southward facing cheek, the cool wind eddied and played against my other side. Across the valley to the west was the magnificent wall of the Front Range with its jagged appliqué of uptilted Fountain sandstone hogbacks. Hazy golden sunlight, the light of fall, poured like treacle syrup through the narrow knife-slot of Eldorado Canyon. The canyon, a deep incision in the massive wall of the foothills, spit the thin white thread of Eldorado Creek onto the flat plains.

Sitting in the sun like that I lose track of time, becoming completely absorbed in where I am. The frantic compounding of seconds to minutes to hours that our time measures falls away and I am drawn into an older, slower rhythm, closer to the flow of geologic eons than to the choppy pulse of human lives. Trucks roared uphill on the highway next to the pullout, passing cars occasionally honked, but their noise faded into the background of my consciousness. I absorbed the warm sun, feeling myself connect to the lives in the soil and the dried bunches of grass around me. I could feel the fungus in the lichen under my back slowly eating the sandstone I leaned on, dissolving its matrix and liberating the individual grains of sand. My skin boundary ceased to define me. I became part of the landscape, the rough sandstone against my back, the golden haze of light, the warm dry soil, the expanse of space. I was no longer an intruder admiring as if from outside; instead I flowed along, part of the pulse that beat in web of life around me.

Curiosity drew me to this class—I wondered what "Contemplative Natural History" involved. At first I was skeptical of the professor's "touchy-feely" approach of teaching by experiencing a place without naming plants, rocks, animals. I wondered how to resolve the tension between the traditional scientific "facts are all" approach to teaching natural history and her attempt to teach by deliberately withholding the facts, encouraging emotional and intuitive nonlogical learning. Sitting in the grass by the roadside today I answered my question. The two approaches are complementary, not exclusive. Knowing a place must involve having a working knowledge of the facts about it—who and what live there, how the plant and animal communities are distributed across the land, the bones that form the surface, the climate that shapes those bones, the processes that nurture and decay the intricate web of life that inhabits the place. But those facts are only a framework, a pencil sketch with no shading or color. The emotional experience, the sensing of a place, is what fleshes out our knowledge of it, gives it life and sound and breath and soul.

Saturday, 17 October ❧ Richard and Molly and I
went hunting snow today. When we woke this morning, we could see what looked like snow up on the upper flanks of the foothills, coming down as far as the saddle between Flagstaff and Green Mountain, just under the lower edge of the clouds. The first snow within walking distance of town!

We dressed in our warm jackets, hats, and mittens, piled into the Volvo, and drove over to Chautauqua Park to hike up towards the ridgetops, eager to touch the first snow of the season.

We hiked up Gregory Canyon, following the tumbling stream in the narrow valley bottom, past autumn-scarlet clumps of smooth sumac, their leaves bright as dripping blood, their clusters of velvety, rust-colored fruits stiffly raised, plush as Victorian parlor ornaments. Molly stopped to climb the tangled branches of a wild plum tree. Her small face soon grinned down at us like a cheeky wood sprite from the branches over our heads.

We hiked on upstream past pale cornstraw-yellow clumps of needle-and-thread grass, the wiry leaves dry and brittle. The loose seed heads looked like victims of electric shock—the long awn protruding from each seed twisted into a tight corkscrew. The twisting awns are part of an ingenious self-sowing process: the hygroscopic cell walls in the awn shrink differentially as the awn dries, causing it to curl like a pig's tail. Later, the seeds drop to the soil, some first carried long distances in animals' fur or humans' wool socks. In spring when the air is humid from melting snow, the hygroscopic cells absorb moisture and expand again, uncurling the awn and literally screwing the needle-tipped seed firmly into the damp soil where it can germinate.

We crossed the creek on a wooden footbridge and turned to climb steep switchbacks between two fingers of the drainage. We trudged up the steep grade silently, heads down, hands in our pockets to protect them from the damp chill, heading for the snow. At the top of the switchbacks the trail leveled off again. The saddle with its snow-white ponderosa pines was just above us—we were nearly there. We stopped to catch our breath and, puffing, turned around to look at the view. Boulder and the plains spread out far below, the regular pattern of houses and streets seeming distant and unreal in the frame of ragged, rocky slopes. The only noises in the silent morning were the swooshing wind and the rushing creek. We turned again and climbed upwards with renewed vigor, boots crunching on the frozen soil, eager to touch the snow.

It wasn't snow at all. Once we drew near the saddle, we realized that what looked like a fresh dusting of snow was hoarfrost, a fake-fur coating of long, intricately branched crystals. Over every exposed surface—the slender ponderosa needles, blades of dried grass, the Oregon-grape leaves, even the grains of the sandy soil—grew delicate crystalline hair. The whole world might have been dipped in saturated sugar water, spawning the sparkling threads. The air in the frosty forest was so moist that we spoke in clouds of dragon smoke, the exhalation for each word crsiply visible.

We hiked on. Across the saddle between Flagstaff and Green Mountain, we perched on a mound of granitic boulders and unpacked our lunch. Grey patches of fog drifted around us, fingering between the trees. Soon the chill of the cold rocks seeped through our clothes, and we gobbled our lunches, drank steamy cocoa, and turned back.

As we crossed the saddle again, the sun appeared in the fog, a silver disk glowing through a thin spot in the worn cloud fabric. In moments, the clouds rose slightly, revealing the back side of the long ridge of Boulder Mountain across the valley. Above an altitudinal line sharp as any drawn with a rule, the forest was powdery white with hoarfrost; below, dark green. Suddenly, the sun broke through the clouds. We blinked and squinted in the unexpected brilliance. The trees and grass around us flashed and sparkled like cut crystal. While as we stood in quiet awe, the sparkling brilliance began to disappear and soon vanished—the ephemeral crystals melted by the warmth of the very sunlight that lit their flashing splendor.

Monday, 19 October ❧ After a cloudy, grey morning, this late afternoon is drenched with brilliant sunlight. From my perch on the bench in the pocket park at the edge of Mapleton Hill, Boulder spreads out like a patchwork quilt of gloriously bright fall colors. The tree canopy is ablaze with gold, amber, burnt orange, chartreuse, Chinese red, scarlet, and even dusky purple. This patchwork of autumn colors is comprised of two completely different forests: the native cottonwood riparian forest growing along the veins of Boulder Creek and the larger irrigation ditches, and the planted forest of street and yard trees.

The overstory of the native riparian forest is dominated by deciduous trees whose leaves in fall turn sumptuous hues of yellow: big plains cottonwoods shimmering gold, box elder bright chartreuse, and peach-leaved willow trees lemon-yellow. Underneath this gaudy canopy, the dense understory is a jumble of subtler colors: dull magenta wild plum, yellow-brown chokecherry, orange-red wild roses, pale buttercup yellow hazelnuts, shiny brown alders. This slender, golden, tweedy ribbon of riparian forest traces the waters' course from foothills through town and out onto the plains.

By contrast, the urban forest, the trees we have planted in our yards and along our streets, is truly a crazy quilt—a randomly chosen patchwork of individual taste. It reveals little about soil type or moisture regime, much about human whim and landscaping fashion. On Mapleton Hill, University Hill, and the university campus, the old silver maples flicker like fat yellow and orange candle flames. Their vivid background is dotted with the occasional deep gold of a big cottonwood, the scarlet and orange-red of Norway or red maples, and the dusky purple of green ashes. A brilliant crimson maple pulses like a neon light in the Mapleton School yard. Only the oak leaves retain late summer's green, but their time will come. As the maples shed their brilliant color, their leaves fading and dropping in chromatic drifts on lawns and streets, the oak leaves turn soft colors, more like the sandstone and granite above town, muted oranges, rusty reds, and then tawny amber or mahogany brown. Oaks hold their leaves on the tree all winter, dry brown and rattling in the winter winds like dens of wary rattlesnakes.

Fall is progressing. On my walk here, I scuffled through drifts of leaves, listening to the dry rustling as my feet pushed along. Above the patchwork quilt of autumn color, the sky is clear cerulean blue. The peaks are dusted with crisp white new snow, and the cool down-valley breeze smells of dust and sun-warmed pine needles.

Tuesday, 27 October ❧ It was cloudy when I woke, low clouds, more like fog actually. But now it is beautifully sunny, with just the beginning of the winter inversion-haze casting a veil of blue air around the ridges.

When I heard the snarl of a chain saw engine this morning, I knew without even going outside to look that the sound meant the end for the big old silver maple at the corner of Maxwell and Ninth. The large blue "X" spray-painted on its silvery trunk meant that the city forester's crew had given it the death sentence. It was a "hazard tree," a tree in danger of falling. Its fat old crooked limbs were hollow, the rot-brown

47

innards revealed by gaping holes where limbs had broken off in Boulder's frequent windstorms.

Silver maples dominate the urban forest of shade trees planted in most of the older neighborhoods of Boulder. They are the grey-trunked, slightly shaggy-barked trees that give Mapleton Avenue and Mapleton Hill their names. Their arching limbs add to the dignity of the big Victorian houses, and their green, leafy branches in summer cast a dappled shade that gives the neighborhoods a cool, lazy feel. I remember vividly my introduction to the big old maples of this remarkable urban forest on a visit to Boulder about twelve years ago. My brother-in-law and his family proudly drove us around Mapleton Hill one hot June day. Accustomed to the arid, treeless basins of northern Wyoming, I was amazed at the steep hills and narrow streets with the green, overarching trees. They took me back to memories of my Midwestern childhood: the sound of my bike tires thumping down brick streets, the dappled shade thrown by a cool tunnel of trees, the hot summer sun far away.

Silver maples were once popularly planted for shade trees in Front Range communities because of their ability to survive in the arid climate (with additional water), their speedy growth, and their spreading form. The latter qualities were to prove a problem as the trees matured: fast growth equals soft wood, soft wood and spreading form equal long, weak branches. Long, weak branches mean structurally unsound trees, a poor choice for an urban forest in Boulder's windy, snowy climate.

Silver maples' heartwood, the tissue that provides structure and support for the tree, is so soft that unlike other maples, it can't be used for furniture and veneer—it doesn't even make good firewood. The cells that form the trees' wood, providing the structural strength to hold up the massive trees, are noticeably less dense than cells that form the wood of slower-growing hardwoods like Norway maple. Consequently, as silver maples grow large and become susceptible to heart rot and other kinds of decay, they are quite liable to shed branches—or come crashing down.

However, because silver maple wood is less dense, and so rots quickly, decomposers like fungi and insects find a congenial habitat in the big old trees, resulting in ideal nest trees for cavity-users—raccoons, woodpeckers, flickers, bluebirds, and owls, as well as aggressive colonies of starlings.

Silver maples' native habitat—the wet soils of streambanks, floodplains, and swamps in the eastern part of the country, east of the Great Plains—also makes them a poor choice for Front Range urban forests. Trees native to riparian forests are not particularly drought-tolerant, requiring watering to survive Boulder's arid late-summer and fall, and they grow most of their roots above, or close to, the surface of the soil. Rooting at the soil surface allows the roots to breathe in waterlogged riparian soils but is not a felicitous characteristic for urban trees. The flowing grey platter of roots radiating several feet out at the soil surface from large silver maples trunks is death on paving. Seasonal swelling and shrinking of the roots as they take on water and pump sap creates wildly undulating sidewalks and, eventually, broken sandstone pavers, or cracked driveways and streets. Further, without deep anchoring roots, silver maples are quite susceptible to windthrow.

Despite its problems, the forest of arching silver maples is a grand part of the community. Unfortunately, it is not long for this world. Like most fast-growing trees, silver maples are short-lived: after 80–100 years, they literally begin to decay from within and fall apart. Since many of the trees in Boulder were planted around the turn of the century, they are due to die off within ten or twenty years, leaving Mapleton Hill and other neighborhoods denuded. In a natural forest, new trees would grow up to replace the fallen overstory. Here in town, the city forester's staff must stimulate a new generation of forest, encouraging landowners to plant a young "hard maple" (sugar, red, or Norway maples) each time an old silver maple is removed.

I walked by the corner of Maxwell and Ninth this afternoon. All that remained of the hoary old silver maple were its snake-like roots flowing out from around where the shaggy trunk had risen, and a pile of fresh wood chips. The air still smelled like chain saw smoke, mixed with the too-sweet odor of rotten wood. Good-bye, old tree!

Thursday, 29 *October* ➤ It hardly seems like late October. These last two weeks have brought Indian summer: each day's skies are indelible blue; the chill, dry morning air splashes my skin awake when I walk to the corner paper machine; the warm noon sun lures me out to spread my work on the bench in front of the apartment; gusty afternoon winds strip the last few leaves from the thick finger-like twigs of the green ash trees in the front yard and blow a scarlet whirlwind of leaves from the tall sugar maple in the school yard; evening breezes bring the winey smell of fermenting apples in our bedroom window.

Yesterday, on just such a sparkling clear afternoon, I walked home from the post office, my head uptilted to watch the clouds form and grow into castles over the foothills, my feet scuffing slowly through crinkly yellow and brown cottonwood leaves, stopping in a patch of warm sun to watch magpies chase each other through the bare branches of a silver maple.... A strange look from a fellow pedestrian snapped me from my reverie. I realized how odd I must look, dawdling along, face turned up to the sky, grinning so hard my face ached. Indian summer fever.

But this halcyon weather is beginning to make me uneasy, sending prickles of unease to my sun-drugged brain: this month has brought only a trace of snow, and a few days of morning fog and rain. Today, a month past the autumnal equinox, the afternoon temperature is in the mid-seventies. Not only has this month's dry weather not added to the snow pack, the warm days have drawn down the balance. If this winter's precipitation is skimpy, we could be facing a drought next year. Next year's water supply, whether streamflow or ditchflow, comes from this winter's snowpack, melting slowly to tide us through the dry summer. Arapaho Glacier, from whence issues Boulder Creek and Boulder's drinking water, is wasting away, along with the rest of the mountain snowpack. (Although most of our annual precipitation falls in spring, it comes as wet snow and rain, tending to melt rather than augment the snowpack.)

Drought or just a dry spell? It is too early to tell. Here, west of the hundredth meridian, we live in arid country. Our fifteen-inch average annual precipitation is a fact of life, a literal boundary. We can allocate that annual precipitation to a certain extent—it can all go to irrigating lawns, flushing toilets, running washers and dishwashers if we wish, although that means none for the trout, the cottonwoods, the kingfishers, the farmers—but what we cannot do is change the weather to make more water, any more than we can control our orbit around the sun, nor should we try. The system that brings our precipitation is part of a complex web of interactions with other systems: the balance of gases in the atmosphere, the exhalations of the world's plant cover, the cycles of minerals and nutrients.... As part of the system, we cannot see it well enough to tinker with it. We can however, learn the boundaries and live within them, and direct our creative energies to being productive, rather than destructive, planetary citizens.

I sit in the lazy warmth of the afternoon sun, listening to the squirrels scold in the box elder tree across the yard, and squint at the cloudless azure blue sky, wondering if there will be enough snow this winter to provide next year's water.

November

Monday, 2 November ᴥ "I think I smell deer," I said quietly to Richard as we walked up the alley in the gathering darkness. Something rustled in the bushes on the other side of the irrigation ditch.

"Over there," said Richard, pointing at a large shape half-hidden in a clump of wild plum across the dry ditch "See it?"

We stopped under a box elder tree, but we had already disturbed it. I had a quick glimpse of sleek hindquarters as the deer slipped through the shrubs and disappeared into a dark Mapleton street backyard.

The concentration of deer on the west side of Boulder in winter is about sixty-five animals per square mile, double the average for deer habitat along the Front Range. That is a lot of deer. Oddly, the winter range in the lower foothills and mesas around Boulder is not considered good natural winter deer habitat—other areas on the Front Range, for instance, the area west of Colorado Springs, rate much better. Deer depend on certain deciduous shrub and tree species for their entire winter diet (deer are ungulates—the bacteria living in their multiple stomachs allow them to digest woody material). Several of these crucial browse species are missing entirely from the Boulder-area winter range. How then can twice the normal population flourish on less than the optimum habitat around Boulder? Urban landscaping, with such delicacies as rosebushes, apple and other fruit trees, aspen, not to mention succulent vegetable gardens. Boulder's toothsome urban landscaping and its geographic position in a stream valley combine to make it deer heaven.

By making Boulder a pretty place for humans to live we have inadvertently improved the habitat for deer, artificially raising the carrying capacity (the number of organisms a certain unit of habitat can support) by replacing the native vegetation with our yard plants. The increased carrying capacity doesn't come free. (There truly is no "free lunch" in our environment. Every change we make involves some kind of trade-off—usually more than one.) Because our landscaping plants are mostly imported from other geographic regions, places with more rain and/or more fertile soils, they require subsidies of scarce water and potentially polluting fertilizers. And the increased carrying capacity means increased deer-human conflicts. We kill deer on the dark roads at dusk, our dogs chase them (yes, sometimes they chase our dogs, but usually in self-defense. More often the aggressors are our pets, hunters still.); sometimes we shoot them in exasperation or out of fear.

Deer can distinguish and do prefer browse that is more nutritious—like shrubs that have been watered and fertilized all summer—over other browse of the same species. For instance, people who live near the open space and have Rocky Mountain juniper planted in their yards report that deer browse their juniper, but leave unwatered, unfertilized juniper in the adjacent open space untouched.

In addition, Boulder was built at the mouth of several canyons, smack in the way of wildlife transportation corridors. Deer and other animals migrate along the riparian areas from summer range in the mountains to less snowy winter range in the foothills and plains. This routes them right through Boulder, past acres of juicy yards.

For those who enjoy seeing deer in and around town, and don't mind donating some of their yard plants for deer food, this is good news. Others do not appreciate the deer. Various solutions have been proposed by those who see the deer as a problem, ranging from shooting the deer, to transplanting them, to fencing the west side of Boulder in order to keep them out. The trouble with these ideas is that they only treat the symptom—the deer..

The problem is our own landscaping. We have modified the natural habitat so that it can support artificially large populations; now we have the problem of how to keep those populations away from our gourmet yards. We can attempt to physically exclude the deer, attempt to modify their behavior, or change our plantings. Excluding the deer with fencing or netting is expensive and chancy. Fencing seems like a challenge for wildlife—like putting a lock on a cookie jar. Deer are fully capable of jumping six-foot fences if so motivated. Besides, fencing our yards smacks of zoos, but with a twist—the humans are inside the fence.

Behavior modification involves repelling the deer from preferred plants or areas—convincing them that they don't want our juicy plantings—not an easy task. Tactics from scaring away deer with noisemakers to hanging up bags of human hair have their adherents. However, the only method successfully tested under research conditions involves applying a preparation made from rotten eggs—available from commercial forestry suppliers and the county humane society, among other places—to the branch tips of plants and tying bright-colored surveyor's flagging near the repellent. Because the repellent is true to its name, deer avoid plants so anointed. At first both repellent and flagging are used, then after a year or two, just flagging. Deer and other wildlife apparently associate the bright-colored flagging with the presence of the foul-tasting repellent and avoid plants with flagging, whether or not they are actually sprayed with repellent.

The most effective long-term solution is to remove the plants that deer come to eat. This may not seem like a viable option for those with yards full of mature and highly edible landscaping. But for those just planning their landscaping or with just a few problem spots, landscaping can be designed to minimize conflicts but still attract butterflies and hummingbirds, for instance. A simple rule of thumb: Plant native species, and water and fertilize sparingly. Any plants that aren't lush and heavily fertilized are less likely to attract wildlife in unusual and undesirable numbers. Yards planted with natives and other drought-resistant plants offer the additional benefits of needing much less water, requiring less fertilizer, and generally being easier to care for. If we must plant things that deer really love, each plant should be fenced until it grows past browse height. A full-grown deer can reach pretty high, especially when standing on its hind legs to nibble on a choice bit.

Boulder is not the only urban area supporting a large population of wildlife: for instance, deer and black bear populations are high in northern New Jersey and other eastern urban areas, and coyotes have moved into the Los Angeles area and many other western desert cities from surrounding habitat. But Boulder residents' generally tolerant attitude may be unique. According to a recent city survey, the majority of Boulder residents do not consider deer grazing their yards enough of a "problem" to warrant drastic measures—two-thirds support the current "monitor the population, watch for trouble spots" approach.

Urban wildlife populations raise interesting questions for urban dwellers and local governments: If by building homes, roads, and towns, we humans displace other species from habitat necessary for their survival, is it ethical and responsible to just shrug and figure that is the price for "progress," or do we attempt to somehow replace that habitat, perhaps somewhere else? When urban areas provide desirable habitat for wildlife populations, do we regard these other species as a nuisance to be removed? Or do we attempt to find a balance and share the resource with them? Our answers depend in part on how we view ourselves—whether we see ourselves as top dogs, the most important beings on this planet; or whether we consider ourselves part of a intricate and complex natural system whose other parts have an equal right to the resources.

Thursday, 5 November ⅏ Tonight's full moon was an

owl moon. When we walked outside at about half past five in the evening twilight after Molly's fall teacher conference at

58

Niwot School, the moon was rising over the hill to the east of the school. We crossed the dark parking lot and stood for a minute watching the huge, pale disk slide into view in the velvety dark sky. As it cleared the houses and cottonwood trees on the hilltop, Richard spotted a large, dark shape hunched atop a telephone pole right across the field. A great horned owl. What a lovely sight! Richard hooted, imitating a great horned's call, and the bird quickly swung its head around and watched us. Its big yellow eyes glittered like twin moons set in the circular feather pattern of its facial disks. After Richard hooted again, it slowly gathered itself up, extended its long pale wings, and flew away silently into the darkness.

Owls are among my favorite birds, partly because they are somewhat mysterious and are seldom seen—they usually hunt at night, flying silently with flight feathers specially adapted to reduce the noise of passing air, and roosting by day. Great horned owls are one of the largest and most imposing owls in North America, sitting about two feet tall, with three- to five-foot wingspans. Front Range great horneds weigh between 2.5 and 3.5 pounds, not very heavy for a bird with a four- to five-foot wingspan. Like all owls, great horned owls have proportionately large heads, which make them appear hunched or stocky when sitting. Their eyes are also large, located in the front of the head like human eyes (most birds' eyes are on the sides of their heads), and have a large proportion of light-gathering rods to help them see in the dusk or dark. Their ears too, are specially adapted to help them locate prey better at night. Larger than normal ear openings and asymmetrical placement in the head (one higher than the other) as well as asymmetrical structure help the bird distinguish which ear the sound is coming to, and therefore help it triangulate the location of its prey. Owls can also swivel their heads nearly all of the way around on their necks to look behind them. It is distinctly eerie to look at the back of an owl, only to have the head swivel to face you without the body moving.

Great horned owls are adaptable owls, found all across North America from forests to urban areas. So it was not surprising to see this one hunkered down on a hunting perch between a school yard and a subdivision surrounded still by farmland. They often hunt over open areas, perching or flying along silently, listening for prey. (One dark night I was buzzed by a great horned owl in a dense Douglas fir forest as it hunted the pitch-black airspace over the trail I was hiking. It flew so low over my head that I felt the rush of air moved by its large wings, but never heard a sound. After I recovered my breath, I saw it silhouetted dimly against the starlit sky as it flew on.) The phone pole used by the owl in Niwot overlooked a stretch of mowed ground between the school parking lot and the close cropped subdivision lawns—a good nighttime vantage point for spotting mice, shrews, ground squirrels, rabbits, or skunks (or the neighbors' cats) hunting the urban/farmland edge.

Numerous cultures believe that owls foretell death or some kind of disaster. Country wisdom says that owls hooting in the daytime mean bad luck. Many Native American traditions equate an owl's hoot with an impending death, or see owls as a form taken on by dead people's spirits. However, owls are also thought of as wise birds (for example, "Owl" of the Hundred-Acre Wood in Winnie-the-Pooh), perhaps harking back to Greek mythology, which associates Athene, the goddess of war and wisdom, with owls.

Tuesday, 10 November ➤ It is still Indian summer— warm, dry, sunny days and chill nights. We leave our bedroom windows open at night, drawing in smells with the cool breeze: the winey perfume of fermenting apples, the dusty tang of drying leaves, the musky odor of raccoons. Night noises pour in as well: first the sound of cars accelerating up the hill and the occasional faraway wailing siren; then, the woods noises, the trees creaking in the night breeze, the last few leaves rustling on the Virginia creeper vine. Finally all is quiet enough that we become aware of faint squeaking and rustling as small rodents forage in the dry leaves, the high-pitched squealing of bats hawking in the air, the crack of dry twigs snapping under hoof as deer pass by.

Last night I woke to the oddest cooing and moaning noises right outside the window. I sat up, moved over to the window and peered through the screen into the near-blackness. I couldn't see anything. Richard woke also, sat up and shined the flashlight out the window, illuminating the dark tangle of wild plum, chokecherry, box elder, and neglected apple trees. The bright light showed a cluster of pale grey raccoons, five of them, two bigger and three smaller. They froze for a moment, startled by the sudden spotlight, and then continued foraging, rooting like pigs in the apple and plum drops. We watched as they snuffled and shuffled about, squeaking and cooing and moaning at each other, a constant dialog of queer noises, distinctly wild.

Our iron cross begonia is beginning to recover, two months after it lost most of its leaves on a frosty night at 7,000 feet above sea level in Laramie during our move. Now, eight weeks after the move, its thick, red-hairy stalks sprout a forest of bright silver and green leaves, splashed with dull red stain where each stem joins a large, ragged leaf blade. Soon it will look like the bushy, healthy plant it was when we left its humid home in Washington State.

We too are recovering from the move. No matter how eagerly desired, moving is wrenching as we sever roots in one place and grow new ones somewhere else. Our apartment now feels like home, two months after we emptied the contents of our rented truck and Volvo station wagon into its bare rooms. Our favorite prints, paintings, and stained glass all hang on walls and catch light in windows; the Persian rugs my great-grandparents brought back from their travels to the Middle-East and Asia brighten the floors; the small found and inherited objects that I stubbornly insist on bringing along on our moves have all found places on windowsills, shelves, tables, and even the top of the hard drive next to my computer. These things say that this is our home, no one else's.

And we have settled into daily routines. Each morning just after rising, I walk to the paper machine at the corner of Ninth and Maxwell, as much to be outside and see what the day is like as to buy the paper. When Richard leaves for his office, I walk him over the hill towards the pocket park. Always that walk gives me something to think about—a new bird seen, the sound of the wind pouring off of the slope of the Front Range, the look of winter in the frost on the sandstone slabs of the sidewalk, the smell of leaves decaying. I walk, absorbed in seeing, smelling, listening, thinking. Then I come home to the quiet apartment and write. By midafternoon I am restless, lonely for the sound of other's voices. I walk downtown to collect my mail at the post office and often have a cup of tea at one of the cafes on the pedestrian mall before returning home. I follow a regular route, not the most direct, but one with plenty of wild pockets and variety. It takes me downtown by quiet side streets and alleys, past old houses with interesting gardens, and through an untamed tunnel of shrubs and trees along a bit of dry irrigation ditch that will burble pleasantly come spring.

On weekends, Richard and I regularly walk right out of town, up Mapleton Avenue past the hospital into the spacious wildness of the city-owned parklands that keep Boulder from sprawling over the foothills. We either climb the dinosaur-spine ridge of Mount Sanitas or wander the gentler trail up the grasslands of the shaley valley sandwiched between Mount Sanitas and the Dakota hogback that edges the plains to the east. Both hikes have become part of our neighborhood, familiar enough that we've begun to notice the changes from month to month, the passing of time and seasons. Settling in.

Friday, 13 November ❧ Yesterday afternoon was made spectacular by the clouds. Late in the afternoon, velvety bands of clouds appeared over the Front Range, forming over the mountains and floating downstream (east) on the winds as they grew and changed. They began as low, fluffy, cumulus-type clouds hugging the peaks, but as they drifted over the plains, they soared higher and merged into a long grey band that hovered above the valley that parallels the swell of the Front Range. High winds aloft shaped the band into a smooth ribbon of altocumulus lenticularis (*alto* = "high", *cumulus* = "heap"; *lenticularis* = "lens shaped"). Its windward edge was unusually smooth, satiny as a fine wood sculpture, forming an aerodynamic, undulating margin. Small, sleek, flattened ellipse-shaped clouds clung to its underside like spaceships or baby whales nursing. One cloud stretched forty or fifty miles north to south, but only four or five miles east to west above Boulder and the edge of the Front Range, probably extending as far south as Colorado Springs, though I don't know because I couldn't see that far. Another smooth grey ribbon paralleled the first, but farther east over the plains, also reaching from Fort Collins to south past Denver.

Such long, narrow, sinuous clouds are "föhn walls": long lines of lenticular clouds parallel to a mountain front and associated with the chinook winds (called föhn in Germany, hence the name). They actually do hover in place, at the crest of a "mountain wave," the standing wave of air created when the westerlies come pouring down the east slope of the Front Range like water pouring over a rock in a river. Föhn walls form when air rushing down the slope of the Front Range hits the first standing wave of air and rises to the invisible crest. As it rises, the air cools slightly and its moisture condenses, yielding clouds that perch just downstream of the crest of the wave. The river of wind rushing past sculpts the clouds into sinuous curves. This afternoon, the parallel ribbons of lenticular clouds were somberly beautiful, their velvety surfaces deep grey in the middle, shading to creamy white at their curving windward sides.

But with the sunset, they changed personality, trading sober grey and white for tropical splendor. As the sun dropped into the slot of clear sky between the westerly föhn wall and the high peaks, the slanting rays flared out across the clouds. I looked out the kitchen window at about five o'clock and was startled to see the world aflame—the grass in the front yard, the wall of the condominium next door, the cars, the pavement of the street, the magpies flying past—all glowed with brilliant orange light, as if lit by a forest fire. I rushed outside and was also bathed in the orange glow. Overhead, the föhn wall, a flaming ribbon, reflected the slanting rays of the sun, bathing the earth in eerie light. The vivid color brought the cloud so low that it seemed as if I could reach up and touch it. As the rim of the earth rotated slowly across the sun, waves of gold, orange, scarlet, and magenta washed across the cloud from west to east like a technicolor version of the northern lights. After many minutes, the earth masked the sun completely, extinguishing the brilliant hues. The cloud ribbon faded in the twilight to rose pink and dusty violet. A faint wash of bruised purple remained into the evening, like a funeral bunting lining the long undulating western edge of the great cloud.

Later that evening, we walked out to look at the night sky. The night resounded with roaring wind. Thick, low clouds rushed by in front of the silvery quarter moon, reflecting just a fraction of its light. The slanting rock slabs of the Flatirons glimmered across the valley in the darkness, faintly silvery, the quartz crystals in the sand grains reflecting the moonlight like millions of tiny mirrors.

The days are rapidly getting shorter—rushing towards winter. Today is the last day with ten hours between sunrise and sunset: the sun rose at about 6:40 this morning, it sets at about 4:40 this afternoon. The shortest days of the year, just barely nine hours long, come in December at the winter solstice, not much more than a month away.

We rise before dawn these days and watch the fiery ball of the sun break over the flat rim of the Great Plains. It sets behind Flagstaff Mountain in the late afternoon, long before we are ready to end our own days.

Thursday, 19 November ❧ Yesterday evening at dusk I walked over Mapleton Hill and up Pearl Street to meet Richard at his office. The air was absolutely still and felt warm. Soft clumps of snowflakes trickled steadily from the barely visible clouds. Both snow and clouds shimmered orange in the darkness, lit by the sodium vapor streetlights. The foothills loomed ghostly above the silent street, muffled in the pale clouds. I walked slowly, wrapped in a glowing orange dream cloud of foggy breath, wet, clumpy snow, and gathering darkness.

Later, the air temperature dropped, the snow ceased, and the muffling cloud blanket rose. I walked home in wintry darkness—tingly cold, crisp air and crunchy snow. Pale light reflecting from the clouds illuminated the snowy foothills; stars shone like brilliant diamond chips through cracks in the fluffy blanket. I drew in huge lungfuls of the cold air as I walked uphill, and slowly expelled clouds of frosty breath, trying unsuccessfully to blow frost rings. I scuffed through the snow in my new insulated boots, listening to the sound of the snow the way a child tests out the splash of each puddle.

Wednesday, 25 November ❧ This morning, the ground was dusted with big snowflakes, lacy crystals of frozen dew. The ephemeral powder will melt once the sun touches it; for now it lays in a light tracery on every surface, a pale mantilla covering the morning world. Funny stuff, snow.

The day dawned clear, with a few neon–pink crayon lines

of north-south trending clouds striping the mostly blue sky. But by midmorning, thin altostratus (*alto* = "high", *stratus* = "blanket") clouds had poured across the sky out of the canyons like pale grey crepe batter. Now the sun shines only dimly, a polished silver disk veiled by the clouds. Its warmth is gone.

Thursday, 26 *November* ✣ Today we had a traditional Thanksgiving: we fixed turkey with stuffing, yams, paté, home-baked bread, pumpkin pie; the weather produced a snowstorm. It began snowing last night, beautiful silent snowflakes falling gracefully from low clouds. The big flakes swirled and twirled as they drifted down, landing soft as light bird feet. Soon the lawn, the bare branches of the shrubs, the street, the gravel parking lot, the trees, the cars, the roofs, all disappeared under a thick, untracked white blanket.

Before breakfast, I went outside to sample the snow. It was light and fluffy, a little clumpy. I scooped up a handful and brought it inside to look at it under my magnifying glass before it melted. It must have formed in cold air (somewhere between 0°F and 20°F) since it was composed of classic six-pointed snowflakes, a bewildering array of infinitely detailed, symmetrical crystalline stars. Edges scalloped, toothed, or doubly serrate, the points themselves sometimes edged with tiny crystalline points, and so on, finer than the most delicately woven Belgian lace. Each tiny star revealed a new, exquisitely complicated geometry. As I examined them, the warm inside air erased their detail. One by one the tiny stars blurred and melted into smooth droplets of water.

After breakfast we went to work producing our Thanksgiving dinner. Richard and Molly mixed the bread dough. I stuffed the turkey, chopped the ingredients for paté, prepared the yams. Soon the apartment was cozily warm from all of our cooking, like a cocoon with steamy windows.

Snow continued to fall quietly outside, inviting exploration. While the turkey was baking and the bread rising, the three of us put on our hats, coats, mittens, and boots and went out for a walk in the new snow. The air outside was perfectly still, cold enough to feel good on faces flushed from the heat. The streets were quiet, stilled by falling snow. We seemed the only life in the hushed world.

Up Maxwell Avenue we walked, shuffling gleefully through six inches of new powder. Smoke plumes rising straight up from brick chimneys in the houses we passed were the only signs of life. Inside the quiet houses we imagined turkeys being stuffed, hams baking, people bustling about preparing their Thanksgiving dinners. But outside all was still. A lone crow flew overhead, a silent and dull black silhouette against pale grey clouds. Thickly falling snow soon furred our bulky outer clothes, metamorphosing us into snow people, trolls caught in transition from human forms to rocks. On the warm pavement the snow turned slushy, prompting Molly to test its clumping index. It packed well, compressing into dense coherent balls—perfect snowball snow. Our leisurely walk soon degenerated into a giggling, running game of dodge-the-snowballs. We arrived home breathless and coated with snow: snow on our backs, snow on our heads, snow clinging to our boots. Snowflakes still swirled out of the clouds around us. Inside we went, to warm, steamy air fragrant with rising bread and baking turkey.

Friday, 27 *November* ✒ This morning dawned sunny and very cold. The world glittered in the brilliant sunshine reflecting from quadrillions of fresh crystalline surfaces. Our Volvo station wagon was a giant white mound in the driveway, muffled with the fluffy stuff. When I walked downtown, I was dazzled by the brightness of the light. The tilted henna-colored slabs of Flatirons were edged with snow, all of the trees on the mountains bending under loads of snow, the sky scrubbed clear blue by yesterday's storm.

The urban forest on Mapleton Hill is much quieter at this

time of year—some wild inhabitants have left for the winter, others spend much of the cold weather in dens or nests. The last migrating birds flew south earlier this month, and the groups of winter finches and crossbills have not yet appeared in great crowds. Some mammals, like bats, squirrels, and muskrats, are hibernating, their metabolism slowed to a near-stall until spring arrives. Others, like skunks, raccoons, shrews, and mice, reduce their activity, retreating to sheltered spots when the weather is inclement and reemerging to hunt and forage on warmer, sunny days or warmer nights. Since the first big snowstorm this month, I haven't seen or heard the raccoons, or smelled the skunks behind our apartment.

Sunday, 29 *November* ❧ Today I flew back to western Washington for a business trip. I'm back in the damp, grey air and fog-shrouded landscape of a Puget Sound winter. I feel like I've journeyed back in time.

I rose in Boulder's predawn darkness. But by the time Richard and I sat sleepily in the kitchen and drank orange juice, the sky was a pale dome, lined with a growing flush of rosy light.

When we stepped outside, our first breath of searingly cold air jolted us awake. The thermometer read 16° F. We walked downtown hand-in-hand in the early morning stillness, our breath rising in clouds of diamond chips above our heads. Underfoot, the sandstone sidewalk flags were slick with black ice, edged with crunchy snow. The Flatirons blushed pink, lit by the rising sun, above them the crisp white snowy ridge of Green Mountain rose to meet the pale robin's-egg blue sky.

From Denver, the entire Front Range was visible, each round-shouldered ridge and spiky peak etched against the sky. Rarely is the air this clear in the winter now that the Denver metropolitan area has grown so large. In the cold months, the basin along the Front Range traps a layer of cold air next to the ground, like a lid of glass. In this layer of still air are caught our effluvia: auto exhaust, woodstove smoke, and industrial emissions, forming a persistent blue or brown smudge that clouds the view. Most winter days the peaks of the Front Range are no more than faint shadows in the haze from downtown Denver.

At the airport I walked quickly across the quiet parking lot, swinging my bags to stretch myself before boarding the plane and sitting again. I breathed in great lungsful of the cold, dry air, vividly aware that the next outdoor air I would breathe would be the soft, damp ocean-tinged air of Puget Sound. In front of the terminal doors, I turned for one last look at the spare white peaks of the range, one last breath of sharp, cold air. I turned back, picked up my bags, and went through the automatic doors to the terminal, sucked in on a great rush of warm, stale air.

Despite our two good snowstorms this month, we ended November with lower-than-average snowpacks in the mountains. Oddly enough, most of Colorado received average or above-average amounts of precipitation, but because of warm weather, much of that precipitation fell as rain, not snow.

December

Saturday, 5 *December* ❧ The moon was full and round and silvery last night—the hunter's moon, the last full moon of fall. Low clouds, like puffs of smoke, drifted across the lower quadrant of the sky, collecting and thickening until there were more clouds than dark night sky. The moon, a shining polished disk, danced in and out of the shifting openings as it rose.

The days are warm still, echoes of Indian summer. Yesterday's high was 60° F, but it felt even warmer in the sun. Temperatures in the mid-sixties in December lure us into donning summer clothes, just because it is December; if it were July, we'd be wearing jackets. When I went running, I wore only a tee shirt and shorts.

I ran uphill on Maxwell Avenue five blocks to Fourth Street and turned north along the undulating line of Fourth where it follows the lower edge of the foothills' sharp upsweep. For a few blocks, Fourth defines the uphill edge of town, but soon a row of houses appears above, perched on level pads carved out of the steep slope—Third Street. I turned uphill towards it on a short, straight block that spans the gap between two contour lines on my topographic map of Boulder County, an elevation gain of nearly fifty feet in about a hundred yards. I ran slowly, struggling to breathe as my legs hauled my body up half a foot for each stride forward. Once up on the relatively level dirt surface of Third Street, I forgot about my lungs and legs, absorbed in the exhilarating view.

Between houses on the downhill side of the street, the landscape dropped abruptly and rolled east to the hazy, smudged horizon. Immediately below lay north Boulder. Farther east, past the abrupt edge of town, the green lawns and planted trees gave way to pale sienna grasslands, rich umber plowed fields, and scattered strings of skeletal cottonwood trunks lining ditches and creeks. East of town, Valmont Reservoir shimmered in the sunlight like a ruffled blue pancake, the tall stack of its power plant interrupting the level line of both reservoir and plains. I traced the winding course of Boulder Creek. First the creek wanders east across the plains, confined by the bulge of Gunbarrel Hill; past that high ground, it turns north towards its eventual confluence with the South Platte River. Farther east still, the plains faded into a hazy brown line, a smudge of urban exhaust that foreshortened the horizon.

Monday, 7 December ❧ The chinooks began blowing sometime in the night. I woke at about five o'clock, troubled by a vague uneasiness, knowing that something was different. The air felt warmer than usual, odd. I became conscious of a distant roaring, like some great wave approaching, a tsunami wall of water. In the few seconds that elapsed as it roared closer, I remembered sleepily that it couldn't be a tsunami. The only ocean to lap this shore is millions of years gone. The roar approached quickly, accompanied by increasingly loud rattling, banging, and crashing sounds as it shook or swayed or broke things in its path. In just a few seconds it rushed by, the intense noise fading. It was the wind—a wave of air, not water. The moon shone brightly when I looked out the window. I could see the trees swaying, dancing in the swirling eddies of air from the great wave's passage.

I could already hear the next gust coming down the slope from the Front Range. I sat up and looked out the window into the pale night. The gust roared through the trees like a train, closer and closer and closer until it poured around the apartment building, tossing grit against the windows, rattling the bare fingers of the wild plum and apple tree branches that touch the back window, clanging the wind chime, whipping the dry leaves from the yard along with great clouds of urban debris—loose sheets of yellowed newspaper, plastic bags, styrofoam cups, and even plastic plant pots. After each gust passed, the night was still for between ten and thirty seconds, until another wave roared downslope. The rhythm was quite regular, like storm waves crashing up on a beach. Only their velocity varied: according to the National Weather Service, some roared along at eighty to ninety miles per hour, others were mere thirty-mile-per-hour gusts. The big ones tore through the trees, sending branches wildly screeching over the rough brick walls like fingernails on a chalkboard, slamming into the apartment wall with enough force to leave it shaking ever so slightly. I stayed awake for a while, listening, then fell back into an exhausted sleep, my dreams pounded by huge waves.

Alm... bohorok... chinook... föhn... halne... i tien tien... fung... kubang... mistral... puelche... reshabar... Santa Ana... ta ke kata... wisper... zonda. Chinooks are just one of the many downslope mountain winds known all over the world. In the Rockies, we call them chinooks; in the Pyrenees of Spain they are the tramontana; in the German and Swiss Alps, the föhn; in the Caucasus of Kurdistan, the reshabar; in southern California, the Santa Ana.

Downslope winds occur when a high pressure area develops over one side of a mountain range, with a low pressure stalled on the other. The low-pressure area sucks the air over the range from the high-pressure area. As the air rises over the highest parts of the range, it loses much of its moisture. Then as it tumbles down the slopes and canyons, increasing pressure and temperature push it faster and faster and faster until it finally blasts howling out over the plains, a hot and dry chinook. Boulder, built at the mouth of two steeply falling, narrow canyons in the Front Range, is right in the floodway of this torrent of air. The Native Americans who inhabited the plains and foothills carefully avoided placing their seasonal camps at the mouth of Front Range canyons. They understood both floods of wind (chinooks) and of water. But the European immigrants who settled Boulder paid no attention to the local conditions or to indigenous wisdom when they sited the town. As a result, Boulder has suffered periodic damage from chinooks and stream floods ever since it was settled.

Most recently, in January 1982, a chinook toppled power lines, crushed cars, and blew away roofs, resulting in $17 million in insurance claims.

Chinooks are named for the Chinook tribe of the Pacific Northwest, who called these winds "snow-eaters," with good reason. By sweeping away the stable layers of cold air in its path, a chinook can raise the temperature tens of degrees in an hour, or even minutes. In Rapid City, South Dakota, a chinook whipped out of the Black Hills on January 22, 1943, heating the air from -6° to 44° F in two minutes. A snow-eater, indeed.

Partly because of the chinooks, Boulder is often much warmer than Denver, which, although only thirty-five miles away, is too far from the mountains to be affected by chinooks. Denver usually remains cold, mantled by stable layers of plains air. For instance, the high in Boulder today was 58° F; Denver's high was a more wintery 38° F, 20 degrees lower. Further, Boulder's high temperature occurred in the early morning (at 6:30 a.m!), brought by the chinooks—the opposite of the usual daily temperature pattern where the coldest temperatures occur in the early morning hours. As soon as the chinooks ceased, just after dawn, the air temperature dropped.

The prickle of unease that woke me to hear this morning's waves of wind had a physiological basis. Human adrenal glands kick in when winds rise above a moderate breeze (nineteen miles per hour or more), producing a "fight or flight" alarm reaction. Our metabolic rate increases, the blood vessels of our heart and muscles dilate while those of our skin contract, our pupils widen. Even our hair raises, producing prickles of apprehension. Maintaining this state of alarm for hours or days of constant wind places intense stress on our systems.

This, plus the peculiar electric nature of chinooks and other downslope winds, gives them their reputation as "ill winds." Whenever these winds blow, the result is higher rates of mental and physical illness—psychic disturbances, suicides, heart attacks and other coronary illnesses, hemorrhages, ulcer perforations, migraines; as well as higher rates of industrial and traffic accidents; and of crime. When the föhn of the Swiss and Bavarian Alps blows, hospitals defer major surgeries until after the föhn passes. Local lore blames the Rhone Valley's mistral for the bout of depression that caused painter Vincent Van Gogh to cut off one ear. Murder rates in Los Angeles may rise by fifty percent during a sustained Santa Ana.

The winds were still gusting hard when Richard and I walked over Mapleton Hill in the grey predawn light. The gusts were so strong that a few times I was whirled about and found myself walking backwards. The eddies dancing in the wind's wake swirled leaves and trash and dust high into the air, flung my scarf away, blew my hair about, and threw dust into my eyes, making me squint. Still, once I grew accustomed to the feel of it, I found the rhythmic waves of warm air exhilarating.

We stopped at the top of the hill to watch the sun rise, an orange ball above the flat horizon of the plains, then turned (wind gusts increasing the velocity of our spins) to see the slightly-less-than-full moon hanging ghostly white in the blue sky above the ridgeline of the Front Range.

Since Richard has just finished the first third of his dissertation, we treated ourselves to breakfast at a Creole restaurant in a gracefully restored old house. We feasted. Richard ordered eggs with hollandaise sauce and red beans and potatoes and a biscuit, and coffee with chicory. Never a breakfast-eater, I had real tea (in a teapot) and warm beignets, the French squares of dough fried to a crisp puff and dusted with powdered sugar. We lingered over our breakfast on the sunny enclosed porch, reading the morning paper and watching the elms across the street sway in the wind.

77

Walking home, we waded slowly uphill against the rushing wind. A wall of fluffy cumulus seeming surreally still from our gust-buffeted vantage point dammed the head of Sunshine Canyon, like a plug of marshmallow creme. The rising sun tinted the billowy mass pale pink, lending the crowning touch of absurdity.

Thursday, 10 December ✒ Last night the chinooks blew again, but this morning I was surprised to wake to calm, silent air—no wind at all. The quiet at first felt eerie, until my body became accustomed to the absence of wind. The high winds continue aloft though; overhead hung a dark föhn wall, paralleling the mountain front north and south as far as I could see. West of town, fluffy clouds bellied down over the mountains, looking full of moisture. Perhaps they are dropping snow.

By midmorning, the air outside felt as warm as spring.

Friday, 11 December ✒ Last night Richard and I walked over to the university campus to attend a concert in the lovingly restored Victorian theater in Old Main. The three musicians played a wonderful assortment of instruments—four kinds of recorders, a fifteenth-century fiddle, a lute, a guitar, and of course, their voices—to produce a variety of pieces, from medieval carols to modern. The simple music resonated, clear and true, in the intimate theater. Food for mind and spirit.

We walked home quietly, thoughtful, in a light rain of large, widely scattered drops. Dense clouds hung low in the night sky over Flagstaff Mountain and the Flatirons.

As we crossed Pearl and Tenth streets, some lucky impulse drew my attention skyward. I exclaimed and pointed; Richard looked up just in time to see a large, pale, winged shape drift westward above the big cottonwood trees. A great horned owl, hunting right at the edge of downtown Boulder! The ghostly-looking bird flew silently, barely flapping its immense wings, into the darkness over the residential neighborhoods across Ninth Street. I could see its underside quite clearly as it passed overhead, illuminated by the reflected light from the crowded cafes and shops. It had long, wide wings; pale plumage barred with fine, dark horizontal lines; a blunt head with two feathery tufts; and yellow eyes set in a barred facial disc. Its passage was startlingly incongruous. I wonder how many of the people thronging the sidewalk in front of the cafes and bars looked up to see the owl with the four-foot wingspan drift by, its pale shape momentarily silhouetted against the darker clouds, hunting silently?

Three species of owls live in Boulder's urban forest: great horned, barn, and little eastern screech-owls. Boulder's older neighborhoods offer plenty of big trees with rotted cores to provide nest holes and roosting places for owls, and abundant prey—from skunks and cats to mice and moths—to feed big and small owls.

This morning, hard white grains of sleet sprinkled the cars and grass, solid water instead of the liquid that fell as we walked home last night. The dawn sky was clear, intensely blue. We are on the cusp between fall and winter—balanced on that horn between the two seasons, not really part of either one.

Tuesday, 15 December ⁓ As Richard and I walked along Broadway this afternoon, dozens of starlings whistled and screeched from perches in the old silver maples overhead.

The European starling's name means "little stars," a reference to the sparkling dots covering their dark breeding plumage. They are bluebird-sized birds, with short stubby tails and plump bodies (they look something like cigars in flight). Males, like those we saw strutting their stuff this afternoon (breeding season for starlings lasts almost all year) stretch and clatter their beaks and whistle and squeak like squealing gears in need of oil—their breeding song, best described as chaotic. Starlings come from a family of good imitators, including their close relatives, the mynahs. Listening to a tree full of starlings I picked out a few fragments imitated from other bird songs, now a snatch of house finch whistling, now a piece of blue jay alarm call, but most of their musical talent seems to be used to produce the clatter and squeal of metal on metal. Not a pretty sound to my ears, but then I'm not a female starling.

Starlings, not native to North America, have successfully colonized the continent (south of the boreal forest) since 60 individuals were released in New York's Central Park in 1890 by a group dedicated to establishing in the United States all of the birds mentioned by William Shakespeare. A hundred years after their introduction, upwards of 200 million starlings flood the continent from coast to coast.

Starlings can raise two to three broods a year—some that we watched this afternoon were copulating, getting an early start on next year's nesting season. And they are gregarious, roosting and nesting communally—their winter roosts sometimes number in the tens of thousands. Their aggressive, opportunistic behavior and communal habits tend to push out all competitors (except for another "successful" introduced species, the English house sparrow), greatly changing community dynamics wherever they colonize. For example, both urban starlings and the species they compete with and have often displaced—such as bluebirds, woodpeckers, flickers, and flycatchers—eat mostly insects. Starlings forage on the ground, probing clumps of grass for grubs and other ground-dwelling insects with their specially hinged bills, whereas the insect-eating species that starlings compete with eat flying insects like mosquitoes and gnats, as well as ants and tree-boring insects, many of which we attempt to eradicate, since we consider them "pests." Ironically, we who could benefit from the effective biological control that these birds provide have hastened their decline. While starling populations were exploding across the country, we began spraying pesticides in an effort to control mosquito and gnat populations in urban areas. Pesticide spraying affected the insect populations only temporarily—their short life cycle and the abundant available habitat allowed populations to rebuild each year—but it nearly wiped out bluebird and other insect-eating bird populations by lowering their food supplies in the crucial nesting season.

Another irony: European starlings were expected to devour thousands of crop pests; instead, huge flocks concentrate around stockyards and farms, devouring grain and damaging crops. These raucous birds also roost in huge flocks in winter in urban areas. A Denver yard was recently plagued by tens of thousands of starlings. The nightly roost fouled the place and any nearby cars with odorous droppings, literally repulsing visitors to the home. The roosting flocks were finally dispersed (undoubtedly to plague some other yard!) by taped starling distress calls played in the evening as they flew in to roost.

Unfortunately, starlings cannot simply be wished away. Boulder is home to tens of thousands of European starlings—a veritable population boom. These are by far the most common birds I see in my walks around town. The very trees that we are so proud of, the legions of big silver maples that give Mapleton Hill its name and provide shade for so much of Boulder, are part of the reason for Boulder's large population of starlings. Why? Limbs break off in Boulder's windstorms, fungi invade and rot the tree's relatively soft core, and, voilà, you have the perfect nest site for communal cavity nesting birds. If we set out to design the optimal starling habitat, it would be difficult to improve on the easily accessible and numerous cavities of the silver maples, adjacent to one of the starlings' favorite foraging grounds—lawns. We have unwittingly created a starling paradise.

This kind of single-species domination of an area poses questions about our urban ecosystems. Should we be concerned about diversity in our towns and cities? Yes. Diversity is important in urban ecosystems too. Loss of diversity equals fewer options and therefore less flexibility in responding to crises, a maxim nicely illustrated by the effect of Dutch elm disease on Front Range communities. Within two decades after the disease reached Colorado, tens of thousands of magnificent elm trees were dead. Whole neighborhoods, once shady, were denuded.

Thursday, 17 December ❧ I'm cold. It is cloudy

today—the sun isn't warming up the house. Without the sun, the front room loses more heat through the big single-pane windows than the furnace can generate.

This morning I was seized with nostalgia for the smell of evergreens. The winter holiday season is inexorably linked for me with the aroma of evergreen boughs: the pungent smell of western red cedars drooping low around our house in Washington State, the spicy fragrance of Rocky Mountain juniper drying in the sun around the ranger station on the South Fork of the Shoshone River in Wyoming, the sappy odor of the clump of Douglas firs outside my bedroom window in Laramie. In Washington at this time of year, I would take an afternoon off and don rubber boots and gloves, pick up my pruning and lopping shears from the woodshed, and ramble in our woods, selecting an armload of cedar boughs here, hemlock there, and grand fir and Douglas fir boughs, too. A couple of holly trees growing next to the cellar-hole of a long-abandoned farmhouse provided shiny leaves and bright red berries. I'd come home with my arms piled high with wet branches, spread my fragrant burden out on newspapers on the dining room floor, and go to work with wire and clippers, making wreaths and swags until my hands were sticky and black with spicy sap. Some wreaths were packed carefully into boxes to be shipped to family and friends, but we always kept enough to fill the house with their resinous aroma. Here in Boulder, I have no coniferous woods to forage in, and I'm sure that my neighbors would not appreciate me thinning the branches on their carefully nurtured evergreens.

Still, I wanted to make wreaths, and fill the house with greens. I tried to work, but couldn't concentrate. Finally, I turned off the computer and drove to a nursery to look for evergreen boughs.

Inside the door of the nursery greenhouse, the air was warm and pungent with evergreen resin. I found a treasure trove of boughs that smelled of our Washington woods on a dark, rainy winter afternoon: Douglas fir, grand fir, western red cedar. There were boxes of boughs, too, from the Rockies: Rocky Mountain juniper, ponderosa pine, lodgepole pine. I spent a long time looking and smelling, and finally decided to buy mostly pine and juniper, with a scattering of cedar and fir in memory of our Washington woods. I filled my arms with as many boughs as I could afford, and drove happily home with my treasures. The remainder of the afternoon passed quickly. I contentedly clipped and wired, bent and trimmed, shaping wreaths and garlands. Soon they filled the house with their fragrance, the air redolent of sunny ponderosa pine savannas, dry juniper/sagebrush grasslands, wet cedar woods... of winter and holidays.

Tuesday, 22 *December* ❧ Winter begins today, not necessarily the winter of meteorology, but the winter of astronomy. Early this morning was the winter solstice, in Latin literally "sun stands still." The rising sun reached the farthest south point on the horizon in its yearly journey (*apparent* journey, that is). As the earth tilts the other way, the sun's rising and setting positions move north on the horizon until the summer solstice, when the earth tilts back, sending the sun south again. If I could mark the sun's setting position on the ridge of Flagstaff Mountain each evening, the marks would creep farther and farther north with the passing days, until finally, at the summer solstice, the tick marks would have marched across Boulder and Sunshine canyons and the sun would be setting somewhere north of the long ridge of Mount Sanitas. Around the solstice, the sun's position on the horizon changes very slowly; near the equinoxes, it appears to move quickly, each day rising and setting the length of its diameter away from the previous day's mark.

The solstices are the year's hinges, the turning points of summer and winter. Today marks both the beginning of winter and the time when the long nights loose their grip. Many cultures, including our own, hold major celebrations near the solstice. Both Christmas and Chanukah, in their traditional meaning, are essentially celebrations of life and light; so too, the solstice, bringer of spring.

Just before dawn this solstice morning, vivid pink and violet cirrus clouds banded the eastern sky. The brilliant clouds tinted the earth pink, coloring windows, light-colored buildings; even the Flatirons blushed a brighter shade of salmon. Next to the horizon, a cloudless band of sky brightened to aquamarine, like a reflecting pool. As the sun rose, the vivid colors extended across the sky to fluffy clouds perched on the high peaks, tipping them with rose and purple. Close to the rising sun, the clouds flamed orange, then gold, splashing the sky with light. But once the sun pulled above the horizon, the show ended: the colors faded, the dramatic clouds revealed as insubstantial icy wisps.

January

Friday, January 1 ❧ Last night we returned after spending a week in Arkansas with Richard's family. The crowded airport bus deposited us in the shadow of the foothills at about eleven o'clock, exhaling people and luggage together into the cold night with a belch of warm air. Exhausted, but wearier still of inside air, we elected to walk home. We retrieved our luggage and walked briskly down the quiet pedestrian mall and up Mapleton Hill, moving as quickly as our heavy suitcases and tired bodies would allow. The cold night air bit at my lungs and burned my cheeks—a welcome, even rejuvenating sting, after the warm, sluggish southern air of Arkansas.

At the top of Mapleton Hill, three blocks from our apartment, I put down my suitcases for a moment and stopped to look at the night. I breathed deeply of the dry air, inhaling slowly because of the cold, and turned my gaze to the sky. What a spectacle! The depthless black night sky was littered with the silvery bright pinpoints of stars. (It rained for five days and nights in Arkansas, the sky there a grey cotton wool blanket in daytime, a garish orange one at night, lit by sodium vapor streetlights.) The snowy ridges of the foothills gleamed palely in the moon's reflected light.

The sky has always fascinated me, especially here, where it is so clear and so expansive: it dominates the night, infinite, dwarfing us to our real size by revealing the immensity of space.

Looking overhead in the cold air, I picked out my two favorite constellations, my companions since childhood: Orion, the hunter, bow outstretched high in the southern sky; and the Big Dipper in the northeastern sky, balanced on the end of its handle, ladle forever emptying. They are really not hunter or dipper—the dot-to-dot connections that form their figures are just inventions of European culture, with names and stories attached. But I find their familiar patterns comforting in the vastness of the dark universe. Their stories bring them closer.

How odd to remember that when we look at the billions of stars pricking the blackness of the night sky, we are looking back in time. Those silvery bits of light are so far away in our galaxy that the light we saw last night, on New Year's Eve, took years to reach us. Stars visible to the naked eye may be as "near" as Sirius, the bright dog star in Canis major—its light takes almost nine years to reach our eyes. (Last night's bright blue twinkling light left Sirius before Molly was born.) The farthest stars we can see without a telescope are as far away as Deneb in Cygnus, the swan, an incredible 1,600 light years away.

Last night the moon, not yet full, hung almost directly overhead, casting its silvery bright light over town, high ridges, plains. Its light clearly outlined the familiar landmarks: the black, needle-sharp steeple of the Catholic church downhill; beyond that the miles and miles of plains stretching far away eastward; uphill to the west, the rough, serrated ridge line of Mount Sanitas just above town. Overhead, the planet Venus, the evening star, shone bright right next to the moon. Molly and Richard and I stood for a minute, heedless of the intense cold, heads thrown back, suitcases at our feet, cars roaring past, brightly-lit houses all around, lost in time and the deep night sky.

The names I know for the stars are Arabic and Greek, for the constellations Latin, given by astronomers in those cultures centuries ago. Every culture had its astronomers: stars and constellations figure in stories, prayers, and songs from Native American cultures to the aborigines of Australia to the Chinese emperors. We began the New Year as so many others have through human history: looking back in time at the stars revolving in the clear black night sky.

Tuesday, 5 January ❧ This morning is chill and grey, with a steady rain of snow floating from the low clouds. I am cold and tired, my fingers fumble on the computer keyboard because they are stiff. Last night, Richard's allergies flared up and he snuffled and snored and sneezed in his sleep. I laid awake for a long time, then woke early.

The clouds hang so low that the ridge of Flagstaff Mountain, normally framed by the kitchen window, has vanished. All of the foothills are lost in the grey mist and falling snow, the underbelly of today's sky. This even grey blanket is the cloud genus nimbostratus (from *nimbus*, "rainy" and *stratus*, "spread" or "layer"), which, according to Lyall Watson in *Heaven's Breath: A Natural History of the Wind* is "the sombre genus, whose only species has a habit of producing continuous rain or snow." It is behaving true to type.

The pale light filtering through the clouds carries none of the sun's usual warmth. Its feeble glimmer reminds me of the last three winters spent alongside Puget Sound in western Washington. The color of winter there is grey: low grey clouds scudding by from the ocean like a moving blanket; grey rain, driven on the wind; grey morning fog, water hanging in the air on days of no rain. Excellent weather for melancholia. Amazing how different the tone of winters here: all sun and blue sky and bright white snow, the air crisp and dry. In western Washington the grey days were right—part of the place. But a grey day here is disorienting. After only one day without the sun, I am already melancholy and gloomy.

But the snow is beautiful. It floats down out of the clouds in thick clumps, light as goose down. Under my small magnifying lens each clump reveals its composition of individual, lacy six-pointed crystals. In meteorologists' terms, these are dendrites, named for the regular paired branching pattern of the crystals, like tree branches (*dendros* is the Greek word for tree). Dendrites are the classic—but not the only—form that snow crystals take. Snow crystal form depends on the temperature of the cloud when the water droplets freeze. Dendrites form at fairly warm cloud temperatures (for snow, that is!), anywhere between 0° and 20° F. In colder clouds, the freezing droplets still adhere to regular geometry, forming six-sided shapes. Depending again on temperature, they will either form simpler hexagonal plates (lacking the exquisite lacy detail of dendrites), or if temperatures in the cloud are really cold (below -20° F) hexagonal columns. However, if cloud temperatures are *warmer* than 20° F when the water droplets freeze, regular geometry is lost: sharp, needle-like ice fragments form, lacking symmetry.

The light is still grey, the air still cold, and the clumps of snow continue to float down from the clouds. I miss the sun—my fingers are blue and stiff. But my spirits have lifted. The low grey clouds seem less oppressive now that I've discovered the exquisite tracery of their snowflakes. Snow, grey clouds, snow on!

Thursday, 7 *January* ❧ I can see clear blue sky overhead, yet the morning sun hasn't slid past the neighboring condominiums. I am cold. But I must be patient. Soon the sun's rays will pour in the windows; I'll stand in a sun rectangle and soak up its heat until my joints loosen and my fingers regain normal coloring.

When I looked out the bedroom window this morning, I was delighted to see blue sky at edge of the high plains far to the east. (Each morning when I get up, I look out the window to see what weather the day brings. Sky visible at the rim of the eastern plains usually means a sunny morning.) The even grey blanket of the last two days' snow clouds was gone, replaced by long bands of north-south trending clouds with wide swaths of clear blue sky in between.

Later, when Richard and I stepped outside on our morning walk, we found fresh deer tracks crisply marked in yesterday's snow. One set of small tracks and one set of large tracks—

probably a doe/fawn pair—walked right up the path across our tiny front lawn, straight to our front door. The two deer apparently stopped to eat the frozen remains of the pansies in the front step garden, then walked along the sidewalk past our big picture windows (did they stop to peer in?). The footprints stop and tramp around a little next to the hop vine left by the beer-brewing former tenant. The hop vine apparently wasn't good browse—it shows a few exploratory tooth marks, but no serious munching.

The tracks go on past the hood of our old Volvo station wagon, then follow the wheel ruts in the deep snow, treading just whisker lengths from the car. At the tall board fence that bounds the parking lot, they reverse and walk back past the Volvo, past our living room windows and back across the lawn. At the edge of the lawn the tracks show the deer stopped to sniff the ornamental Pfitzer junipers—I wish they'd browse the ugly, prickly things down to the nubbins— but apparently they didn't like the Pfitzers any more than I do; they didn't stop long. The two delicate sets of tracks continue up the driveway, sticking to the wheel ruts to avoid the deep snow, the small deer following (its tracks sometimes fall right on top of the larger tracks). From there the prints are obliterated by the tangled ruts of morning commuter traffic. I like to think that the mother/fawn pair followed the sidewalk along Ninth Street, past the shiny new red Maserati and the two BMWs parked at the condominiums next door, and disappeared down the alley by the irrigation ditch.

It's been a tough couple of weeks for the deer herd that winters in the foothills on the west edge of Boulder. Boulder—usually the "banana belt" of the Front Range because of its frequent, warm chinook winds—has been gripped by an unusual cold snap since Christmas. Nearly a foot of snow remains on the ground from the Christmas Eve snowstorm, causing many grumbling letters to the editor about inefficient city snow removal, and much real hardship for wildlife. The deer usually move down into the west side of town in the winter since winter browse in this part of the foothills is not abundant. Fortunately (so the deer must think) many of the ornamental plants favored by Boulder home owners and landscape architects provide gourmet deer browse. So they come to town, quietly slipping through dark neighborhoods in the evening and early morning, searching out the roses, apple trees, and hardy pansies. They don't usually come as close to downtown as our apartment, but the deeper than usual snow is probably causing more competition for urban gardens.

Last year saw no more than a handful of letters to the editor complaining about the deer "damaging" carefully watered and fertilized plantings. Concern in past years has been so great, however, that the city, in 1984, commissioned a study of Boulder's deer population, including recommendations on how to avoid deer/human conflicts. The city continues to trap, radio collar, and monitor the deer population but hasn't yet decided to do anything drastic about these "pests."

The fuss doesn't make sense to me. I, for one, am perfectly happy to donate my hardy pansies to the deer in return for the pleasure of seeing the delicate strokes of fresh deer prints pressed in the morning snow right at my doorstep.

Monday, 11 January

Banana belt weather has returned. Today the temperature along the south-facing brick front wall of the apartment rose to 59 °F at midafternoon. The snow is beginning to melt back from the sidewalks, exposing the dry grass and damp soil of the lawn. Boulder's three weeks of hard winter appear to be on the wane.

I knew that Boulder's winters were relatively mild for the Rockies, but I am surprised to realize how mild. This winter, with the snow from the Christmas Eve snowstorm preserved by the cold snap, the streets and sidewalks were clogged with rutted snow and ice for nearly three weeks. That seemed normal to me—this is, after all, winter in Colorado. Yet the newspaper continues to detail the terrible inconveniences—like the story of the city councilwoman whose Mercedes was ticketed because she had to park facing the wrong way on her snow-filled street in order to plug in her engine heater—and to print innumerable grousing letters. Could these be the same people who boast of Boulder's proximity to fabulous skiing opportunities? The same folks who crowd the highways headed out of town on sunny afternoons and each weekend, their cars laden with ski paraphernalia, heading for snow? Perhaps they really love snow, just not in their backyard, or on their streets.

Today's weather should please the grousers.

On my walk downtown this afternoon, I spotted a tiny clump of violet leaves melting out of the snow at the edge of the parkway on Broadway Avenue. The heart-shaped leaves nestled close to the warm, dark soil in their own solar home: a southwest-facing curve of a silver maple root. Violets are one of my favorite plants, perhaps because there are so many species, some with flowers colored deep purple, some white, some yellow; some growing loose and sprawling, some clustered, as these were, close to the ground in tiny clumps of heart-shaped leaves. I especially love these last for their subtle growth form and the flowers' intensely sweet fragrance. Romantic Victorian lovers speaking the language of the flowers exchanged bunches of violets to say "of fond remembrance." Today's tiny clump of green and growing leaves set me to thinking of spring.

Spring in January—this is an odd climate indeed, alternating snowstorms with thawing chinooks brought by the prevailing westerlies. In winter, we are in the track of the cyclonic storms that blow east from the storm factories in the Pacific Ocean. Though the spinning cyclones are forced upward (and therefore weakened) by the miles of mountains between us and the West Coast, they often rejuvenate when they slide down the Front Range to meet the plains. The alternating patterns of high and low atmospheric pressure that come with the cyclonic storms bring us our weekly doses of winter, then spring; winter, then spring.

Wednesday, 13 *January* ✦ Tonight Richard was walking home from work along Sixth Street, between Spruce and Mapleton, when he heard a screech-owl whistle. He searched the surrounding trees in the dusky light until he thought that he located the sound in a bushy ponderosa pine next to the alley, then stood and whistled back. It responded, and they carried on a short duet.

Despite their name, screech-owls do not screech, nor do they hoot; they whistle, an odd rolling sound with the cadence of a bouncing ball speeding up at the end. The eastern screech-owl's whistle descends; the western screech-owl's is a series of monotonal notes. Here on the east side of the Rockies, the two species' ranges overlap. This owl sounded like an eastern, its soft whistle boinging down the scale.

Screech owls are small (seven to eight inches long), about the size of a paperback field guide; and surprisingly light, weighing about the same amount as a good imported chocolate bar (about six ounces). Like most birds, their skeleton is very strong, and as light as possible. Some of their bones are hollow, filled with air instead of marrow. They roost in holes or crotches of trees during the day and are most active at night. Dusk is a great time for seeing or hearing them, as they are often at their roost tree at dusk, just beginning their night of hunting.

Owls can hunt successfully at night because their sight and hearing are extraordinarily keen. Their eyes are large and elongated to form a tube. Wide cornea and lens surfaces make their eyes good light gatherers; a high concentration of light-sensitive rods allows them to make the most of low-light images. They even have an opaque third eyelid to protect their sensitive eyes from bright daylight. Owls' hearing is more acute than ours also; their ears are surrounded by feathers that may be used to focus sounds and funnel them into each ear. Even the distinctive concentric rings of feathers (facial disks) around owls' eyes may function as a kind of parabolic reflectors, collecting and focusing sound waves.

What does an urban screech-owl eat? Whatever small animals or insects it can find—at this time of year mostly mice, shrews, and other small mammals. In spring and summer they expand their diet to include spiders, insects (beetles, cutworms, caterpillars, grasshoppers, crickets, ants, cicadas, moths, etc.), and even small birds. They also eat Norway rats, kangaroo rats, gophers, moles, bats, crayfishes, snakes, lizards, frogs, toads, scorpions, and even fish! A screech-owl is a desirable neighbor indeed.

How many owls (the little screeches and the bigger great horned and barn owls) per square mile live in this town of 95,000 people? And how many of the 95,000 people have any idea of the owls living here?

After dinner, we walked out to listen for the owl, along the quiet streets lined by big old houses. Richard whistled like a screech-owl for several minutes, but the tree gave no answer in the quiet darkness.

Sunday, 17 January ✒ Every day a few more appear. I carefully catch and put them outside, but the next sunny morning brings more. I'm afraid that these small black-and-red bugs are lying dormant in each crack and crevice of our apartment. These warm, sunny days are a false spring, prompting them to emerge and bumble about.

Our unexpected guests are box elder bugs, members of the "scentless plant bug" family (what a marvelous name!). Box elder bugs, named for the trees that they prefer, inhabit a very specialized niche: they lay their eggs in the bark of female box elder trees, where the young hatch and grow to adulthood. They spend their whole lives in the vicinity of box elder trees. Around box elders, they are ubiquitous; elsewhere, rare or absent altogether.

Box elder bugs are quite pretty, their bodies and wings mostly chalky black with bright red wing linings peeping out. When they fly, they display the bright vermillion abdomen usually hidden under the somber black wings.

Last summer and fall uncountable numbers of them lived out their larval to adult stages on the south wall of our apartment. On any given day, at least fifty bright black and orange bodies crawled over the warm brick wall by our front door in various stages of wing development, from tiny flightless ones with clownish big abdomens and stumps of wings, to adults, whose fully grown topcoat of wings conceal that garish abdomen. Now they seem to be wintering not just in the cracks in the brick wall, but also inside. On warm days they buzz clumsily around the apartment, always ending up banging into the bright front windows, trying futilely to get out. I wouldn't mind them if only they didn't have the less-than-endearing habit of flying straight into my face in their careening flight around the house. (They really are quite poor flyers, no grace or precision apparent in their erratic, rattling progress. Their wings work so tremendously hard just to keep them aloft that setting a precise course seems to be impossible.) I usually capture them in my hand and launch them into the icy air outside the front door. They are momentarily rendered immobile by the cold, then bounce about until they find themselves a sheltered crack.

Come next spring they will lay their eggs in the furrows of the clump of female box elder trees at the edge of the parking lot. When the box elders are draped with small winged seeds, the eggs will hatch into little red wingless larvae. The larvae will eventually find their way over to the south-facing wall of our apartment and crawl about on this sheltered nursery until their wings are fully grown. As the days grow colder next fall, the next generation will move inside, to spend another winter knocking about in the living room airspace. Such a simple life—no wars, no terrorists, no arms race, no national debt, no worry about pollution and abuse of natural resources, no poverty, no homelessness—just a continuing cycle of life, growth, and death.

Thursday, 21 January ⊛ At dusk this evening, I walked over to Richard's office to pick him up. From the pocket park at Sixth and Highland, each of the waves of rocky ridges stood out distinctly in the clear evening light, with scattered ponderosa pines edging them like shaggy fur. Ponderosa pines growing on the dry, nutrient-poor soils of the Front Range foothills are short and stocky, like muscular character actors. These are tough trees, with their thick platy bark and long slender needles in clumps at the ends of the branches. They seem ageless, enduring, their roots probing deeply into cracks in the rocks, their trunks and branches twisting gracefully to offer the least resistance to the incessant wind. I can trace the path of the wind by the shapes of the ponderosas—here in a sheltered spot the trees grow straight; here on this ridgetop the trees are wind-groomed to a curving silhouette.

By the time I met Richard and we turned towards home, the sun had slipped below the dark ridges. These clear, cold evenings the sky is positively luminescent after the sun sets—the light fades very slowly, leaving a violet-rose-golden glow in the western third of the sky for ever so long. Tonight the new moon, a several-day-old sliver, hung in the sky above the horizon. Its bright silver rim cupped upwards to hold up the remainder, a shadowy globe, in the darkening sky.

Three bright planets were lined up east to west, right in line with the sliver of moon: Mercury in the west, Venus right next to the moon, then the moon, and, farthest east, Jupiter. Richard and I stopped and stood tracing the line of bright planets and moon in the black sky. We spread our arms wide, trying to see if the planets were all in line or if it was just a trick of their dazzling brightness in the darkening sky. We stretched one arm out straight, our fingers pointing directly at Mercury; then we pointed the other arm, fingers outstretched, at Jupiter. As we each slowly raised our arms straight overhead, our outstretched fingers pointed straight at the moon and Venus. They were indeed, in a straight line. I suppose that we seemed to passers by to be engaging in some odd new form of exercise; they'd have thought us odder still if they'd known that we were tracing celestial geometry!

Saturday, 23 January ⚜

Last night's chinook winds blew from the north, instead of the usual westerly direction, producing subtly different noises: rat-a-tat-tatting as the dry Virginia creeper vines banged the bedroom windows, clanking as heaven-knows-what in the vacant lot behind us rolled around, screeching as the Russian olives on the east side of the apartment tore against the metal gutter. Rushing, screeching, crashing, scraping, and moaning of wind-stressed branches, trunks, fences, gutters, and shingles filled the night and continued unceasing. The great gusts blew on and on, roaring by like freight trains speeding through the night.

The winds peaked in a tremendous crescendo at about 6:30 this morning, according to the weather station at the National Center for Atmospheric Research, when ninety-mile-per-hour gusts *blew* seven enormous concrete girders off the overpass under construction over the Diagonal Highway. Apparently the girders, weighing a hefty 45 tons apiece, were positioned almost precisely crosswise to the crashing gusts. No one is sure exactly how they blew off—one theory says that the gusts were strong and regular enough to set up a harmonic vibration in the immense concrete I-beams, until finally their own weight toppled them over. The vibration could have been helped by a sort of lift effect (similar to that which allows airplanes to fly) from the air rushing over the upper surface of the girders. Seven girders times 45 tons apiece equals 315 tons—over 600,000 pounds of hardened concrete crashed down onto the four-lane roadway below, a roadway that carries 50,000 vehicles a day. Fortunately, at 6:30 a.m. on Saturday morning there is no rush of commuter traffic, so no one was underneath when the big I-beams thundered down. However, a car and a semi-trailer, the drivers blinded by the dust storm from the bare soil around the overpass, crashed into the mass of debris just moments after it fell. Still, neither driver was seriously hurt. Eyewitnesses struggling though the gusts to free the driver of the semi-trailer from his cab as the last big girder pounded down onto the roadway said that the ground was shaking like jelly, as if it were the epicenter of an earthquake.

The construction company and the state department of highways are already squabbling about who pays for new girders, and for repair of the cratered road surface. The construction company argues that it was an act of God, meaning they don't have to pay, the highway department maintains that it was part of the "normal, expected weather pattern." Does the wind blow in Boulder? Is the sky usually blue?

Tuesday, 26 January ✒ I left the apartment at around five o'clock this evening to go for a run. The sun hung low, only the length of its own diameter above to the ridges. When I reached the upper end of Maxwell Avenue, I looked over my shoulder at the sky to the north and was so surprised at what I saw that I stopped running. A miles-long, wavering line of dark birds approached from the plains. Coming closer, the moving black dots resolved themselves into an endless line of crows, clumped in groups from ten to fifty individuals each, all headed west over the first ridges of the foothills from northeast of town (the beginning of the line was hidden, so I couldn't see where they came from). As I watched, the head

99

of the group reached the top of the first ridges and spiraled up, up, up into the sky (gaining altitude to rise above the strong ridge crest winds). At an altitude so high that they shrank to dark specks, they exited the spiral, turned west, and flew over the ridge out of view. The rest of the line followed, duplicating the spirals and twists of the leaders like a ragged flying serpent. I turned back to look for the other end of the line over the plains. There was no end in sight. I stood until I began to get stiff. Still they kept coming, flapping past overhead in untidy groups, their long wings almost graceful, coursing an invisible track in the sky.

Crows, like blackbirds, starlings, and some other birds, roost communally in the winter, gathering by the hundreds or thousands in the same area every night. They forage in small groups during the day, returning, often from many miles away, to the communal roost in the evening. This flock of crows (while stopped, I counted 500–600, perhaps half the number that passed overhead) was apparently returning from the day's feeding to their roost. How did they know to gather and return all in one long serpent-like line at the same time? Did the coming sunset trigger their movement? Bird behavior in communal groups is complex—ornithologists readily admit that flock behavior may be much harder to understand than solitary behavior.

As I ran around the corner towards Sunshine Canyon the serpent-line of crows continued passing overhead, climbing as they approached the ridge, then spiraling higher and higher, finally disappearing into the blue sky beyond. I felt as if I were privileged, allowed to view a momentous tribal ceremony. The moving black dots in the sky seemed to spell some great portent—if only I could understand it.

I continued running up the hill past the hospital towards Sunshine Canyon. Here the creek cuts through hogbacks of the Fountain and Dakota formations in a narrow canyon, winding down a slot through the uptilted layers. Tall, crooked cottonwoods edge the canyon bottom, their bleached bark deeply furrowed, as if raked by the claws of a stretching bear.

When I reached the opening in the cottonwoods where the valley between the hogbacks stretches north, I ran through a shower of small birds: chickadees and juncos bobbed about my head like snow. For a moment only, I was part of their flock, airborne with small grey-and-white feathered wings beating a rush of air and bird voices chattering in my ears. Then our paths untangled, I ran on up the road, they flew past me to settle in a ponderosa pine up the valley.

I ran up the canyon until I tired of the steep grade, then turned and floated downhill in great long strides, catching my breath as I let the pull of gravity do the work for my tired legs. Out over the plains, the long, smooth, ribbon-like chinook clouds stretched parallel to the Front Range. As I watched, still breathing hard, they turned orange and then softer pink, their colors limned by the setting sun. From my place up where the old pediment meets the mountain front, I could see the dusty purple shadow of the Front Range rippling eastward to snuff out the golden light on the still-sunny plains. As the shadow's edge stretched farther and farther, I turned around and ran backwards, looking up at the ridges above town. A fluffy grey pile of cloud dammed the sky up Sunshine Canyon. I watched it flame orange, then magenta, then violet, brilliant as dyed silk in the last light of the sun. I turned back around to the plains and saw the bright silvery half moon take shape in the luminous blue sky, almost directly overhead. Cars drove by me, headlights on, rushing home in the gathering dusk.

How many of the drivers looked up to see the clouds above the peaks, bright as gaudy silk banners, or at the moon, shimmering high over the plains? I would have shared my sunset, but they rushed on, none pausing to look.

Sunday, 31 January ❧ Today is the last day of January, and the weather fits my idea of the season: no sun this cold morning, the sky blanketed with low grey nimbostratus clouds. It is snowing gently, a drizzle of ice.

This snow is not the usual snow *flakes*. It doesn't float down the way snowflakes do, wafting on the slightest breath of air, floating sideways almost much as down; this snow plummets like rain. From a distance, on the brown asphalt roof of the condominiums across the street, it appears to be a dusting of regular snowflakes, but up close the difference is clear. It is granular snow, more like a sprinkling of fine sand grains left by chinook winds. Under my hand lens I can see that it is not composed of geometric crystals; what I see are tiny white pellets, about the size of sand fleas, each one a clump of minute rounded grains.

Snow *grains* form when the air temperature in a cloud is just below freezing, allowing the water droplets to coalesce to the size of fine raindrops before they freeze. The cloud cover must also be fairly thin, so that the frozen grains fall before they grow any larger. Apparently this grey layer of nimbostratus clouds is not a very thick blanket, or our snow grains would have grown larger and perhaps taken on a crystalline form. It is, however, dense enough to hide even the top of the Dakota hogback, shrinking the visible world to a very small urban one indeed—not a single mountain in view.

Just yesterday, Richard and I were sitting out on the bench in front of the apartment in the sun, joking about getting tan. Against our warm brick south-facing wall, the air temperature rose into in the mid-sixties. It felt so like spring that we walked over Mapleton Hill to his office in our shirt sleeves. It was a false spring. Winter returned abruptly as we exited Richard's office building. We stood for a minute on the deck, looking south across Boulder Creek, enjoying the warm sunshine. Suddenly the wind came, swirling a dusty, wet gust around us. That first gust was warm, the second frigid and hurling snowflakes. Almost immediately, the air filled with snow. A cottony layer of thick grey clouds boiled out of the canyon, blocking the warm sun. We stood mesmerized for a moment, watching the low grey clouds pour over the ridge and feeling the icy air raise goose pimples on our skin. Our breath blew past us in clouds of frost. The air temperature plunged twenty degrees in those few minutes. Then we raced the storm home, walking the three-quarters of a mile over Mapleton Hill in record time, shivering in our shirt sleeves. At our apartment, the sun still shone.

I phoned a friend who lives up in the mountains to invite her and her family for dinner. "We're not going anywhere for a while—I'm watching a blizzard bury our cars," she reported. As she spoke, I watched clouds pour over Mount Sanitas. The first white snowflakes swirled down around our apartment. Here at the foot of the mountains, spring had just turned back to winter; at our friend's house in the mountains winter was in full blast; east of us the plains basked in warm sunshine. What confusion!

It feels to me like a good day to hibernate, but the business of life goes on for those animals that are active in winter. I hear chickadees outside in the ash tree, gleaning the branches for small insects stilled by the cold. Small grey-and-white juncos chip at each other as they pick up fine grit and seeds from the gravel in the parking lot. And the ever-audible starlings squeak from their warm perches around the chimney pots across the street.

January 13

February

Tuesday, 2 February ❧ Today, Groundhog Day, dawned clear and sunny—hooray! I know that a sunny morning on Groundhog Day means umpty-ump more days of winter, but if they are sunny days, I'll take them gladly.

Just after dawn, the air outside was very cold (10° F), clear as glass, and absolutely still. Even up at the ridgetops where the air is nearly always restless, the ponderosa pines remained muffled in yesterday's bulky snow blankets, not a flake of the delicately balanced stuff disturbed. They looked like crowds of feathered birds standing rank on rank, white plumage fluffed out for warmth.

The stillness and perfectly feathered snow figures weren't destined to survive intact much past sunrise. The air is active here. Once the the sun begins to cast its warmth and melt the snow, the air at ground level positively boils with motion. Air warmed by solar heat radiating from dark buildings and city streets rises in lazy spirals or bubbles, pulling in new cold air, which, itself warmed, begins to drift upwards in turn, and more cool air pours in to take its place.... Soon local breezes are blowing, ruffling the stagnant cold air down here in Boulder Valley. In the mountains, the thinner air warms even more quickly, rising upwards and pulling air up from lower elevations. These updrafts eventually coalesce into regional upslope winds, mothers of the clouds. Puffy white cumulus, like bumptious marshmallows, soon form. They are birthed when moisture from the melting snow on south slopes rises with the warm air and collides with cooler air that bears cloud-seeding dust and pollen particles. The clouds modify still further the local air currents by casting cool shadows, thereby removing some of the land surface from warm air production. Soon the air is dancing, its movement choreographed by the interaction of topography, vegetation, and daily weather. But this morning the air was especially cold. For several hours past dawn, it was dramatically still, a frozen pause.

By afternoon, the air was neither still nor clear at ground level. Breezes twirled the downy snow piles from twigs and power lines, and plucked the ponderosas on the lower slopes of the foothills, whirling away their tidy white plumage. Curiously, above a smudgy blue layer of air about halfway up to the ridgeline of the foothills, the snow-mantled upper slopes remained pristine. Up there, the air looked clear and still. A classic inversion: the blue smudge marks the lower edge of a layer of cold air that has trapped the warm air like a ground glass lens—along with all of the car exhaust, dust, power plant particulates, and woodstove smoke—in the valley. Where rising warmed air hits the lid, gases and particulates, unable to rise farther, form a dense hazy layer, a veil of noxious content. An inversion on a sunny day is like putting a glass lid on a steaming pot, except here the steaming pot is polluted, the normally healthy atmospheric stew laced with the foul exhalations of our urban life. Usually these waste gases and particulates blow downwind and disperse into someone else's air; today, instead, they remained trapped for us to see and breathe.

We are careless with our wastes. We dispose of the unwanted by-products of our lives thoughtlessly. Bodily wastes are flushed "away" down our sewage systems, hazardous wastes trucked "away" to repositories far from our backyards, lawn fertilizers and weed killers dumped in our storm drains to flow "away" downstream, household trash hauled "away" by our trash collector's trucks, auto exhaust exhaled to blow "away" downwind. We send all of our wastes out of sight—downstream, downcounty, downwind—willfully shutting our eyes and our minds, pretending that the wastes just safely disappear. That they don't is becoming abundantly clear. This earth is a globe, a circle in three dimensions. What goes around, comes around—witness this afternoon's blue air.

Friday, 5 February ✒ Last night Richard saw the screech owl on his way home from work. He heard it first as he was walking up Sixth Street, so he stopped to listen near the ponderosa pine in the alley between Mapleton and Spruce. "Boing... boing... boing... boing, boing, boingboing-boing" a soft whistle, barely discernible in the quiet darkness. He scanned the branches of surrounding trees as it whistled again, and finally spotted it in the crotch of a silver maple, directly overhead. Stepping softly backwards, he craned his neck for a better view. He whistled at it and it whistled back, stretching its body to its full six-inch height and looking right at Richard with its outsize yellow eyes.

We walked up the hill after dinner in the evening darkness to look for it, but it was gone. Off hunting, most likely.

Saturday, 6 February ✒ This afternoon we drove to Denver. The twin ribbons of the Boulder-Denver turnpike took us southeast across typical Denver Basin landscapes: level mesas alternating with shallow, rolling stream valleys. Inverted topography—the mesas, once valley bottom flood-plains, now stand above the new valleys. A thick layer of loosely consolidated and permeable stream gravels (deposited when the mesas were valley bottoms) caps the mesas, absorbing rainfall and slowing runoff, protecting the soft shales beneath from erosion. "Modern" streams have cut new valleys in the softer uncapped sediments in the 15,000 or more years since the last glacial age, leaving the former valley bottoms standing high and dry.

From the top of one mesa we looked back over our shoulders at the line of peaks that mark the Continental Divide from above Boulder north to Wyoming. They form a magnificent white wall, the high peaks rising shoulder-to-shoulder in a nearly impenetrable barrier above the mile-high plains. Indeed, for fifty air miles—from 11,314-foot-high Berthoud Pass, west of Denver, north to 10,276-foot-high Cameron Pass—

the white wall is impassable by car in winter. In summer, only two other auto crossings are possible: the long switchbacks of Trail Ridge Road, climbing to 12,183 feet in Rocky Mountain National Park, and the Rollins Pass road, a narrow gravel road that winds over an 11,680-foot-high pass.

Where the divide swings closest to the plains, twenty miles west of Boulder, the peaks rise quickly to dizzying heights. South to north along the divide in close formation we could see Mount Neva (the "tiny" one at 12,814 feet; the rest are at least 13,000 feet); South and North Arapaho peaks (the ice that provides Boulder's "pure cold water from the Boulder-owned Arapaho Glacier," according to the gilt inscription above the drinking fountain in the Hotel Boulderado's Victorian lobby, was concealed in the high cirque between the two Arapahoes); Kiowa and Arikaree peaks; and behind them but only partly visible the rest of the "tribal" peaks—Navajo, Apache, Shoshone, and farther north, set off by a larger gap, Pawnee Peak. Paiute Peak and Mount Audubon mark the corner where the divide takes a wide swing west and disappeared from our view. The next visible cluster marking the line of the divide is also the most prominent group of Front Range peaks besides Pikes Peak: Chiefs Head Peak, Pagoda Mountain, and Mount Meeker, all respectably tall, but dominated by the massive pyramidal shape of 14,255-foot-high Longs Peak. This group, visible as a faint blue lumpy smear on the horizon, gives travelers crossing the state boundary into Colorado along the South Platte River their first inkling of mountains. Around Fort Morgan, halfway across the rolling eastern Colorado high plains, the smears intrude on the traveler's consciousness. Still nearly 100 air miles west, they could be towering cumulonimbus clouds. Closer yet, they grow more substantial, clearly mountains—a whole wall of peaks thrusting high above the plains, dominated by the triangular black wedge of Longs Peak.

Just before we reached the suburban sprawl of Broomfield, a large dark bird flew across the highway, flapping slowly, flying low over the brown grassland. At first I mistook the big bird for a raven, and looked back at the mountains again. In a moment though, our paths crossed and I looked again. The bird flew at car-window level over the barbed-wire fence along the highway just as we drove by—bringing us eye to eye. It was huge—outstretched wings as long as Richard is tall—with a snowy white head and tail. An adult bald eagle. It hung in the frosty air above the highway fence for a long moment, turning its white head and yellow eyes on us. A tuft of fur hung from its sharply curved beak.

The big fish-eating eagles usually winter along the few rivers affording open water (and therefore good fishing). But it has been a colder winter than usual; rivers and lakes along the Front Range are frozen. This eagle was likely out combing the winter grasslands for slow prairie dogs or carrion. As we passed, it flew on up the valley towards the foothills, long black wings beating the frosty air slowly, white head glistening in the weak sunlight.

Tuesday, 9 February ❧ The night's cold north wind had already waned when Richard and I walked over Mapleton Hill to his office this morning. The sun and the wind were now warm, thawing exposed soil and reducing the already tattered remnants of January's snow to isolated grey piles in shady spots. Heavy frost melted from the trees, splattering the sidewalk around us with quarter-sized drops of water. I inhaled long breaths of soft, warm air and hungered for a glimpse of spring, despite the calendar's insistence that spring is months away. Reason wrangled with hope as I walked along. I scanned the ground under the shrubs and in the other sheltered spots for signs of growth, but the plants were still brown and dormant. Then, in a lawn past Mapleton Avenue, I saw loose clusters of tiny, heart-shaped green leaves, close to the ground in the winter-bleached grass—violet leaves. Hope won. My heart swelled, I skipped in place, grinned, and called to Richard to come and share my discovery. Although they looked wilted after the night's cold, they were green, alive. Richard and I walked along happily, hands clasped, swinging our arms wide in the morning sun.

In the next block, I nearly tripped over the upraised edge of a sandstone flag when I spotted a bit of purple close to the ground next to the sidewalk. I pulled Richard to a stop and bent down to look. My excitement bubbled up again—a violet flower! One tiny purple flower, about the size of my little fingernail, the edges of the petals wrinkled from the frost, but still blooming. I squatted down to examine this unseasonable bit of spring.

Violets are asymmetric flowers, with four unequal-sized petals. The largest petal—the lowermost one—is swollen into a small sac at its base, just above where the flower stalk attaches. Sugary liquid filling the sac attracts insects, who brush the pollen-covered stamens when they burrow into the flower to reach the nectary. The load of pollen acquired by each insect travels with it to the next flower it visits, thus neatly cross-pollinating the violet flowers. This morning's tiny violet flower was out of sync, several months early for the spring insect hatch.

Later in the day the chinooks blew in. I struggled against huge billowing gusts of air and dust as I walked west up Canyon Boulevard in the afternoon. Wading against the current left me breathless and panting—several times I was simply stopped in my tracks and once nearly knocked backwards by a particularly strong gust. My slender Scandinavian anatomy is all wrong for this wind: the resultant surface-to-mass ratio is better suited to a kite than a human. (Richard, ever helpful, suggests wearing lead ankle weights.) I've discovered the technique for walking against the chinooks, though. I walk quickly forward in the intermissions of still air between the crashing gusts, covering as much ground as possible. As the next gust approaches, I walk more slowly, pressing determinedly forward until it becomes impossible to wade against the rushing air, then turn my back to the wind and brace myself against its thrust. Once it washes over me and slackens, I turn about again and walk quickly forward until the next wave grows too strong. My instinctive about-face response as the gust strengthens is characteristic of the universal response to winds rising above the biological wind threshold (over thirty-one miles per hour). Women and men, regardless of culture, react predictably but differently to rising winds. Men tend to face into the wind, even when it rises above the biological threshold, leaning into the stream of air with their chests, the layers of muscle insulating their bodies from harm. We women, on the other hand, with chests fronted by nerve-rich breast tissue, tend first to cross our arms protectively over our chests, then once the wind passes the biological threshold, turn around, facing our less-sensitive backs to the rushing air. Beyond simple comfort, this behavior has evolutionary value: nursing mothers may quit producing milk if their breasts are suddenly chilled.

Two crows rode the waves above me with the ease of surfers. They flapped swiftly towards the foothills in the still air between gusts, then rode the gusts back, black wings stiffly curved, feathers outstretched like airplane flaps to maneuver on the stream of air. I wished for a measure of their airy grace as the gusts buffeted my earthbound body.

Wednesday, 10 *February* ❧ Yesterday brought the first wild violet flower, today February's first big snowstorm. I woke in the night, my sleep disturbed by the queer, orange glow lighting our bedroom. Billions of snowflakes drifting through the night air reflected and magnified the penetrating light of the streetlights, creating a sort of false dawn.

We rose to a white world, only the low clouds grey, the still air dense with tiny snowflakes pouring straight down like rain. About six inches were already piled up on the ground and the flakes still sluiced down. Beautiful fluffy stuff, perfect for skiing—oh, to be out on my wooden boards, kicking and stepping up the hills, turning and gliding, swooping down!

Strange weather, but so typical of February's extremes. The past twenty-four hours' weather has bounced from end to end of the possible range: Yesterday morning before dawn, a high pressure brought a cold north wind, hard frost, and dry, clear skies. From midmorning to midafternoon yesterday, gusts of high wind thawed the air and brought spring, but also knocked out our electricity for about two hours. Now this morning is still, the air cold and wet, blizzarding. Snow piles a thick, crystalline blanket over yesterday's violets.

If outside is winter again, inside is spring. From my seat at my computer, the view is bright with crimson, pink, and scarlet flowers; the air spicy sweet. A column of rosy pink hyacinth blossoms rises from a mahogany bulb in the enameled Japanese mug on the bookshelves, loosing threads of intense, sweet fragrance. The blue-and-white porcelain rice bowl on the kitchen table holds three tall, slender green narcissus stalks, each terminated by a cluster of creamy white, fragrant flowers. Crimson ivy geranium flowers dot the riot of shiny green leaves that cascade from the hanging pot by the kitchen window. Next to the geranium, the crab cactus (a close relative to Christmas cactus) is a burst of vivid color with scarlet and magenta flowers hovering at the end of each angular stalk like a cloud of feeding hummingbirds.

In full bloom, the crab cactus is by far the most exotic of the houseplants. For much of the year it is unobtrusive, a cluster of green stems, each made up of nearly identical strap-like flat segments with toothed edges. (Two pincher-like teeth at the end of each segment give the plant its name.) But twice a year (near Halloween and Valentine's Day), globular red buds appear at the terminus of each stem. They grow and swell for about three weeks, until finally, when they are nearly as long as my little finger, their pointed tip flexes downward like a parrot's beak and the petals open, peeling away from the tightly furled bud. Once open, each flower resembles a gaudy praying mantis poised to pounce, the petals reflexed and the flower arched up and backwards, powdery yellow stamens and velvety magenta pistil sticking far forward like an elaborate protruding tongue. The petal colors are splendorous: each one creamy at the base, gradually deepening to scarlet and orange at the middle, the edges brilliant magenta—a tropical sunset gone wild. Their surface sparkles like satin sprinkled with quartz sand. The whole flower, from the waxy green ovary to the protruding velvety stigma surface, is about three inches long, just the size of a hovering hummingbird.

Although spineless, crab cacti are true cacti. They are epiphytes, tropical plants that grow on tree trunks in the rain forests of Central and South America—they look very little like our native cactus, the sprawling prickly-pear and globular corypantha that stud dry grasslands of the foothills and mesas.

Snow still pours out of the leaden sky. I am as fickle as this weather. Yesterday I was all spring fever after seeing the first violet; today I dream of skiing and cheer the snow on.

Saturday, 13 February ❧ The sickle moon hung overhead this morning just before dawn, a ghostly crescent in the bright golden-blue morning sky. A soft warm wind blew around me as I walked to the corner newspaper machine.

Later, as Richard and I walked up the hill on Broadway Avenue towards campus, a bird kited overhead, arcing its wings and twisting and canting its tail to maneuver in the gusts. I watched it zip past on the wind, thinking it was a pigeon—until I noticed the finely barred plumage of its underside. That barring, plus the long, maneuverable tail and the short, stubby wings with primaries outstretched at the ends like fingers said "hawk!" I tapped Richard's shoulder excitedly, pointing up at the bird, now sailing swiftly westward over the houses across the street. We both stopped, heedless of the roar of passing traffic, and watched the hawk as it glided easily on the eddying wind. It followed the wind currents west towards the foothills and then, catching a thermal, spiraled up and up and up, that long tail tilting just like a rudder to make the tight turns without straying out of the bubble of rising air. After several more turns it exited the thermal and with characteristic quick flaps headed west again, riding the upslope winds. It grew smaller and smaller until we lost sight of it against the ponderosa forest above the Flatirons. After a moment we turned and headed up the hill, abruptly conscious of the city around us.

It was an accipiter, one of a group of short-winged, long-tailed hawks, probably a Cooper's hawk. Accipiters are hawks of woodlands, with broad wings ideal for quick bursts of speed and easy maneuvering among dense tree trunks in pursuit of their avian prey. Crow-sized Cooper's, and sharp-shinned hawks, the size of a domestic pigeon and the smallest of the accipiters, are the primary predators of small and medium-sized birds. Their predation helps balance populations of birds from small creepers and chickadees to large pigeons and woodpeckers. Cooper's hawks have even adapted to farm woodlots and urban forests, where their major prey is starlings—we need more Cooper's hawks living in Boulder.

Accipiters may migrate long distances each year, nesting from the southern parts of the U.S. to the northern forests of Canada, then moving south as far as Costa Rica in the winter. (Not all migrate far: some Cooper's both nest and winter in Colorado.) Like other North American birds that winter in Central and South America, accipiter populations are hard pressed on their wintering ranges by a variety of factors: human population growth, wholesale rain forest destruction, excessive pesticide use. In *The Birder's Handbook*, biologist Paul

Ehrlich and coauthors warn that "the greatest threat to the preservation of many North American birds occurs south of the U.S.-Mexican border." The world is indeed a global system, and problems do not respect our imaginary political boundaries.

I bless whatever good fortune brought the accipiter coasting over the Saturday morning traffic on Broadway just as we walked past. It was a welcome bit of wildness on the gusting morning winds.

Monday, 15 February ❧ I sat outside for a while around noon today, my back leaned against the warm bricks of the south-facing wall, my legs stretched out to reach the sun. Soon I had company—a mud-dauber wasp explored the wall around me, landing and flattening itself against the bricks, then stretching and flying around again. At first, because I am allergic to stinging insects, its proximity made me nervous. I gathered up my writing, preparing to go indoors. But I felt silly running from a wasp, a neighbor really, and since it seemed to be ignoring me, I stayed where I was and watched it.

Mud-daubers are big wasps, nearly as long as a tube of chapstick, with slender, shiny, dark amber exoskeletons. Their upper body is marked with bright yellow highlights where the plates of their skeleton join, their head sprouts long black antennae, their wings are translucent amber, their legs yellow. Mud-daubers' shape gave rise to the phrase "wasp waist": in between the flattened ball of their upper body and their short, fat, sausage-like abdomen, they narrow like an hourglass to a thread-like connector. If my proportions were similar to this wasp, my waist would be small enough for me to easily encircle it with one hand.

It flew about as if searching for something, casting randomly around the wall, ignoring passing insects. Once it banged smack into the glass of the big picture window behind me.

Then it spent several minutes hugging the brick wall, flattening its body right against the warm bricks. Was it taking warmth from the bricks? Searching for nest sites? My insect books held no enlightenment about this particular behavior. Except for very common insects and insects of economic value, knowledge of insect behavior is spotty.

Wasps are predators on other insects. Most wasps either parasitize other insects by laying their eggs in or on the bodies of hosts (the larvae then eat the hosts) or hunt, stinging their prey to stun it and then provisioning their nests with stunned prey for the larvae to eat. Except for colonial wasps like paper wasps, whose tastes are necessarily more catholic since they hunt for large numbers of larvae, each group of wasps hunts one kind of insects. For instance, ampulicid wasps prey only on immature cockroaches; scoliid wasps parasitize white grubs; spider wasps (true to their name) prey on spiders; aphid wasps prey on leaf hoppers; thread-waisted wasps (the subfamily of my mud-dauber) are split into several groups, one group nests in holes in the ground and preys on grasshoppers; another, also hole nesters, preys on caterpillars; the group of my mud-dauber makes nests of mud and preys on spiders. A precise set of relationships indeed.

The mud-dauber clung to the warm bricks of the wall, its dark body still. We each basked in the sun peacefully, respectful of the presence of the other. Finally it flew off to the corner of the parking lot where greying mounds of snow languish in the shade, seeping trickles of water. It landed in one of the dark muddy spots there, perhaps to gather mud for a nest. I gathered my work and went inside, leaving it to its perambulations. The warm south wall of a brick building near a good muddy spot is probably good nesting habitat, although February seems early. I'll watch and see.

Wednesday, 17 February ✒ It snowed again yesterday evening. As I was leaving Kinko's to walk to the bus stop

and wait for the bus downtown, the low grey clouds began leaking big fluffy clumps of snow. The air was choked with soft, wet snow, snow on my eyebrows, snow clumps on my face, snow coating my jacket... snow everywhere. I felt as if I were wading through a storm of feathers, except that the feathers melted on contact with my warm skin, dripping cold drops of water down my neck, in my eyes, and in my nose when I pulled them in with my breath.

In the ten-minute span of my bus ride downtown, several inches of snow accumulated. Still the storm continued. By the time I reached Richard's office, I'd collected so much snow that I looked like a yeti. The weather forecast predicted only a chance of flurries. Some flurries.

Although the *season* of spring does not begin for another month, yesterday's was a spring snowstorm. It came from the northeast, unlike our usual westerly winter storms. Spring snowstorms get their moisture from warm, wet air masses moving north from the Gulf of Mexico. The wet air masses tend to follow along the eastern (plains) side of the Front Range, directly in the path of dry, arctic air masses moving south. When the two air masses collide, they swirl around in a huge counterclockwise storm that hurls moisture at the Front Range. Hence yesterday's northeaster.

What a contradictory month. Here we are in February, still winter by the calendar. Our season of heaviest precipitation (usually falling as snow) is just beginning. Yet the lilac buds are so swollen that they look like they could burst, the violets are putting up new green leaves, and the silver maples are blooming with abandon.

After yesterday's spring storm, today is winter again, the sky blue and distant, the air bitingly cold, the light brilliant. Crystal planes in the new white snow reflect the waves of light in all directions, dazzling my brain. A day for sunglasses and skiing.

Sunday, 21 February ✒ The chinooks began to blow as we walked Molly down to the bus station this afternoon. Cold gusts blasted downhill past us, raising goosebumps on my bare knees, hurling trash and grit high in the air, adding a crunchy layer to Molly's cracker and cream cheese sandwiches. The main streets in our part of Boulder—Mapleton Hill and downtown—run west to east, funneling the downslope winds like so many Corps-of-Engineers-straightened stream channels. Dust devils trailed the waves of wind, whirling like small, ghostly tornadoes, their funnels palely outlined by whatever dust and debris they'd ingested. They form downcurrent of obstructions in the winds' torrential flow (in this case, houses, and tall trees). Like the eddies and whirlpools in a rushing stream, they spin downstream until they lose momentum, spiraling slower and slower.

Even the normally ineffable wind was visible this afternoon. From the shelter of the bus station, I watched the big gusts billow out of Boulder Canyon in rounded foggy waves, colored by their load of road grit. They flowed swiftly down Canyon Boulevard, their pale brown crests high above the crowns of the tall trees.

After putting Molly on the bus, Richard and I waded slowly home, hand-in-hand, eyes squeezed half-shut against the grit storm. Unusually oblivious of my surroundings, I concentrated instead on tacking upwind against the big gusts, intent simply on getting home. Still, my senses nagged at my attention. By the time we crossed Broadway to walk uphill on Maxwell, I recognized the cause—the air smelled like forest fire smoke. A peculiar smell of smoldering duff and sappy, green wood burning that raises the adrenaline level of every person who has ever spent time on a forest fire. I know the smell well. My nose sniffed the torrential air flow and said, "forest fire." Logic responded, "This isn't fire season—there is snow on the ridges, the fuels are wet." An old silver maple overhead groaned in an especially fierce gust, distracting me.

I forgot the smell entirely when we turned the corner by our apartment and I remembered the income tax forms awaiting my attention.

After sunset, the winds picked up. Gusts blowing as fast as 100 miles per hour roared past the apartment, thrashing through the ash trees out front and whipping our four-foot-long wind chimes about like oversized steel drinking straws. We sat in the living room and worked—Richard on his dissertation and I on our taxes. Occasionally a particularly violent gust slammed into the apartment building, rousing us briefly from our work. The night was alive with crashing and creaking and screeching noises. Smoke leaked in under the door sill with each gust. I noted it distractedly, but had no attention to spare from negotiating the convolutions of income tax forms.

Not long after we went to bed, a tsunami of a gust blasted past, causing a tremendous crashing noise from the front of the apartment. Richard and I started up out of bed and toured the apartment. We found nothing broken. As we peered out into the darkness past the front picture window, the stainless steel pipes of the wind chime hurtled towards us, nearly cracking the pane—there was our noise. I pulled a chair outside and braced Richard against the wind while he hauled them down, the pipes crashing and banging in dreadfully discordant clangor. It was the first time we've taken them down in the wind.

Tuesday, 22 *February* ❧ This morning the smell of smoke was strong enough that I remarked on it to Richard when I walked outside to get the newspaper. The front page of the paper blared the cause—an out-of-season forest fire, started by a hiker's campfire and whipped by last night's winds along the ridge just west of us between Sunshine and Boulder canyons. My senses were right.

We missed the entire crisis. At its height early this morning, just before the winds fueling it died down, the fire blew rapidly eastward through the sparse ponderosa pine forest and dry grassland towards Boulder, moving close to two subdivisions at the west edge of town. Fire officials sensibly took the precaution of alerting residents and even evacuating a few people. But the winds died, and without their momentum, the fire, a low-intensity ground fire, began to subside. By dawn today, most of the fire fighters were sent home. When snow began falling at midmorning, the fire was history. It had touched an area of about 200 acres, only actually burning a third of that, and fire fighters were simply mopping up the remaining hot spots.

Boulder residents and the local news media reacted to the fire with incredible hysteria. "Snow Halts Forest Fire Short of City," and "Fear, Not Fire, Took Greatest Toll on Those Near Fire," cry the *Daily Camera* headlines. One story begins: "Was Boulder going to burn? When the flames leaped above the mountain that shades the homes in the 100 block of Pearl Street, residents' hearts began to pound...." Indeed! A four-column wide picture of the fire, "Flames of Destruction," with orange flames leaping about three feet in the air (almost reaching the lowest branches of the ponderosas) splashed across the front page. An earlier issue of the paper carried a dramatic telephoto picture of the fire at night, shot from across the canyon atop Flagstaff Mountain. The darkness was lit with hundreds of points of orange flame. On closer inspection, the flames turn out to be the creeping tongues of a ground fire. Reporters described the fire in war-like terms: fire fighters from volunteer departments and various agencies "joined forces" in the "battle to control" the blaze, which "consumed" forty to fifty acres in a "trial by fire." Officials hope to minimize the "destruction" of the forest.... Sensation surely sells newspapers; it does not always serve readers well.

Most of us rightly fear fire. As children, we were instilled with the picture of Smokey the Bear's charred forest with Bambi, Thumper, and other cute animals either burned up in

the forest fire or wandering sadly through the resulting "wasteland." Who could argue with such powerful images? Wildfire
was clearly "bad." But Smokey the Bear and Bambi misled us—
the picture is not nearly so simple. Just as not all thunderstorms trigger a Big Thompson Flood, not all fires devastate
the landscape. Further, value judgements like "bad" or "good"
have no place here. Like summer thunderstorms, wildfires are
normal to the Front Range, an integral part of foothills forest
and grassland ecosystems. Fires and thunderstorms are inti-
mately related, products of the arid climate and dissected
topography. Fires play a crucial role in forest and grassland
processes: speeding nutrient recycling, thinning weak trees to
keep the forest healthy, and promoting the diverse stages of
vegetation that provide deer and other wildlife with a variety
of habitat and food sources. Without fire, these ecosystems
lose diversity esential to their balance.

The question then, is not whether natural fire is good or
bad, but how to reintegrate it into an area with dense, but
scattered, concentrations of flammable structures. Present
policies require that all fires, accidental or natural, be suppressed. Ironically, one effect of the past eighty years or so of
fire suppression in Front Range forests has been to set the
stage for a really catastrophic fire. Without periodic ground
fires, shed needles, twigs, branches, and fallen dead trees—all
natural fuels—pile up. (Decomposition is painfully slow in
arid climates: a large tree trunk may lie intact on the forest
floor for two hundred or more years.) High fuel loadings
guarantee that when fires do occur, they will be bigger, hotter, more catastrophic fires, the kind of fires that fire fighters
dread because even the best modern fire fighting techniques
and equipment can in no way "control" them. These big fires
burn until they either run out of fuel or weather conditions
put them out. Unless fuels in Front Range forests are reduced,
a catastrophic fire—with many homes, and perhaps lives,
lost—is inevitable.

Present fire management policies carry other problems. Fire suppression is very expensive. Last night's small fire cost the county $27,000, not counting overhead; the city spent $5,500 in salaries only, plus the cost of disrupting regular work. Costs to fight larger fires quickly soar into the million- or billion-dollar range. Even if we could suppress fires cheaply and effectively, we have no technology that will duplicate fire's role in forest and range ecosystems as a recycler of nutrients, a culler of weak plants, and a maintainer of diversity. The lack of frequent fires helped set up the conditions necessary for catastrophic insect and mistletoe epidemics—thousands of acres of even-aged, even-sized trees, which all become susceptible to insect infestation at nearly the same time. Hence, pest levels build up to epidemic proportions and the densely packed trees, already stressed by the intense competition for space, light, water, and nutrients, are less resistant. Recent insect epidemics have left forest stands in some foothills canyons more dead than alive. The lack of fires has also resulted in monotonous habitat. Frequent ground fires in the dry forests and grasslands would leave a patchy pattern of burned and unburned areas, resulting in more diverse vegetation, and more niches for wildlife. The City of Boulder's deer report cites long-term fire suppression as one factor in why the dry ponderosa forests in the foothills west of Boulder provide very poor deer habitat.

The past three decades of accelerated Front Range development have compounded the problem. Houses have sprouted throughout Front Range foothills and canyons like toadstools after a rain. Understandably, each is built to take advantage of splendid views and/or wild solitude, with no thought of the inevitability of fire. Hence, they are often firetraps: built of kiln-dried lumber (drier than fuels rated "extreme" in the U.S. Forest Service fire danger rating system), with shake roofs and decks that wrap around trees; explosive propane tanks and dry firewood piles located next to house walls; winding, often narrow access roads; and limited water supplies. Moreover, fire fighting responsibilities are pieced among a crazy quilt of government and volunteer fire departments. No matter how willing and able, all are hampered by the rugged and difficult topography, inadequate equipment, and insufficient water supplies. Add in the fuel accumulation from nearly a century of suppression, the mortality from bark beetle and budworm cycles, the regular occurrence of successive dry years, and what do you get? A disaster waiting to happen.

Reconciling natural fire and other forest processes with development is no simple problem. Fire ecology is a relatively new field of study—we have a lot to learn. Any solutions require a shift from reactive to proactive fire management, and must involve coordinated changes on several fronts: controlled burning plans to reduce fuels, thin forests to healthier conditions, and begin restoring diverse habitats; zoning regulations and building code changes to discourage development in especially fire-prone areas and encourage less-flammable structures; formation of a regional fire-fighting authority to coordinate planned burning and suppression activities. First, however, we must replace our emotional image of Smokey and Bambi's devastated forest with a realistic view of fire's role in Front Range ecosystems.

Front Range land management agencies, local and regional governments, and the public are currently playing the proverbial ostrich; we're sticking our heads in the sand, hoping the problem will go away. Unfortunately, unless we face reality, we are likely to singe more than our tailfeathers.

Saturday, 28 *February* ❧ Tonight, when I walked out to meet Richard, I heard the screech-owl. At Mapleton, I stopped for a moment to look at the long row of spreading maples that split the street into a boulevard. The shaggy grey bark of their fat trunks and long branches glowed in the silvery, liquid moonlight.

Past the ranks of maples, I walked slowly, listening intently for the owl. At first I heard only small mammal rustling and squeaking noises in the dry maple leaves underfoot. I stopped and "looked" intently with my ears, turning my head to locate the sounds. Two, or perhaps three, shrew- or mouse-sized mammals scurried about in the leaves right near my feet. The peculiar cadence of their movements was what attracted my attention: rustling and scratching and squeaking, then a silent pause, then more rustling and scurrying and squeaking, then a silent pause.... Why the pause? I listened closely in the next pause, straining my hearing to sift out any other sounds from the background of city noises: cars passing several blocks away, a door slamming, the wail of a faraway siren.... There! A low, rolling whistle, barely audible, lasting for perhaps five seconds. Then about twenty or thirty seconds of small mammal scurrying sounds, then silence at another low, rolling whistle. The small mammals paused, silent, each time the screech-owl whistled. And for good reason—they are prey for the little owl. But where was the screech-owl? The whistle was so soft that it would be difficult to pinpoint.

I moved a few steps down the sidewalk towards where I thought the whistle originated, then stopped again, listening. Now it seemed to come from the other side of the street, per- haps farther down the block. I walked forward slowly, then stopped to listen. Yes, definitely the opposite side of the street. But where? Just then I saw Richard's tall shadowy sil- houette approaching.

"Can you hear it?" I called softly. He stopped and cocked his head, listening. I could see his delighted grin in the moon- light as he heard the next low whistle. "I think that it's across the street, not in its usual perch," I whispered.

We crossed the street and stood in the quiet darkness under a silver maple. There it was again, quite near. I craned my neck and squinted at the dark maple branches overhead. Screech-owls are quite hard to see, even in the bright moon-

light. In addition to their small size, they are well camouflaged, their feathers colored and patterned quite like the
peeling silver maple bark. It whistled again. I was positive this
time that I knew where the sound came from. "It's in the other
side of this tree," I whispered excitedly to Richard, pointing
up towards a crotch on the far side of the dark tree, just a few
feet away from the second–story windows of a big brick
house. It whistled again, and we scanned the dark shadows on
the back side of the tree. We couldn't see it, but it clearly was
right there next to the house. We were tempted to knock on
the door of the house and rouse the residents. But we lost
courage, imagining their reaction to a summons from two
strangers to hear an owl, and simply walked home.

Sunday, 29 February ❧ Today, leap day, our extra
day in this 366-day year, we drove over the mountains to the
"other Colorado," the less-developed, rural Western Slope.

Over two passes, through a succession of ranges that
together comprise the Rocky Mountains, and past budding
colonies of condominiums and ski areas, we followed the
Eagle River downhill, then the Colorado River. Urban
Colorado seemed far away. Towns were small, surrounded by
space. Even clusters of ranch buildings were far apart, tucked
in sheltering valleys or on the leeward sides of rounded shale
buttes. The pale blue sky and varied landscape dominated the
view. Mule deer grazed in olive-green pinyon-juniper forest,
magpies' black-and-white wings flashed among the gnarled
brown limbs of the shrub oak stands. The bottomlands were
silvery with sagebrush, the high ridges white with snow.

Western Colorado is geology revealed as poetry. Downstream from Avon, thousand-foot-thick grey, gypsum-laden
shale layers formed from the muddy sediments deposited by a
long-ago evaporating inland sea, and later buried by thousands of tons of new sediments edge the river channel. During
those eons of burial, the overlying weight caused the shales to

soften and flow like plastic, creating patterns in the rock like marbled cake batter. Now, river erosion reveals queer, giant swirls and loops in bare, sloping hillsides sculpted into softly voluptuous forms. A few miles downstream, between Edwards and Wolcott, the shales bend in a sharp, vertical syncline, a down-arching fold, and disappear below the surface of the ground only to reappear twenty miles farther downstream, brought above ground again by the opposite, more gently dipping, leg of the fold. Still farther downstream, where the Colorado River cuts through the last mountain arch of the Rocky Mountains, east of Glenwood Springs, is Glenwood Canyon, a rhythmic alteration of thin layers of shales, limestones, dolomites, and quartzites in varying shades of brown, tan, and grey, stepping steeply upwards to the narrow thread of sky above the muddy brown river. Upstream on the Roaring Fork, the skyline burns deep red, its edge of cliffs and peaks formed from layer upon layer of iron-rich sand and mud washed off the ancient Rockies. Burial by later deposits hardened the interbedded sediments into sandstones and shales. The upheaval of the modern Rockies thrust the massive layers, rusted blood red, up to form these gaudy ridges.

The abundant variety of western Colorado landforms is a gift of the rocks themselves: sensual valleys and curving contours result where easily eroded shales form the surface; sandstones, limestones, basalts, and other hard rocks dictate angular breaks, sheer cliffs, and steep, stair-stepping mesas; crazily tilted hills result where the once-level sedimentaries were folded and bent by pressure from crustal warping. Faults slice through it all like the cracks in settling plaster walls, disturbing the layer-cake order of sediments. Much of the color in this landscape is itself also a product of the rocks: brilliant vermillion sandstones, older, dull blood-red sandstones, hard steely grey magnesium-laden dolomites, soft yellow-ochre sea-bottom shales, olive green and dusky purple swampy shales, umber and buff limestones.

We spent the sunny afternoon and early evening hours closeted indoors in a newspaper office in Paonia, a small town in the wide valley of the North Fork of the Gunnison River. Our job was to assemble a functioning computer system from a tangle of hardware and software. Connecting the old computers to the new network proved to be a task not unlike teaching algebraic logic to dinosaurs. Finally, exhausted, we drove up the hill to the house of the paper's editor and publisher for dinner. Above the braided channels of the river bottom, the level shaly benches are carpeted by hay fields, cattail marshes, and orchards; these, in turn, give way to a mosaic of shimmering white aspen groves and dull chestnut oak brush on the jumbled foothills. Above rise the regular, stair-stepped slopes of the steep mesa sides, and, punctuating the level mesa tops, a pointed snowy peak or two.

We sat outside on the deck as the light dimmed. Puffy cumulus clouds glowed gold, rose, and violet, then dissipated in the crystalline evening air. Wild turkeys chortled and gobbled from the shadow-filled trees of a neighboring orchard. Downhill, the cattail marsh released a swelling cacophony from hundreds of red-winged blackbird throats. The liquid burbling songs of a dozen meadowlarks threaded the occasional collective blackbird pause. Shadows dimmed the brilliant snowy whiteness of Mount Lamborn, standing by itself 12,000 feet high above the rounded shale foothills to the southeast. In a reverse of earlier cloud behavior, a thick cloud formed and lowered itself over Lamborn, completely shrouding the peak as darkness clothed the land. The sky remained luminous and clear. Tiny pinpoints of light blinked on down below in the valley, sketching the few streets of town, marking scattered farmhouses. Save those few lights, the immense landscape faded to near-obscurity, only faintly lit by a wash of silver from the rising moon.

March

Thursday, 3 March ❧ This morning dawned in a blanket of white. The night air must have been completely still, since yesterday night's wet snow remained just where it hit. The neighborhood was coated with meringue: each maple tree iced with soft white, each house limned with white, each dark evergreen now white; a sticky stripe plastered the north side of each light pole, blobs bowed the juniper branches and insulated the crocus from the cold; lawns, sidewalks, streets, cars all covered in a white foamy blanket. The day warmed up quickly though, and the meringue melted—liquid again—running and ripping and chuckling downhill to Boulder Creek. As the sun-warmed air stirred in twirling currents, long spongy snakes plopped off of the phone wires. Soft blobs bombed pedestrians from roofs and trees. The air was wet. Great steamy clouds of breath followed us as we walked across Mapleton Hill. Our friend Brooke, visiting from his home on Puget Sound, said as he pulled his knitted watch cap low over salt-and-pepper eyebrows, "I feel like the ocean must be out there somewhere nearby, as if I never left home."

March is a soggy, snowy month. But between storms the weather is balmy, warm enough to melt the snow, sending water rushing to gutters and drains, creeks, and rivers. After a few such spring-like days, the next storm blows in and dumps more heavy wet snow, and so on through the month. These wet snows—averaging over an inch of water in each foot of snow—provide the moisture for spring. Plentiful snows mean moist soil and flourishing new growth; few snows mean droughty soil, a poor start for spring.

The full moon rose high in the dark sky tonight, lighting our evening walk with Brooke. The moon seems far away at this time of year, distant and cold and silvery, like ancient Egyptian mirrors—polished metal disks held up by outstretched arms of the moon goddess. Only we are too distant to see our reflections.

133

The moon's bright reflected light overwhelmed the stars, leaving only the planets clearly visible. In the west, Venus and Jupiter shone together, two bright spots of light past the middle of the sky, on the way towards Flagstaff Mountain. Venus, the brighter of the two, seems to be overtaking Jupiter in a planetary race, gaining ground night after night. Appearances are deceptive, however; the two planets are actually quite far apart in space. It is our perspective, our vantage point from earth that makes them seem close together as they orbit the sun. Planets closer to the earth, like Venus, appear to race faster along the ecliptic, passing the more distant planets. A month ago Venus and Jupiter were far apart, lined up one after another along the ecliptic with Mercury first, each planet about the width of one of my fists apart. But last night Venus and Jupiter shone not even a finger-width apart, two sparkling racers frozen neck to neck in the inky black sky.

Silvery moonlight threw our dim shadows on the ground as we walked up the hill to home. The ridges above town beckoned, glimmering palely in the moonlight, given depth by black velvet shadows. Cloudless nights on the plains are surprisingly bright and spacious. With no dark forest to absorb the moon's bright light, the night is just a dimmer, shadowy, silvery-pale other sort of day.

Sunday, 6 March ≈ The days are warm again. Thursday's snow has already melted and soaked into the thirsty soil. It feels like spring. Each morning, when I step outside to collect the newspaper, I examine the shallow clay bulb bowl on the front step, searching for signs of growth to brighten our still-winter-brown yard.

A few days ago, the crocus bulbs pushed delicate green leaf tips up through the pale conical sheaths that hood each bulb's growing tip. The sheaths look like miniature hothouses, their pale tissue sufficiently translucent to let light reach the growing tip, yet insulating enough to protect it from the cold. The sheltered sunspace under the shield probably allows the new leaves to begin photosynthesizing before they push through, giving extra nutritional umph to their already fast growth. Each day, after the sun melts the frost and warms the dark soil surface, the crocus leaves stretch further upwards, sometimes as much as an inch or two.

This morning brought a surprise: a fat translucent flower bud case about as long as my thumb thrust from the dark soil of the pot. No crocus produced this giant; this comes from a dwarf iris bulb. Dwarf iris are flamboyant plants, reckless gamblers, expending their stores of food to produce bright-colored, outsize flowers first thing. They throw their resources at ensuring the survival of their line, gambling on successful sexual reproduction, before they grow leaves and begin feeding themselves. Crocuses are more conservative, growing leaves and photosynthesizing to restore the energy used in leaf production before expending energy on sex.

After breakfast we four—Richard, Molly, our guest, Brooke, and me—lounged on the bench outside in the warm sunlight, reading the paper and drinking coffee. The rough bricks warmed our backs, the sun shone steadily, box elder bugs crawled in their endless trek up and down the wall. A mud-dauber buzzed around us, exploring, its long legs dangling.

At mid-morning, the iris bud case suddenly split open, revealing a slender yellow flower bud rising from a delicately green half-inch-tall stalk. The pale lemon tissue-paper petals were tightly furled to an acute point. A butterfly suddenly splitting its chrysalis could not have seemed more miraculous than the appearance of that elegant two-inch-long bud.

The miracle continued: ten minutes later, I looked up from the editorial page just in time to watch the flower come to life. In one sudden motion, the first yellow sepal unfurled from the pointed bud, popping away from the tight whorl like a bright bird waking up and stretching. The rest of the flower soon opened, the yellow petals and sepals stretching away

135

one-by-one from the furled spiral until the graceful iris flower fluttered, fully extended, taller than the pale green crocus leaves. Three pairs of petals and sepals—each pair opened out like a set of smiling parted lips, yellow, and dotted with pale green freckles—thrust outward from the joining of their three throats.

Richard, Molly, and Brooke bustled about, loading skis and lunch into the car for our afternoon trip into the foothills. I sat absorbed, entranced by the magic of life that produced a delicate yellow iris flower, the first flower of spring to bloom in our yard.

Monday, 8 March ❧ Oh, yellow iris, why did you bloom! Yesterday afternoon, our friend Pamela died, caught in an avalanche while skiing near Mount Rainier in Washington. Her companion skied it out; Pamela didn't. They found her body early this morning, buried in the white mass of snow at the foot of the slope, face frozen in surprise.

Pamela was like a younger sister to Richard and me in our days in Washington State. She lived down the road from our house in the woods and often stopped by on her way home, bicycle panniers loaded with books and vegetables from her garden. She adopted us into her circle of family with a passion out of proportion with her small frame: one day her donkey-bray laugh split the sound barrier in our kitchen, another, her dark eyes flashed as she struggled to explain her anger. An adventurer who strayed to western Washington from a solo bicycle trip through Nepal and China, she seemed vividly, uncontrovertably *alive*. When Richard and I bid her good-bye before our move, she sang us a farewell song as we drove away. I can still hear her clear, bell-like voice and see her standing there, hands held palm-to-palm in a Buddhist prayer salute, tears trickling past her singing mouth. I saw her only once more, on a damp, grey day last November in Olympia. As I was leaving, I commented about the irony of visiting her at her house in Washington, our old home, when we now lived near her old home in Colorado. "Yes," she said and nodded, grinning a wise woman's Cheshire-cat-meets-Buddha grin, "Things change." We hugged each other in a hard goodbye. "Say hello to the Flatirons for me!" she called as I sprinted to my car, hiding my tears in the rain.

The wind is sharp, out of the northeast, the sky intensely blue. The air is so clear that every detail of the uptilted sandstone slabs of the Flatirons is visible. An indecently beautiful day. I want mourning weather—chill grey fog and dripping rain or howling winds and leaden grey skies.

Still, spring approaches: A striking butterfly flew across the sidewalk in front of me as I walked downtown. It fluttered fast but erratically. Its dusky black wings, each cut by a vivid red-orange stripe said unmistakably, "red admiral." Red admirals overwinter either as chrysalises or adults in mild winter areas and migrate north as far as Central Canada to breed. They are common in open woods, meadows, pastures and other areas where nettles grow. It is early for such a fragile insect to be migrating: the nights are still below freezing, and the winds strong and cold; few flowers are blooming to feed it.

The scrawny young horse chestnut tree in the alley by the irrigation ditch has grown chestnut-colored buds, fat and long and pointed and sticky with sap. Horse chestnuts grow absurdly large buds to accommodate their big compound leaves, which span ten inches from leaflet tip to leaflet tip. The fuzzy buds are already almost as long as my thumb. Below each bud a heart-shaped monkey face grins from the twig where last year's leaf stem broke off in the fall winds. Four or five dark brown dots (scars of the leaf veins) form a semicircle along the lower part of the scar, that ghostly grin all that remains of last year's leaves. The leaf buds above each monkey face are so swollen, the cells stretched so tight, that they look ready to burst, revealing the bright green leaflets, folded and pleated tightly, like butterfly wings in the chrysalis, to fit in the confines of the bud.

Across the alley, the twisted grey branches of an old tangled lilac are studded with buds, each sprouting tiny, pale green, heart-shaped leaves. The air is moist and warm, fragrant with life.

Life and death. Death makes possible new life by returning the materials needed to build life: the calcium of bones, the carbon, nitrogen and phosphorus of our flesh; all are returned to circulation to give birth to others. Yet that makes it no easier to bear the loss of a loved friend, who died so far away, buried under a flood of snow.

Tuesday, 15 March ❧ Last night brought winter again, the temperature dropping into the teens. This morning when I walked with Richard toward his office, the air in the shadows was so cold it felt heavy, dense. Despite the warm sun, our breath puffed out in clouds of white frost. The night's cold held the air unusually still; no stirring of sun-warmed eddies whispered through the silver-grey maple branches.

The cold also froze the top layer of soil wherever the surface was bare and uninsulated. Meltwater from Sunday's snow contorted the saturated soil into bizarre shapes as it froze. The water expanded when it changed from liquid to solid, pushing the dark soil into inch-high pedestals, like hobgoblins, black with icy fringes of water crystals. The bare ground under the front yard ash tree was transformed into a miniature ice-sculpted landscape: narrow twisting passages between fantastically eroded rock columns. The crocus and daffodil bulbs must indeed be firmly anchored to have resisted being heaved right up out of the freezing soil.

March weather is living up to its crazy reputation: the past ten days have fluctuated from near-tropical sunny days to dense, wet snow; then sub-freezing nights. Through it all the delicate yellow dwarf iris flower has continued to bloom, crisp and fresh. Its three-part blossom stands alone, bright and fragile, the solitary flower in my bulb bowl. Each night it closes tight and each day opens wide again, the sepal lips curved back like a smile. A line of golden fuzz leads down each throat, aiming insects towards the nectary. On their way to the banquet, the tight passage forces them to brush the golden stamens, picking up pollen. I bent close to the bright flower this morning, to see if it had attracted any early insects. I was astonished to smell a sweet, faintly musty scent in the air above it—of course, pollinating insects have keen senses of smell. The delicate fragrance is its advertisement. But its blandishments were so far unsuccessful; its stamens remain pristine, untouched by insect guests.

This afternoon, Richard directed me to an oasis of spring on Fifteenth Street: a yard dotted with vivid purple clumps of dwarf iris. The clumps, each packed with a dozen or so flowers, were such an intense hue that it was difficult to bring them into focus, as if their color lay just at the edge of the visible spectrum. Surrounded by the bleached greys and tans of winter, they vividly proclaimed the overture of spring.

Snow flurries drifted from the low grey clouds. The north wind cut right through my jacket, chill and sharp. My ears stung. But I stood still, taking in the irises' message.

Wednesday, 16 March ✒ This afternoon we bundled up in our jackets and hats and scarves and mittens and walked down the hill and across town. Grey clouds hung low above town, their drooping underbellies smothering the foothills. Walking up the hill to campus we heard, then saw, two ravens soaring on the updrafts at the edge of the hill, two very black shapes against the pale grey sky. They soared over us, wings stiffly outstretched and wedge-shaped tails spread wide, circling each other, crossing paths in the air. They croaked as they soared, their voices an unlikely mating of rasp and bell, like wooden percussive blocks knocking together.

Common ravens, with a four-foot wingspread, are the largest perching bird, much larger than their relatives the crows. Ravens pair for life, engaging in courtship with agile, dance-like aerial displays: soaring together, wingtips touching; wheeling around each other, scribing spirals in the sky like these two; the males sometime tumble like clowns, diving and climbing. Ravens winter in small communal groups, and leave the roost at this time of year to nest.

Snow flurries swirled against our backs on the chill northeast wind. The big birds soared, black against grey, a monochromatic scene from a Japanese brush painting, backed by the chill wind.... Black ravens croaking, warning of snow.

When we started home the clouds hung even lower, already beginning to hunker over the tops of the trees. Big white clumps of snow swirled like drifts of feathers on the wind. We walked quickly, heads down against the sharp wind and the blinding snow as it twirled faster and faster.

Later, after dark, I walked over to the Naropa Institute to hear a lecture. About four inches of snow had collected and it continued to pile up. I walked in a quiet world, all noises damped by the thick blanket on the ground and the quadrillions of flakes swirling from the low clouds. The streets and the usually jammed pedestrian mall were both deserted. The snow fell thick and fast. Soon, I too was covered. Under the streetlights, the shadows of the clumps of snow swirled and flurried like a blowing sandstorm.

After the lecture I walked home in a very quiet night. The snow had ceased. About six inches lay on the ground, light and fluffy and wonderfully soft. The thump and rattle of a snowplow blade passed behind me on Arapahoe Avenue, transporting me home to rural northwest Wyoming. I remembered lying awake and hearing the fleet of Highway Department snowplows rumbling up the highway above my little cabin outside of Cody, their six-foot-tall, V-shaped blades slicing through each wind-crusted drift.

The snowplow rumbled on up Arapahoe Avenue, the heavy blade rattling as it hit holes in the pavement. I wiped my eyes with a mittened hand and walked on home through the quiet, dark neighborhoods, scuffing in the snow.

Thursday, 17 March ✒ The yellow iris blossom is finished. After last night's snowfall, the clouds dissipated and with no insulation, the air temperature plunged. This morning, the delicate petals of the iris lie wilted, crumpled like wet tissue paper. Goodbye Pamela!

Sunday, 20 March ✒ Today is the vernal equinox. This morning's sunrise brought spring. Today the sun will be above the horizon exactly as many hours as it is below the horizon, but soon daylight will gain over darkness, growing longer and longer until the summer solstice. The dates of the vernal and autumnal equinox vary from year to year because our calendar does not exactly coincide with the rotation of the earth around the sun. The vernal equinox usually falls on March 21, but this year it fell on March 20. This year's seasons all begin early, the earliest seasons since 1896–7.

Spring has begun already for the plants, regardless of March's fickle weather. This morning early, Richard and I walked down Mapleton Avenue, past the big houses that line the brow of the hill. The ground was soft and damp, without a trace of frost. Violet flowers peeped through the litter of last fall's leaves, crocus bulbs sprouted clumps of vivid yellow and purple flowers, new bright green leaves colored bare honeysuckle branches.

In our own front yard, purple-and-white crocus blossoms circle the ash tree, dancing lightly as the breeze stirs the air at ground level. Each fragile, vase-shaped flower is formed from six petal/sepals, rising directly from a short stem. Thread-like purple veins stripe the white tissue of the petals; inside, chrome-yellow stamens terminate pale anthers just below a brilliant orange stigma. A ring of slender, grass-like green leaves surrounds each cluster of silky flowers.

Although most garden crocus bulbs are probably grown in the flat fields of the Netherlands, wild crocus, from which this graceful circle of plants in our yard descended, are native to the desert mountains of the Mediterranean and Southwest Asia (including Turkey, Iran, Iraq, and Pakistan).

Saffron, the dye and spice of Mediterranean and Asian cultures, comes from another cultivated crocus, likewise native to Asia Minor. Saffron is actually the dried stigmas (the surface where pollen lands to fertilize the flower) of saffron crocus flowers. The flowers must be harvested by hand, the feathery orange stigmas picked, separated with tweezers, and dried. Collecting an ounce of saffron powder requires some 4,000 crocus flowers! Imagine how beautiful saffron farms must be, their fields carpeted with millions of purple crocus flowers, the tissue-like petals stirring in the breeze.

Thursday, 24 *March* ❧ I *listened* this morning, as Richard and I walked across Mapleton Hill towards his office, hearing and feeling instead of seeing the day.

As we left the apartment, a chill gust blasted down the walk, dashing the pipes of the wind chime together in clashing disharmony, swooshing the dry leaves and scraps of old newspaper against the fence. The force of the gust slowed our forward progress but we plowed on, furrowing the moving air. As the noise of the gust subsided, the notes of a house finch song rose above the wind, coming from the top of the cottonwood tree across Maxwell Street. My eyes pressed tightly shut, I imagined the small, streaky bird, perched way out at the end of the branches at the very top of the tree, dull reddish head upraised, warbling as loud as it could, riding the swaying branches like a ship rolling in heavy seas. Another gust blew across the street, stinging my face with its load of grit. I grabbed Richard's elbow for support, and we walked on up the street.

In the next pause between gusts, the starlings' cacophony reigned above other noises, wheezing and whistling and croaking like an orchestra tuning up for a concert of discordant modern music. Through the starling's noise, I thought that I heard a killdeer. I stopped, letting go of Richard's arm in surprise. My eyes popped open unbidden, I looked up, searching for a slender brown-and-white plover with pointed wings flying overhead in the bright blue sky. I saw none. I heard the plaintive *kill-deer* again, nearby—coming from the outstretched throat of a male starling.

Disappointed, I shut my eyes and walked on, momentarily angry at the starlings for tricking me, and for taking over our neighborhood. Hundreds of birds live here, mostly starlings. Habitat that could support more common flickers, hairy woodpeckers, tree swallows, western bluebirds, warbling vireos, chipping and song sparrows and other birds is populated with a surfeit of European starlings. It is not the starlings' fault, though; their abundance is not some plot they have hatched to reduce the diversity and beauty of the bird community here, they are just being starlings. We humans have created the conditions that allow starlings to dominate.

As we continued up Maxwell Street, the wind roared downhill, eddying around us as it passed, nearly drowning out the starling orchestra. I concentrated, tuning my ears like antennae to hear other bird songs through the wind and the starlings. From across the street somewhere came the two-note alarm call of a common flicker. Up the hill farther, chickadees called from low in a backyard: "Phoe-be... Phoe-be... Phoe-be." I couldn't resist looking for them. The plaintive two-note whistle sounded again, and I spotted two small birds foraging on the whippy twigs of a forsythia bush. Their grey-and-white plumage, with neat black cap and black-and-white face mask, seemed sober in contrast to the yellow forsythia buds.

Forsythia bushes studded with chrome-yellow buds, crocuses blooming in fragile clumps—spring is indeed here. Even last week's swollen lilac buds have popped open. The tiny reddish leaves have curled back, revealing tight clusters of flower buds, like so many miniature purple ears of corn—if corn grew purple. Each fat cluster is only about half of the size of my thumbnail, but each flower bud is already distinct, packed together tight as corn kernels. The embryonic flower buds are scored at their upper ends by two lines crossing at right angles to each other—the ends of the four petals, which will open, releasing their sweet lilac scent, when the buds grow big enough.

We turned the corner on Sixth Street and walked straight into a southerly gust. Momentarily blinded and deafened, we grabbed each other's hands and waded upstream into the wind, our upper bodies canted forward to counteract the force of the gust. When the gust passed, the starling orchestra filled the air again, chirruping and whistling and squeaking from the branches of the old shaggy silver maples lining the street.

At the edge of the hill, we turned the corner into a calm patch of air, momentarily sheltered from the wind's roar behind a screen of tall spruces. We stumbled for a moment, off-balance without the force of the wind. The sudden quiet was deafening.

Friday, 25 March ❧ Here in Fort Collins, this afternoon's wind is especially lively, blowing down the streets like a mad thing, gusting wildly, flapping awnings and banners like sails, whirling around corners making kites of newspaper, leaves, hats—and disheveling my hair so that the loose tendrils dance, red-blond and sparkling, around my eyes. Between gusts, the air is still and sun-warmed. Then another chill blast raises goosebumps on my pale skin, rattles the canvas awnings, setting leaves and papers in flight.

The gusts, blowing directly from the edge of the snowstorm that trails white wooly clouds over the ridges west of town, feel fiercely cold. Up around the divide is a driving snowstorm; here on the plains we catch the edge of the wind, but not the storm.

Like Boulder, Fort Collins is a small city. Also like Boulder, it was laid out and built by European immigrants in the late 1800s; both towns are now home to large state university campuses. There the similarity ends. Fort Collins is clearly a rural town, a place where traditional values are strong and change comes slowly; where cafes keep farmer's hours, where bill caps and cowboy boots are still considered work clothes, espresso is a rarity, and pickup trucks with stock racks out-number BMWs. The downtown shopping area sports a JC Penney's, a Rexall variety store, a Miller Stockman western store. Fort Collins seems comfortable as a farm town grown big, built to serve an agricultural population, set solidly on the flat plains, several miles from the mountains. The original town plan is rectangular. The streets are boulevards built wide enough to accommodate the most unwieldy of farm imple-ments, intersecting at right angles. The Victorian houses are solid and square, almost Calvinistic in their simplicity. They are direct descendants of the farmhouses that dot the rural Midwest—the larger ones massive, ornamented simply; the smaller ones spare.

Boulder, in contrast, sees itself as a sophisticated and rich city, as proud of its liberal traditions as it is of its dramatic set-ting—the kind of place where tourists come to gawk at the mountains and the inhabitants; where cafes keep stockbroker's hours and serve espresso brewed with fresh-roasted beans; where cellular phones, portable computers, and briefcases are essential tools; and Buddhists are as common as Baptists.

Built by those who aspired to make their fortunes mining or taking miners' money, Boulder straddles the edge where the plains tilt into mountains. It flows upward over the rumpled topography, aiming towards the hills. The main streets of the old town radiate like the spokes of a wheel, following the drainages that gave access to the mountains and the mines. The street pattern bows to the form of the landscape, never quite achieving the rectangular symmetry of a town imposed on a flat site. Architecture in the old parts of town—and the modern "Boulder Victorian" style elsewhere—is exuberantly self-aggrandizing, unabashedly declaring the wealth of its builders, the buildings adorned with towers, gables, curved porches, a multitude of details from whimsical to frilly.

The afternoon cumulus clouds blow swiftly past, an uncountable flock of sheep pouring east on the incessant wind. Usually I love the wind, but this afternoon I am tired and cold, so I am out of charity with it. Above me, a rock dove sails, wings dihedral, balancing on the wind for a moment, hanging in the air as if it were still. Then it tips one wing and drops suddenly, gone behind the worn red brick wall of the building across the street. I brush the loose hair out of my eyes and snug my coat collar up around my neck as a flurry of icy snow skims by on the wind.

Thursday, 31 March ❧ Today is the last day of March; tomorrow, All Fool's Day. The National Weather Service predicted a twenty percent chance of snow showers for yesterday. About mid-afternoon yesterday, the hills disappeared as the clouds lowered down over town and began to snow, and snow, and snow…. Eight inches of snow fell, and it is still snowing this morning. Perhaps the forecast was the weather service's April Fool's joke, one day early.

Last night I walked out in the storm to the nearby grocery store. Wet snow swirled heavily in the air, piled up on the ground and on my coat and in my face. My skin was soon misted with droplets. But by the time I walked home, the air temperature had fallen and the half-melted snow on the sidewalks was freezing in pebbly popcorn bumps.

This morning the world is quiet, muffled in white fluff. I haven't yet heard a car go by on Ninth Street.

If I were a rancher or farmer, I wouldn't be so delighted with the snow. It is calving and lambing season for domestic stock. Every year ranchers gamble on the weather, breeding their stock so they will give birth in early spring—the season of spring snows—in order to have the longest possible time to fatten up their stock before fall markets. And each year brings a wet spring snowstorm, and anxious stock raisers watching the snow fall, worrying about whether the newborns can survive the cold, wet weather. I wonder about the calves we saw on the way home from Fort Collins the other day. Are they sturdy enough to survive two or three days of exposure to this weather? It is no accident that the native grazers, the pronghorn antelope, deer, and elk that have flourished on these plains and in the foothills through thousands of spring snowstorms, calve or fawn much later.

Paradoxically, the snow is also a boon to ranchers and farmers. It brings much-needed soil moisture to pastures, fields, and rangelands, ensuring spring growth. Our 25 inches of snow this month contained 2.5 inches of precipitation, or ten percent water—good wet snow to begin the growing season.

April 16

April

Saturday, 2 April ❧ April's full moon came last night, the pink moon, the first full moon of spring. I saw it when I woke before dawn this morning, a round and silvery disk hung in the pale sky above the dark ridges west of town. It set behind the high peaks just before the copper disk of the sun burst over the low eastern horizon. If the western horizon was as flat as the eastern, the two disks would have been in opposition, the pale silvery one disappearing just as the brilliant golden one rose.

Monday, 4 April ❧ Spring is not a static season. Each day brings new buds swollen almost to bursting, new flowers, new insects, new smells, life in abundance. Clumps of tiny, intensely purple violets bloom in every lawn, each crack in the sidewalks, each crevice between gnarled silver maple roots. Daffodils wave gently in the breezes, bright yellow trumpets at the end of long green stalks. Clumps of dwarf tulips bloom with vivid splashes of scarlet and yellow above stiff blue-green leaves. Floppy yellow blossoms cover the slender brown twigs of forsythia bushes.

Mourning cloak butterflies are beginning to emerge from their chrysalises and flutter through yards around the hill. Their velvety bright-colored inner wings, dusky brownish-maroon bordered with a band of iridescent blue spots and a wide creamy yellow edge, contrast with their drab, bark-colored outer wings. Butterfly emergence signals mating time. For mating to be successful, spring must be far enough along that when the resulting eggs hatch, the host plant will be available to provide the voracious little caterpillars with tender green food. The cycle is a precise one—if the caterpillars hatch too early, they will die of starvation; too late, they do not have sufficient time to mature and build their chrysalises.

This morning's altocumulus clouds were a pod of smooth, grey whales swimming slowly in the blue sky just east of the divide. Over the day they metamorphosed into altostratus opacus, an even grey cloud blanketing the entire sky, obscuring the sun. I much preferred the whales.

Friday, 8 April ❧ We drove from Boulder to Laramie this morning so that Richard could give his dissertation seminar. All too soon he will finish his degree, bringing our stay here to an end.

The highway route from Boulder to Laramie crosses the Rocky Mountains in open country—the whole 110-mile route lies in grasslands, passing through only a smidgen of forest. Between Boulder and Fort Collins, the route crosses farmlands and skirts suburbs, running parallel to the Front Range. The snowy peaks rise above the regular furrows and roads where once stretched unbroken midgrass prairie. Past Fort Collins, the highway cuts west through the sedimentary hogbacks that edge the Front Range. Here it passes through a bit of forest, then quickly back into grassland, now unplowed dry bunch-grass range. Cultivated land and urban development fall away, no longer dominant. The road climbs up onto the core of the mountains, swooping up and up and up through shortgrass rangelands stretched like a thin skin over the irony red soil of the Fountain sandstone formation. Higher still the road goes, passing through scattered dabs of forest as it climbs onto the rounded backbone of the range. Here the arching sedimentary formations are eroded away, revealing the harder, crystalline granitic core, and drier, sparser grasslands dominate.

The grassland communities that cover the core of the range from west of Fort Collins to the Laramie Basin are a continuously varying mosaic, their relative height and density changing with the topography. On the deep soils and flat surfaces of stream bottoms grow dense riparian grasslands with bunches of taller grasses, topped by the four-foot-tall, coarse bunches of wild-rye. Upslope from these grassy jungles, both height and productivity drop quickly as soils thin and available water becomes limited: wetter north-facing slopes and sheltered pockets of deeper soils support taller, foot-and-a-half-high bunchgrasses; shorter, drought-tolerant grasses grow close to the ground in wide-spaced tufts on the windswept, exposed high surfaces.

As I drove, I scrutinized the grassy landscape with interest. This time of year the continuum is still winter brown—golden-brown where prudent grazing management leaves some of the previous year's production to protect the grass rootstocks from winter's searing drought; deathly grey-brown where spendthrift management allows grazers to nibble plants right to the rootstocks. Most of the range was grey-brown. It looked shabby, like a fraying carpet, worn so thin that the soil showed through. Worse still, the steeper hillsides were pocked in many places by crescent-shaped erosion scarps, where grazing has worn the grassy pile away completely and the soil has sagged, leaving an eyebrow-shaped "cliff" one or two feet high. These embryonic gullies channel normally gentle sheet flow to fall abruptly over the lip, like the drop basin below a waterfall. Instead of flowing evenly across the ground surface and sinking in to nurture plant roots, the runoff, flowing faster and harder, picks up surface debris and soil, gaining more cutting power. It eventually erodes a channel in the soil and pours downhill into the nearest stream, increasing its speed and power as it goes, carrying its load of soil. The channel deepens as it gathers water and soil from all around...and the gully cycle is well on its way.

The streambanks of existing drainages also showed signs of wear. Once-rounded and grassy banks were steeply gullied, with small cliffs cut deep in the red sediments. Beneath the gnarled old cottonwoods, instead of lush stands of tall grass, the productive riparian grasslands were grazed as smooth as bowling greens, cropped almost bare.

What are we doing to our rangelands? These grasslands looked abused. Each year's grazing seems to have consumed the whole of that year's crop, leaving no savings account to draw on for the next season's growth, and no organic matter to insulate fragile rootstocks or enrich thin soils. Once this ecosystem begins to unravel, the damage accelerates: the thin soil, with no network of roots to hold it, no mat of organic matter to protect its surface, will quickly erode away, damaging other ecosystems—choking streams, clogging ponds, suffocating fish and other aquatic life. Do we not remember the lessons of the Dust Bowl years? Where are the caretakers of this rangeland?

I once spoke with a Nisqually Indian leader who has spent years working for enlightened resource management in the Pacific Northwest. Native American cultures knew, long before we biologists came to our cautious conclusions, that salmon are reliable indicators of the health of the whole mountain/river/forest/ocean region west of the Cascades. Where the salmon populations are abundant and in balance, the water is clean, the river flows steady, the forests healthy, the whole system in good shape. Once the salmon begin to disappear, something is wrong. When this Indian leader presents his resource management plans to legislators, timber company managers, or other groups, he points out the window towards a river or the Sound and says, "I speak for the salmon—he is out there, swimming around; he cannot come in here and speak to you about these things. So he sent me here to speak to you." He looks his audience right in the eye and says calmly, "I speak for the salmon." No one snickers; people listen.

I have trusted those who use these grazing lands to be good and wise stewards, like my Nisqually friend and the salmon. It seems that they are not. Who speaks for the rangelands?

Thursday, 14 April ⟐ This evening I drove to Denver to pick Richard up at the airport. The sun set behind a hazy thundercloud towering over the high peaks of the range. Other thunderclouds built and billowed, clogging the sky.

Gusts skittered across the mesas, saturating the air with dust and water, scattering the evening light into a golden haze. The outlines of the nearest peaks, brown, jagged shapes slightly more solid than the diffuse thundercloud bottoms, were just barely discernible. Those massive clouds—like hands grasping for the middle of the sky—bubbled upwards, hazy and gaseous, their tops smeared eastward by the high winds coming off of the peaks. All were silhouetted by the setting sun so that the light pouring through blurred the lines like a drawing smeared by the artist's dragging hand. The air was translucent, not transparent, an amber veil. To the south, where the storm clouds were thickest, grasslands, foothills, sky, clouds all merged into golden haze.

It was an evening landscape worthy of Thomas Moran and the other romantic landscape painters, charged with a sense of great spiritual power. Intense slanting sunbeams pouring through the storm clouds, the hazy amber light, each mote of dust in the air sparkling, suffused the scene with grandeur. The twin streams of traffic on the parkway rushed by. The light faded, losing its amber glow, the clouds dissipated; dusk fell, the glorious evening gone.

This time of month the moon is a daytime creature, a ghostly sliver shimmering in the blue sky. It rises in the early morning, slightly less than an hour before the sun, and sets in the evening three-quarters of an hour before the sun sets. This morning, the sun rose at about quarter to seven; this evening, it set behind the dark spine of the foothills at eight o'clock. That makes today just a bit longer than thirteen hours—the days are now longer than the nights, and lengthening fast.

Saturday, 16 *April* ✒ Tonight, Richard, Molly and I walked homeward across campus in the early evening. At the edge of campus, we stopped on the brow of the hill to look north along the line of the foothills, then we descended the hill on the worn sandstone steps. At the creek, we turned

155

upstream to walk the creek path through town. The evening light was golden and hazy. The willows along the creek sprouted tiny green leaves. And the cottonwood buds dangled long catkins that waved in the slightest breeze, either dispersing or catching pollen. (Cottonwoods are dioecious—each tree is all male or all female.) The creek was very low, studded with inviting stepping stones. Molly practiced creek crossing, wandering down the banks to test each likely ford, absorbed in the pleasure of hopping from rock to rock.

Just before the path goes under the Broadway Avenue bridge, a loud, warbling, wren-like song sounded over the roar of auto traffic and the rush of the stream. Richard and I walked ahead quickly, curious to find the singer. The song seemed to issue from the creek on the far side of the bridge. From under the bridge, we saw the source of the music—two plump dark birds, about the size of starlings, balanced one atop the other on the diversion dam, the top one twittering loudly—unabashed avian sex. At first we thought they were starlings, and turned to walk on. Then the male bird hopped off of the female's back and walked with a curious bobbing motion towards the stream. We stopped, riveted. "Dippers!" I exclaimed in surprise.

When standing still, dippers are amazingly nondescript: small birds with steely grey-black plumage, rounded bodies, and short tails. In motion, though, their eccentric character is revealed. Dippers are the only truly aquatic songbirds, making their living catching aquatic insects, and occasionally small clams, snails, and trout fry from beneath the surface of swift-flowing mountain streams. (Their food preferences overlap with those of trout.) They can actually swim (using their wings), dive, and even walk on stream bottoms, picking up insect larvae from the rocks and logs. Like ducks and other waterfowl, they have an extraordinarily large preen gland, which provides oil to keep their feathers waterproof. A flap over their nostrils keeps water from entering their respiratory system; a third eyelid protects their eyes from sediment in the water. Dippers are related to both pipits and thrushes—they act like pipits, with quick jerky movements and fast flight; their long warbling song may owe its melodic quality to thrush songs. And of course, they "dip," the curious bobbing motion that gives them their name.

One of the pair walked right off the top of the diversion dam into the cascading stream, descending under the surface. Richard and I watched with as much excitement as Molly. Its plump dark body was visible underwater as it walked around the rocks, probing with its bill and bobbing up and down, searching for food.

We watched them until the light faded, then we walked on. Dippers are common on mountain streams, where they build their football-sized nests in the shelter of waterfalls. Yet here were dippers mating along Boulder Creek next to downtown! As we walked away, their warbling song threaded through the urban noise, touching the evening air with wildness.

Saturday, 23 *April* ☙ Evening clouds, grand towers of cumulonimbus, pile miles high in the sky over Flagstaff Mountain. Underneath, untouched by the slanting sun, they are dove grey; above, the sun paints their puffy heights pure white. These popcorn-like mounds are summer clouds, their bulging heights undisturbed by winds, like those that build high in the still air at the end of hot summer days. In contrast, spring clouds are usually wind-shaped—smeared or honed or otherwise sculpted by the high-altitude westerlies. Yet to-night's clouds are crisp in puffy detail, declaring the stillness of the lower atmosphere.

Earlier, Molly, Richard, and I went searching for spring wildflowers up the trail behind Richard's office. Uphill from the fragrant rank of tangled wild plum lining the irrigation ditch, the south-facing slope was dotted with swollen prickly pear pads and sulphur yellow clumps of mustard flowers. The prickly pear's tissue reservoirs are fat with water from recent rain, stretched to capacity. Between the swollen green pads, small, silvery green rosettes of leaves dotted the bare soil, each issuing forth a slender stalk ending in a cluster of tiny, intense, sulphur-yellow flowers. The small, four-petaled, cross-shaped flowers (the size of a pencil eraser worn to a nubbin) are mustards—the scientific name for the family is *Cruciferae*, for the cross-shaped flowers. Leaves and stems alike are rough, covered with stellate hairs (hairs branching in a star shape from a single stalk) that give the plant its silvery-green look. A few of the flower clumps had already produced fruit. These twin bladders attached to the flower stalk reveal the plant's identity: double bladder pod mustards, one of the first spring flowers in the dry grasslands.

We climbed up behind the Dakota hogback where the sandstone stands on end, sticking up like ancient, lichen-crusted giant's bones. Under the scattered ponderosa pines were more pale yellow blossoms—Nuttall's violets, named for Thomas Nuttall, a self-taught English naturalist who in the 1830s published the first field guide to North American birds. Nuttall's violets are quite tiny (the size of a cough drop) and easily overlooked. Close examination shows that each flower is different and exquisitely detailed, with varying amounts of purple shading the backs of the petals, and purple veins threading a lacy pattern on the yellow upper sides. Some flowers are nearly lemon yellow, contrasting sharply with deep purple backs; others are pale cream shaded with lilac; still others are almost entirely yellow with just a blush of purple around the nectary at the base of the sepals. Their leaves are long and spatulate, not heart-shaped like most violets.

Impressed in the clayey red soil was a clear trail of delicate deer prints, leading from violet clump to violet clump. Abruptly truncated flower stalks stood in mute witness to the nibbling teeth that had nipped them off. Deer are not alone in their taste for violets: insects search them out and drink the surgary liquid in their nectary, ants unwittingly distribute the hard seeds as they nibble at the sweet "tail" attached, even humans are rediscovering violets and other edible flowers.

Up the street from our apartment, the line of Norway maples has sprouted tiny leaves (the biggest about two inches across) from swollen buds. The vacant lot behind us is full of blooming crab apples and wild plum sprouts. At night the sweet scent pools along the ground like a snowdrift, pouring into our bedroom window in dense, intoxicating clouds.

Wednesday, 27 April ✌ The green grass is here—suddenly the grasslands surrounding Boulder have metamorphosed from faded winter-brown to a bright green carpet.

We went wildflower hunting again this afternoon, this time on the slopes of Chautauqua Park. All around, the lush new green was dotted with flowers. We walked uphill until the town noises receded, then sat on the hillside looking north towards Wyoming. From Chautauqua Park the foothills roll away westward like green waves from the flat plains, long gentle swells breaking over the ragged snowy shore of the Continental Divide.

Close to the soil the earliest of the spring flowers bloomed, their short flower stalks bearing a tight cluster of pinhead-sized cream-colored flowers. Black anthers that look like pepper sprinkles on the creamy clusters give the plant its name: salt-and-pepper. The silvery-green, fern-like leaves grow nearly flush to the soil surface in the sheltered microclimate between the taller bunchgrasses, warmed by solar heat stored in the soil surface, allowing salt-and-pepper to begin photosynthesis long before taller plants.

Downslope, the thickets of wild plum were bursting with ivory flowers, like pencil-thin drifts of snow lining the ravines. Wild plum grows from two feet to about five feet high, its tight branching pattern and stout, spiny twigs forming formidable tangles. Spring transforms the thickets when the plum blooms, releasing its fragrance in clouds of sweet mist.

A patch of chokecherries grew nearby, its stems neatly hedged by browsing deer teeth. Unlike the other shrubby islands of chokecherry patches that dot the grasslands, this patch was completely bare, but it hummed with activity. Its short, thick branches sported cobwebby "tents" crawling with inch-long, hairy grey caterpillars and sprinkled with their grainy scat. The colony of tent caterpillars, among the most voracious grazers of the insect world, had already denuded their host. Still the hungry caterpillars crawled slowly up and down the bare stalks, searching for more food. To reach new food from this isolated patch, they would have to abandon their protective webs and crawl across several hundred yards of open grassland exposed to a variety of predators. The burgeoning colony faced a problem familiar to humans: that of balancing population size with resource supply. I wonder if the caterpillars will survive long enough to pupate.

Deer scat abounded on the soil around us—both solid, neatly cylindrical winter pellets and wetter, loose piles from spring grazing—testifying to the popularity of these slopes for Boulder's deer herd.

A cumulus cloud grew between us and the sun, sweeping chill air over the hillside with its shadow. We roused ourselves and walked on uphill.

On a northeast-facing slope, near the top of the mesa, the green carpet was splotched with ragged patches of bare soil, flattened dead grass, and looping mounds of rodent tunnels. Late snowbank spots, where the winter's accumulation of snow had just melted, revealed the bare beginnings of spring in the newly warmed soil. Each patch was dotted with new leaves, bright green and red against the brown soil. Even here, flowers were blooming, delicate pink-veined, cream-colored flowers—spring beauty, herald of the new season in mountain meadows. Their fat stems and leaves are succulent and nutritious, full of energy stored in a Jerusalem artichoke-type corm the season before. In other parts of the Rockies where grizzly bears still survive, the big bears search out spring beauty corms to eat when they emerge, thin and hungry, from winter hibernation. A meadow harvested by grizzlies is a queer sight, the dark soil pocked by dozens of holes where the bears' long curved claws have excavated the plant, corm, soil, and all.

At the lip of the mesa, a strip of desert grew on soil so thin that the bones of the sandstone outcrop showed through. This miniature desert is a microsite, a small area within another ecosystem that, because of radically different environmental conditions, grows a whole different community. A linear foot down slope were relatively lush bunchgrasses; a foot behind us the rest of the mesa top was forested with ponderosa pines. In the arid microsite grew widely spaced mats of blue grama grass, characteristic of the arid, sandy soils of the shortgrass prairie. Between the low pile of the blue grama protruded a scattering of half-dollar-sized, bumpy plants. Corypantha cactus, each plant comprised of about ten breast-like bumps, each bump terminated by a tight whorl of businesslike spines, the whole clustered into a mound (the plant's appearance is much better described by the old scientific name, *Mammalaria*, "breast-like").

Downslope, sandlilies bloomed, their starry white flowers almost hidden by the fast-growing clumps of wiry needle-and-thread-grass and junegrass leaves. Sandlilies look like wild crocus, with clusters of white, six-petaled flowers rising from the middle of a clump of slender, crocus-like leaves. They bloom early, their starry flowers dotting foothills and plains grasslands even before the snow is completely melted.

Dusk fell, bleaching the color from the towering cumulus clouds overhead. We walked down the hill to town as the shadow of the Front Range stretched east, snuffing the day.

April 23

May

Wednesday, 4 May ❧ May began with rain here, and wet snow in the mountains. I hope it will continue similarly. May is usually our wettest month, providing crucial moisture for the growing season. We need the moisture: April was drier than usual, bringing 1.5 inches of total precipitation, about two-thirds of our normal total. Although last calendar year was unusually wet (Boulder had 25 inches of precipitation, 7 inches more than normal) much of that fell as rainfall in the unusually wet spring and early summer, sustaining last summer's growing season. Then September and October were drier than normal, November about average, December a little wetter. January precipitation was about half of the normal amount, February and March up over normal again. Then came April, drier and much warmer, to melt snowpacks early. We need a good month of rain.

It is a beautiful sunny day, the blue sky partly veiled in the west by high, thin cirrostratus clouds streaming over the summits of the foothills.

The horse chestnut tree on Pine Street has sprouted tall spikes of creamy-colored flower buds. First, the new green leaves unfolded, metamorphosing from punk Mohawks to bright green hands, fingers widespread. And now, big conical flower clusters stretch up past the palmate leaves. Soon the fat buds will open to tubular flowers speckled orange and yellow inside, endowing the whole tree with a profusion of blooms. Now, though, the flowers are still buds, covered with the same rusty felt that insulates the surface of the new leaves and stalks. The cobwebby fuzz scrapes off easily under my fingernail, revealing brilliant green cells. As the cells grow and their walls harden, the fuzz drops off, shed when the danger of widely fluctuating temperatures is past.

The flowers mature into greenish, spiny capsules, each bearing three smooth brown nuts. The nuts, easily gathered once the spiny capsule dries and splits, are not edible. But their silky smooth surface, deep chestnut color, and odd three-cornered shape make them ideal for "worry pebbles." Tradition says that the Turks fed the nuts to their horses (hence "horse chestnut") as a stimulant. (The scientific species name, *hippocastanum*, also commemorates that belief. It has nothing to do with hippopottami—*hippos* is Latin for horse, and *castanum* for chestnut.)

Although horse chestnut trees are common shade trees in the older parts of North American cities and urban areas, they are not native. They come from the forests of the Caucasus and Balkan Mountains of Eastern Europe, and have long been planted in urban forests, beginning in Vienna in the sixteenth century. They were commonly planted in North America beginning in the early 1800s. They are magnificent trees, growing up to seventy feet tall, with a single trunk and a gracefully rounded crown. In spring, they carry torch-like clusters of flowers; in summer, the palmately compound leaves cast dense shade. Further, they thrive despite the poor air of urban and city streets. Thousands of tall, mature horse chestnuts planted in the last century still grace urban and city streets. Horse chestnuts are currently out of favor with landscape architects because the trees are untidy, shedding both leaves and spiny fruits. Imagine how monotonous indeed our urban landscaping will be if we restrict ourselves to trees that never shed their leaves and have tidy fruits!

Thursday, 5 May ❧ Today was rare bird day. Walking home this afternoon along the irrigation ditch between Mapleton and Pine streets, Richard and Molly and I stopped to look at a small, plain bird quietly gleaning the ends of the branches and the new leaves of the wild plum and chokecherry. It was about the size of a house sparrow, but with the thin, almost needle-like bill and gleaning behavior of a warbler. Warblers, small, usually colorful insect-eating birds, migrate north at this time of year from their wintering areas in

Central and South America to their breeding ranges in forests throughout North America.

Its behavior convinced us that it was a warbler, but not a typical one. For one thing, compared to the fidgety darting about of most warblers, this one was positively clumsy and tortoise-like. It crawled over the leaves and twigs like a sparrow. For another, it was very plain, with a dull olive-green back and buff-colored breast; its only pattern a crown of parallel dark brown and yellow-tan stripes on the top of its head. And it was silent, lacking the fussy calls, trills, and buzzes of most warblers.

Our bird was a worm-eating warbler, not a common bird even in its regular summer range in the deciduous forests east of the Great Plains, a real oddity here nearly a thousand miles west. One or more of these unobtrusive, sparrow-like warblers regularly appears along the Front Range in spring migration, for reasons unknowable to human watchers. Most likely they are occasionally blown far off course by spring storms, but perhaps they, like humans, are pushed by an urge to explore new territories. But the Rockies, lacking large areas of deciduous forest and associated insect fauna, are not a particularly hospitable habitat for these odd warblers. Like most warblers, worm-eating warblers eat insects almost exclusively; however, worm-eatings seem to specialize in small, smooth caterpillars (spanworms or inchworms, hence the warblers' name).

We watched it glean the branches of the wild plum until it worked its way across the ditch and disappeared in a thicket. We looked for the little bird again when we walked downtown in the early evening, but couldn't find it. Likely it had continued on its solitary journey north, far from the others of its kind.

Monday, 9 May

Summer seems near. The urban forest is clothed in a green canopy; even the tulip trees and the oaks have tiny leaves. (They are the last trees to put out leaves besides the locusts.) Clumps of voluptuous bearded irises bloom in a panoply of Victorian colors: violet, blue-purple, maroon, mauve, mustard, gold, pale peach.

I walk the alley along the irrigation ditch with my eyes closed, breathing deeply. The air is so heavy with sweetness that it makes my nose ache. Clusters of tiny white or purple flowers exude scent from the twisted old lilac bushes. Sweet-smelling pink blossoms hover on the tall honeysuckles like tiny single-engine planes. Bees hum around the sticky-sweet-smelling creamy flower spikes on the chokecherry trees. The old apple tree leaning over the far side of the ditch contributes a thread of scent from its last white blossoms, the petals falling into the ditch like clumps of snow.

This evening, daylight lingered in the sky and reflected from the low clouds when we left the apartment for an evening walk with our houseguests. We strolled slowly uphill and along the streets that cling to the steeply dipping hogbacks, talking as we walked. By the time we climbed up to the edge of town it was nearly dark, but the eastern horizon was still visible where the level line of the faintly darker plains met the lighter sky. Above us, a long altocumulus banner stretched parallel to the Front Range like pulled taffy. Its windward edge, directly overhead, was honed sensuously smooth by the west winds. Its trailing edge, east of us, was diffuse, like a water-worn sandbar spreading downstream. As the light faded, color spread across the cloud from east to west, first luminous violet, then pearly grey; finally the color faded, leaving the banner a darker shadow in the still-light sky. The rippling western edge held the light longest, dancing satiny bright like the Northern Lights.

We turned towards home, tuning in our noses and ears as darkness obscured our sight. Fragrant, blossom-scented air pooled in the low spots, held in heady perfume-puddles by the cooling night air. Unmanicured corners of yards were alive with small animal noises: soft rustling and scratching and squeaking. In the darkness we couldn't see any of the perpetrators of the noises—mostly likely mice, voles, shrews, or weasels—but we could hear them energetically going about their nighttime lives.

Crossing the irrigation ditch on the footbridge at Ninth Street, we heard soft rustling, then scrabbling as if one small animal pursued another. We stopped to listen. Next came a squealing screech quick as an indrawn breath, then abrupt silence—most likely a shrew, successful in its hunt. What would it be like to be a shrew, smaller than a mouse, tiny body weighing less than a handful of paper clips, quivering with energy, whiskers vibrating, all senses alert as it listens for prey in the dark? Here in the dry leaves, under the overhanging wild plums along the irrigation ditch fallen branches and tree trunks provide the topography of a shrew's landscape, its home a teacup-sized burrow in a rotted limb lined with dry leaves. A few yards away, thundering machines shake the ground as they pass; but a tiny shrew's attention would be focused on its prey, and on the threat of owls hunting overhead in the night, or on neighborhood cats foraging.

A shrew is little more than a bundle of nerves—its pulse 1,200 heartbeats per minute (twenty beats per *second!*) and its respiration far higher than the human point of hyperventilation. Its life is a blur of movement, even in sleep. In order to stoke the fires, a shrew is an eating machine, catching and consuming several times its own body weight in food in a twenty-four-hour period. Shrews turn food into energy at a rate comparable only to similarly hyperactive hummingbirds. Driven by the quivering need to eat, shrews are efficient hunters, foraging for insects, mice and other small animals, and seeds, day and night. Their lives are simple: hunt, eat, sleep; hunt, eat, sleep....

Female shrews accomplish the Herculean task of raising one or two litters of two to ten young each year. They are single parents, hunting food not only for their own ravenous bodies but for their young ones also. Shrews must surely be the most stressed of mammals—besides humans.

We looked up one last time at the night sky, clearly visible from the relative darkness of the thread of woods along the irrigation ditch. The altocumulus cloud stretched its now-velvety shadow in the sky above us. On either side of it, bright, sparkling pinpoints of light marked the distant stars in the hard black sky.

Thursday, 12 May ✥ The sun dropped close to the ridge of Mount Sanitas as Richard and I walked up the hill this evening. Golden light poured through the leaves of the silver maples like treacle syrup. Purple finches sang from the tops of the evergreen trees. Starlings squeaked and whistled from the silver maples overhead.

We climbed the short, steep slope of the hogback behind the hospital, and followed the ridge crest, walking between rounded rock outcrops. Partway along the ridge, we cut downhill through the narrow band of open ponderosa forest that lines the west side, on well-drained soils eroded from the sandstone. We walked down into the valley between the hogbacks, a trough between two reddish waves of rock. The eastern (and lower) wave is uptilted Dakota sandstone, the western, higher wave the uptilted Fountain sandstone that forms Mount Sanitas. The valley's simple trough shape and north-south orientation reveals it as a strike valley, eroded in the near-vertical sandwich formed by the tilted progression of resistant sandstone–soft shales–resistant sandstone. Surface water flow is slowly eating the soft shale filling, working north along the axis, or strike, of the dipping formations to form the valley. The water-miserly clay soils weathered from the shales grow bunchgrass grasslands, now flushed with pale green spring growth.

At the head of the valley we crossed the Dakota ridge again and perched on a sandstone ledge overlooking Boulder and the plains. The rocky slope tumbled abruptly from under our seat to the verdant yards of the north part of Boulder, five hundred feet below. The shadow of the Rockies crept across town and slowly extended itself out across the plains until only a bright golden line rimmed the eastern horizon.

Around us, plants grew sparsely in miniature tapestries colored by bright spring flowers, flourishing in spots of soil on ledges, clinging in clumps to the steep slopes. Nearby, spreading phlox formed pale green patches of tufted carpet, studded with lavender five-petaled flowers. Unlike the tall phlox of Boulder gardens, this phlox adapts to its extremely dry site by hugging the ground, growing only a few inches high but spreading outwards in a dense mat. Between the phlox, drifts of starry white chickweed flowers bloomed from their loose tufts of silver foliage. Silvery-green bunches of junegrass sprouted slender flower stalks. The minute flowers, comprised only of male and female sexual parts—no colorful petals or sepals—are each enclosed in two scaly pen-point-size green bracts. When the flowers bloom, the scales open, exposing both waving anthers and feathery stigmas to the pollen-dispersing breezes. (Wind-borne grass pollen is one of the most irritating allergens to hayfever sufferers.)

Despite the unusually hot weather, the grasslands remain spring-green, touched with the color of their ephemeral growing season. The delicate green, and the season of growth, last only as long as the moisture from melted snow and spring rains wets the soil. Both end when soils dry out enough that plants transpire more water—losing it through their pores to the thirsty air—than they can pull in from the soil through their roots.

Perennial grassland plants have two basic strategies to deal with summer drought: avoidance or resistance. Drought avoiders are opportunists, growing when moisture is available, shutting down when it is not. They mature early (in May-June), growing, flowering, and setting seed in the wet months, then go dormant during the late-summer drought. They may grow again in September and October if cooler fall days yield sufficient moisture. Drought resisters, on the other hand, are conservative. They grow very deep roots (up to ten feet long in some species) and mature more slowly. Their roots reach into the subsoil to tap moisture even when the upper soil is dry. This allows them to grow through the drought of late summer. (Little bluestem and the other midgrass prairie remnants fall in this group.)

As in most arid ecosystems, moisture stress is exacerbated by extreme fluctuations in temperature. Daily temperatures during the growing season ride a roller coaster, from daytime highs of 85–90° F to nighttime lows of 55–60° F, a spread of at least 30 degrees. At the soil surface, where the plants grow, the spread may be wider. Without the cooling breezes that blow at human head height, daytime temperatures near the soil may be 10 or 20 degrees higher. To survive these extremes, most perennial grassland plants take refuge in the relatively constant climate of the soil, storing the bulk of their biomass underground as extensive root systems, bulbs, or rhizomes (underground stems). Above-ground parts are usually divided into narrow segments to minimize heat gain and moisture loss. For example, native grasses' narrow leaves align vertically, equalling less surface area to lose moisture and gain heat from the hot midday sun. Many plants are also insulated: their leaves and stems are covered with mats of fine hairs, helping to reflect drying heat and to provide a boundary layer of still air that helps lower evaporation of precious water from the plant's pores.

In stark contrast are the urban plant communities, the emerald green lawns and green, leafy forest, nourished by sprinklers and irrigation ditches. These plants are not adapted to Boulder's arid environment. We subsidize them. When we decide to grow lawns and other water-consumptive vegetation, we have to "borrow" water from somewhere else to do it. There is only so much water in the global cycle—we can decide to allocate it however we want, but we cannot make any more of it.

In effect, each time we water our lawns and our gardens, we make a value judgement. Hoses in hand, we declare that it is better to have thirsty lawns in Boulder than to let water flow downstream and maintain the rich plains riparian ecosystems. Would we support that collective choice if it were made consciously? Our current value system asserts that humans have a greater right to water and other resources than the host of other lives that make up this world. Some believe that our right stems from a divine appointment as stewards over all the globe, according to the Christian Bible, having "dominion over the fish of the sea, and over the fowl of the air, and every other living thing that moveth on the earth." However, new information about the earth points to what may be a self-regulating global system: for example, the complicated interactions of biotic and abiotic processes that, with no assistance from human brains, maintain inherently unstable atmospheric gasses in the exact proportions necessary to sustain life. The seductive chimera of humans as benevolent stewards, tending the earth as if it were a verdant and dumb garden, fades in the light of this new model. If the earth is indeed a self-regulating system, it is much harder to argue our superiority as stewards; if not superior, we have no more right to resources than any other life.

Streetlights were flickering on by the time we walked down the ridge towards town. A swift fluttered by, its bubbling song trailing through the twilight. The night air flowing downhill around us was cool, and carried the cloying sweetness of chokecherry blossoms, just like children's cough syrup.

Monday, 16 May ❧ Early this morning we watched a MacGillivray's warbler out the bathroom window. It was feeding in the wild plum tree, not five feet away. It puttered in a spiral fashion out to the very branch tips, probing each square centimeter of the leaves and twigs for insects. Its movements were strikingly different from the worm-eating warbler; this bird climbed delicately, moving quickly and lightly, the barest flutter of leaves revealing its presence. MacGillivray's warblers are regular migrants and nesters here, summering in shrub thickets along the Front Range, wintering from Mexico to Panama.

Warblers have developed interesting diet and habitat specializations. In order to avoid energy-intensive competition, different species occupy distinct horizontal niches: some warblers feed on insects living in the upper forest canopy, others on insects living at mid-level in the canopy, still others in the tops of tall shrubs and trees under the canopy, others close to the ground. MacGillivray's are of this latter group, foraging on or close to the ground. They are nicely camouflaged for this niche: drab olive-green and dark grey above to render them invisible to aerial predators; their flashy, sulphur-yellow belly visible only from below. A sober grey hood and thin white ring outlining their eyes make them look like British magistrates in horsehair wigs and wire-rimmed spectacles.

The little warbler puttered about in the branches of the wild plum, now and then uttering a soft, single-note call. By midmorning it was gone, the plum thicket silent. Warblers migrate in the night when fewer of their predators are active; they feed and rest in the daytime.

This month feels like summer already—we broke a heat record one 89° F afternoon. The sun slides up over the level horizon before six o'clock, and two hours later, the air is summer-hot, all traces of nighttime coolness vaporized. I no longer sit outside during the scorching afternoons; instead, like a hot lizard, I seek shade. It is dry, too. We've received only half an inch of precipitation this month, a third of the average. Despite receiving near normal precipitation this calendar year (6.5 inches, as opposed to the normal 7 inches), the hot days have already baked the soils. If this unseasonable weather continues, we are headed for a drought.

Still, the water in the irrigation ditch chuckles and gurgles as it runs by, a welcome sound. And, although the apple and chokecherry blossoms have loosed their petals to the wind, the hawthorns are blooming. The new leaves on the tall cottonwood trees are still small and shiny, colored vivid chartreuse. From a distance, they look like green clouds, a shimmer of new leaves hovering around their crooked old skeletons like pale green fog.

Tuesday, 17 May ❧ An intense half-hour thunderstorm this evening brought a dose of much-needed spring precipitation. I was so absorbed in the intricacies of writing when it began, intent on painting pictures with words, that I paid little attention—until a power surge from an especially close lightning strike turned my computer off. I gave up writing, unplugged the computer's delicate electronic innards to protect it against another jolt, and swiveled my chair around to give full attention to the storm.

Enormous raindrops splattered from above, veiling the foothills in ragged grey curtains. A brilliant fork of lightning flashed through the bottom of the cumulonimbus cloud directly overhead, illuminating the early dusk, loosing the timpani of thunder. Cool air rushed in through the screen door. The rain accelerated to a torrent, drumming on the roof of the car, the sidewalk, the dry ground. The raindrops were so big and hurled so hard by the wind that they bounced like hail. The smells of lightning and wet soil, wet grass, and wet air blew into the house.

At last the cumulonimbus cloud expended its energy. The

rain slowed to a drizzle, then stopped. The lightning flashes ceased to light the dusk, coming less frequently from farther away; the throbbing boom of thunder subsided to a distant rattle of small snare drums. The big cloud dissipated, revealing clear blue sky. Warblers resumed gleaning for insects from the tangled shrubs out back. Their soft chatter mixed with a multitude of water sounds—the hollow plopping of water dripping from the balcony onto the cement sidewalk, the gurgle of water rushing down the gutters, the slap and splash of water rising in the irrigation ditch.

According to the National Weather Service, an inch of rain fell on Boulder in that half-hour thunderstorm. Unfortunately, since it was hurled so quickly and violently at the ground, most will run off the surface instead of soaking in. But the storm did cool and clear the dusty air. And I am grateful for the lightning strike that turned off my computer, nudging me to watch the grand show.

Thursday, 19 May ❧ Late this afternoon, while wading across town in the pouring rain to pick up the Volvo, I crossed an irrigation ditch and stopped to watch the water. The muddy brown torrent looked to have risen at least a foot from its level this morning. As I watched, turning my umbrella to shelter my face from the blowing rain and splashing stream of traffic, I spotted a mottled brown form preening itself on the bank at the edge of the flow. It was raining hard, and the sodden animal was all curled up, so I couldn't tell what it was. I wiped my rain-soaked glasses and peered harder, trying to discern details through the streaming downpour. The whatever-it-was solved the mystery by uncurling itself in one lithe movement and pushing off from the bank, swimming upstream against the muddy torrent. It was brown all right, and about the size of a cat, but with a long scaly tail. A muskrat. I stood on the bridge watching it struggle upstream. It half-swam, half-crawled against the flood, staying close to the edge and pulling itself along by grasping the sparse vegetation protruding from the bank.

Muskrats look like large rats (their name commemorates that resemblance and the fact that they have a set of glands near the base of their tail that secrete a strong, musky odor). Seen up close they are much prettier than rats—their fur is two-layered, with silky dark brown guard hairs over a thick and soft, almost downy, grey-brown underlayer. Their plump bodies are from ten to fourteen inches long, their bare tails nearly equal; they weigh two to four pounds.

The resemblance to either rats or house cats ends there though—muskrats are aquatic mammals, spending the majority of their lives in and around water of lakes, ponds, streams, and irrigation ditches. Depending on the available habitat, their homes are either conical structures of cattails and other aquatic vegetation that stick out of the water in lakes and ponds, or are elaborate tunnel systems dug in banks of streams or irrigation ditches that lack good dome-building habitat. (Either way, the entrances are underwater.) Along the Front Range, muskrats inhabit nearly every aquatic habitat from the irrigation ditches of the Great Plains up to ponds and streams above timberline. They are nocturnal, grazing on roots, stems and bulbs of cattails, pond lilies, arrowhead, and other aquatic plants; but even their diet varies, expanding to clams, frogs, and fish.

The muskrat continued to crawl/swim upstream. Suddenly it vanished, disappearing under the brown water. I wiped my glasses again and peered intently at the rushing water in the early dusk, concerned, until I realized that it must have found an underwater entrance to its burrow—unless it drowned. A passing truck splattered me with cold water, bringing me back to the driving rain and splashing roar of the traffic. I hunched my shoulders, attempting to shrink under the shelter of my umbrella, and waded away, hoping that the muskrat had found its burrow and was curled up inside, dry and warm.

Friday, 20 *May* ❧ My wish for rain has been filled to overflowing. Stratus clouds, brought by a cold front pouring over the Front Range, oozed across the sky on the heels of Wednesday afternoon's thunderstorm, and the real rain began. By last night, a total of 2.4 inches had fallen, bringing May's precipitation to nearly 3 inches. The creeks are bank-full again, pouring silty torrents into the ditches. Yesterday's high was a chilly 53° F. I turned the furnace on for the first time in nearly a month.

Late this morning when the rain finally ceased, I walked downtown. Whenever I step outside, I automatically look up at the sky and the mountains above town and evaluate what the day is like. This morning, what-the-day-is-like brought a shock. The low grey blanket had lifted enough that I could see the ridgeline for the first time since Wednesday. White stuff dusted the trees and ground above town. Fresh white snow, enough snow to make the top of Flagstaff Mountain and the long undulating ridge line of Green and Boulder Mountains glitter.

For a moment, time folded in on itself, and I couldn't remember if it was spring or fall. I was back in October, feeling the excitement as the low grey clouds lifted on a chill day to reveal the first dusting of winter snow. The clouds lifted and there it was, the first snow I'd seen close up in three years, frosting the ridgetops above town. I was excited all over again, eager for winter—then I remembered that this is May, not October. Winter is past, summer up next. I shook myself and walked over the hill towards town.

Tuesday, 24 *May* ❧ Today is a warm day, the first really sunny morning in a week. Already, fluffy white pillows of cumulus pile over the Divide. Higher up, veils of wispy cirrus clouds stretch eastward over the foothills and Boulder, their long filmy plumes of snow disappearing behind the cumulus like hazy tails of a thundering herd of horses.

It is summer—not by the calendar, but by the vegetation. The leaves of the spreading silver maples, just last week still new-green and fragile, are subtly different, tougher, less fresh, darker green, older. They have become the leaves of summer. The grasslands above town, too, have lost that soft green with a spark of neon lime; they are summer green now. A week ago, all was spring; now it is summer. I didn't see the subtle transition happen, but I recognize the results.

June

Wednesday, 1 June ▸ This morning's weather is windy, sunny, and not nearly up to the forecasted seventy degrees except in sheltered, south-facing spots. The air is already hazy, full of particulates, the airborne waste of our society. Different indeed than the crystalline air of our camp-site last weekend under a western Colorado mesa rim. Starlings screech over the rush of morning traffic.

I am exhausted, physically and emotionally, from the bar-rage of landscapes and images of last weekend's trip to western Colorado. My memories of the magnificent land-scapes, normally vivid and detailed, are a blur, as if seen and sensed through dulled receptors. My emotions are shut down, locked tight in in the knowledge that since Richard is nearly finished with his dissertation, we are leaving the Rockies. My heart simply refuses to respond to the mute appeal of the landscapes that usually pluck its strings. To respond would only add to the coming pain. We are leaving at the end of August, going, gone.

Sunday, 5 June ▸ After walking Molly to the bus sta-tion for her bus to Niwot, we headed down Pearl Street for coffee at Haagen Dazs. The afternoon was still and hot, the air sticky, the sky grey and hazy, billowing with tall cumu-lonimbus thunderclouds. It could have been a midwestern summer afternoon, hot and close, the air muffling the land-scape like a heavy blanket. The clouds towered overhead like enormous sailing ships becalmed in the stillness. The world seemed to be stalled, waiting for rain, but none came to break the spell.

By the time we left Haagen Dazs and walked down the Mall towards home, the cumulonimbus were moving, under full sail again, merging to form a bumpy grey ceiling. Their frothy white tops streamed eastward above the plains. Lightning flickered, touching a rocky ridgetop beyond Green Mountain. A whisper of cool breeze heralded rain. As we topped Mapleton Hill, the first drops splattered the flagstone sidewalk, raising puffs of dust. We hurried home, pushed by gusting winds. The real rain—big soft drops pouring from the clouds—began just as we reached our driveway. We ran down the driveway, laughing, and made it to shelter before the shower became a thundering torrent. Once inside, we stopped and stood at the screen door to enjoy the storm: feeling the cool breeze blow in, watching the curtains of rain waver as the gusts pushed them, listening to rolling thunder from invisible flashes of lightning, absorbed in the *sturm und drang*. The smells of renewed life poured in with the rain, the verdant fragrance of lush new leaves, of water gurgling in the dry washes and creeks, of damp soil waking dormant seeds and spores.

Our regular walking route to the neighborhood grocery store passes a thicket of peculiar trees, with twisted grey trunks rising out of the soil like serpents swaying to a snake charmer's flute. Each smooth-barked stem branches only at the top, ending in clusters of long, pinnately compound reddish-green leaves that look like sumac leaves.

The thicket of serpents are ailanthus, also called tree-of-heaven. Ailanthus are native to China, but were introduced to eastern North America in 1751 by a Jesuit priest. Once widely planted as ornamentals, they took enthusiastically to their adopted habitat and are now common volunteers in urban, industrial, and inner city areas. (They are the tree of *A Tree Grows in Brooklyn*.)

Ailanthus' extraordinary ability to tolerate poor soils and air pollution enables them to germinate and flourish in city and industrial deserts—even growing up through cracks in cement. Thus, they are pioneers in urban wasteland rehabilitation: their feathery crowns shade the soil, mitigating the desert-like conditions and allowing less tolerant species to become established; their long roots break up and help enrich compacted ground; their respiration cleans the air…. They are not, however, miracle trees: their very tolerance and ready adaptation labels them "weeds," because they establish themselves so readily; their pollen causes hay-fever-like symptoms in some people; their fast-growing branches are weak and break easily; and their snakey roots are poisonous. Ailanthus are the tumbleweed of city landscapes—indicators of abuse, pioneers in recovery.

Tuesday, 7 June ❧

Another breathlessly hot, humid day. By eight o'clock this morning, when we walked home across town after leaving the Volvo at the mechanic's east of the parkway, the sky was impossibly clear, not a cloud around, any scrap of shade welcome. A tiny, wavering breeze trickling from the still-green foothills helped mitigate the blazing heat, but it was too fickle to provide much relief. High above town, a smudge of haze tinted the shrinking snowfields by Arapahoe Pass a sickly shade of pinkish brown.

Once past the commercial sprawl of Thirtieth and Twenty-eighth streets, we headed for the cool tunnel of trees along Walnut Street. Walking was pleasant again in the shade of the spreading trees. Silver, Norway, and red maples; pin, bur, and red oaks; horse chestnuts; catalpas; black and honey locusts; green ashes; crab apples—the very same trees planted along suburban and town streets on the east side of the plains. Walnut looks just like a quiet, tree-shaded street in Genesee, Illinois, or Red Oak, Iowa. Except, that is, for the purple wave of mountains rising high above.

The shady tunnel of midwestern forest trees planted along Walnut Street, together with millions of other trees, form the Denver/Boulder metropolitan area's vast urban forest, the collection of trees and other plants growing along city streets, in yards, in parks, and in open spaces. Although "urban forest" at first sounds like an oxymoron, it is not. City and community forests may not be "wild," since they are largely the products of haphazard individual plantings, but collectively these plants comprise a forest. Like other forest communities, the urban forest is a key part of its ecosystem: it interacts with and affects local climate, wildlife populations, air quality, water quality and quantity, and human behavior.

Looking at urban vegetation in toto, as a part of an ecosystem whose parts and processes are interdependent, is a new idea. Traditionally, city and urban trees have been planted and cared for individually, without considering their cumulative effect. But over the past two decades, foresters, municipal officials, and private citizens have shifted their perspective and begun managing the forest, as well as the trees. The old approach simply could not cope with threats to community tree cover from shrinking wild or open land, increasingly scarce water and other resources, liability judgements for damage caused by urban trees, nor with catastrophic events like Dutch elm disease. Since Dutch elm disease reached Colorado in 1948, tens of thousands of American elms in Front Range forests have succumbed—Denver alone lost at least 15,000, over half of its American elms—leveling whole neighborhood forests in just a few years.

The new approach recognizes urban forests as valuable community resources. In many ways, some obvious and easy to assess, others less tangible, they improve human-designed and built habitats.

Contrary to former President Reagan's belief, trees do not pollute—quite the opposite. In the process of making and using their food, trees release oxygen, without which we could not survive, and take up and fix carbon dioxide, one of our primary industrial pollutants. Urban forests can help offset the increase in atmospheric carbon dioxide: healthy, fast-growing trees fix from twenty-five to fifty pounds of carbon dioxide per year. Trees also clean the air in other ways: they trap dust and other particulates on their leaves and release pleasant fragrances, overcoming urban odors. Urban forests act like sponges: they can provide sound breaks, absorbing noise pollution the way windbreaks absorb the force of moving air; their leafy canopies intercept precipitation, helping to stabilize urban water cycles, routing runoff through the soil to slow and cleanse it on its journey to streams, rivers, and lakes.

Urban forests save energy. Acres of paving and heat-absorbant surfaces make urban areas simmering heat islands in the summer, when urban temperatures average 5–10° F hotter than surrounding areas. Enter trees. One deciduous tree shading the south side of a structure can have the cooling effect of five average air-conditioners running twenty hours per day. Less energy used to cool or heat buildings equals less carbon dioxide released by fossil-fuel burning power plants. Trees planted for shade or thermal barriers can reduce carbon dioxide releases by as much as fifteen times the amount that each tree can fix per year.

Urban forests have other benefits. They increase property values; they soften the often-harsh lines of human developments, making them more liveable.

Welcome as their shade may be on a hot June morning, urban forests have drawbacks too.

Trees and humans do not always coexist peacefully: trees inevitably grow, changing dimension with passing time, and then just as inevitably disintegrate with age. Growing tree roots can break up sidewalks and driveways, crack foundations, or interrupt sewer or water mains; limbs can tangle with utility wires or roof overhangs; decadent trees can fall in wind- and snowstorms, crushing whatever they land on— cars, houses, people.

In arid areas like the Boulder/Denver metropolitan area, urban forests pose special problems. Here, forests of largely deciduous trees have replaced the drought-adapted native plant communities, and therefore displaced the native fauna. Boulder's urban forest reflects our national taste for turfgrass lawns, shade trees, and shrubs, rather than reflecting the vegetation indigenous to the Boulder area. Hence, Boulder's forest is home to the thousands of European starlings, house sparrows, and the other denizens of the homogeneous urban forests across the continent. Further, trees not adapted to the arid climate, like maples, locusts, lindens, oaks, elms, and others, are heavy consumers of scarce water supplies because they are leaky, losing an astounding amount of water vapor in respiration. A deciduous forest in summer acts much like a humidifier. No surprise then, that the air this morning in Boulder felt more like the sticky Midwest than arid Colorado.

Ideally, we should plant native vegetation around our shopping malls, offices, and houses in order to minimize use of water and fertilizers and disruption of the local environment. For much of Boulder that would mean short- or midgrass prairie, with threads of riparian forest tracing the course of streams, and ponderosa pine/grassland savanna on the uphill side of town. But the people who settled the town of Boulder planted shade trees, willing us this hundred-year-old forest. It would be foolish to cut it down and start over.

However, we do need to plan for its future. Like other urban forests in the nation, Boulder's urban forest is facing stressful times. As Mapleton Hill's venerable, and decadent, silver maples demonstrate, it is an aging forest. Nationally, for every four trees that die, only one is planted. Those that are planted face increasingly shorter lives—an average of only twenty-five years—in evermore stressful environments characterized by polluted air, competition for scarce space and light, compacted and poor soil, moisture stress from surrounding heat absorbing surfaces, vandalism, poor maintenance, diseases, and other ills. As Boulder's population grows, and development fills in "empty spaces," trees give way to paving and structures. Surprisingly, Boulder has never mapped the city forest—although street and park trees have been inventoried—nor developed a master plan for its continued maintenance and growth. Urban forests, planted and designed by humans, are not stable, self-sustaining communities. If we simply take them for granted, we could be in for a rude shock.

Today's high was 92° F. And it is only June—what will summer bring?

Wednesday, 8 June ☙ We stopped to look for wildflowers this evening on our drive home from a soak in the hot waters of the bathing rooms at Idaho Springs' Victorian bathhouse. The mesa-top grasslands are already beginning to lose their green look, and the profusion of spring wildflowers have gone to seed early. We did find a few stalks of violet-blue penstemon blossoms, and the occasional sky blue face of a flax flower among the clumps of needle-and-thread grass, but the rest of the flowers are long past. Except for the Spanish bayonet.

Spanish bayonet, a kind of yucca, gets its name from its clumps of pointed, foot-long, dagger-shaped basal leaves. The dark green clumps are especially visible in the winter, protruding, stiffly erect, above the bleached grasses of the shortgrass prairie. This time of year the tall flower stalks are the prominent landmarks, rising about two feet above the dark green leaves. Large, ivory-colored flowers, the size of a small child's fist, hang like waxy bells from the stalk.

Most shortgrass prairie plants are either wind pollinated or pollinated by insects searching for nectar. But the stigmatic surface of Spanish bayonet flowers is buried so deeply in the pistil that neither wind-dispersed pollen or pollen carried on traveling insects can reach it. Instead, Spanish bayonet depends on a night-flying moth in an intricate kind of mutual cooperation. The moth lands on the flower, pierces the fleshy ovary, and lays an egg inside. Then, apparently to assure a source of food for the growing larva, the moth collects a mass of pollen from a nearby anther and stuffs it deep into the funnel. The pollinated ovary grows hundreds of seeds, plenty to ensure new life both for the growing larva and the plant.

Saturday, 11 *June* ⮿ These sunlit, fifteen-hour days make the dark winter days seem so distant. Today began at 5:30 a.m. when the sun slipped above the line of the eastern horizon; the sun set just before 9:00 p.m. I walked to the store in the golden light of the warm, languid, summery late evening. The sun had dropped behind the ridges but the sky remained luminous blue and the air sparkled with light. Swifts, dark cigars with curved wings, chased insects through the air above the treetops. Their songs burbled, the cadence of flowing water.

High above the swifts, a bird glided by on the north wind. Its boomerang-curved wings, narrowing to a point at the ends, and long narrow tail identified it as a falcon, one of a group of hawks noted for their agility and speed. Falcons are spectacular flyers—fighter jets mimic falcons' aerodynamic feats—able to overtake their prey on the wing or on the ground. They usually either speed low to flush ground-dwelling prey, or hover once they spot a movement, then stoop in a breathtaking dive, first propelling themselves downward with a few quick wing beats, then folding their wings to pick up speed, plummeting headlong at the ground, braking with their wings only at the last moment. The force of their dive kills or stuns their prey instantly. Falcons are among the fastest birds known—peregrine falcons can dive as fast as 200 miles per hour.

I watched the falcon pass overhead, my errand forgotten, standing in the middle of the sidewalk with my head craned upwards, totally absorbed. Just before it disappeared behind the leafy silhouette of a cottonwood tree, it tilted on a gust, revealing pale brown streaking on its ivory-colored under-feathers. Then it was gone, a dark silhouette against the aqua-marine evening sky. It looked about the size of a crow, much larger than the small, elegant American kestrels that hover, hunting mice, over the mown verges of rural highways. It was a prairie falcon.

Prairie falcons are birds of the arid West. Unlike peregrine falcons, recently successfully introduced in the steel and concrete canyons of downtown Denver, they are intolerant of human disturbance, preferring inaccessible cliffs for nesting, near grasslands, shrublands, tundra, or other open hunting country. In Colorado, prairie falcons nest from the foothills to as high as 10,000 feet in the mountains. Here at Boulder's elevation, nesting pairs should be raising young now, after laying eggs in April and incubating them for about a month. They are skilled hunters, catching a variety of small to medium-sized birds and mammals, from sparrows to mourning doves, mice to jackrabbits.

Prairie falcons wear typical falcon plumage: brown to grey feathers cover their back, the top of their wings and tails, and head; and pale whitish feathers with darker horizontal barring cover their underparts, their chest and belly, lower wing surfaces and tails. But prairie falcons are paler than most other falcons, as if sun-bleached, their upper bodies weathered brown, their lower parts dusty as dry clay. (The only other pale falcon is the larger, nearly white, Arctic-dwelling gyrfalcon.) Prairie's coloring is well-adapted to the hot, arid western deserts and grasslands: their upper body plumage is just dark enough to absorb the sun's heat and therefore conserve energy in cool weather, but not so dark that they bake; the very pale feathers on their undersides reflect the intense heat radiated from the ground, helping them to stay cool.

The falcon reappeared farther away. I watched its silhouette until it flicked those curved wings once and sped out of view again, still gliding south on the fast wind.

By the time I walked home, the last light had faded from the sky. Cool night air washed over town as the stars twinkled into view.

Tuesday, 14 June ❧ This unusually hot weather has brought summer before the calendar. The box elders and other maples are hung with thousands of pale-green, twin-winged seeds. Crickets chirp into the night, grasshoppers and cicadas rasp and buzz during the day. Bees hum and drone around the penstemons, delphiniums, and scarlet runner beans in our front yard garden. In the night sky, Orion, Taurus the bull, and Leo the lion have been replaced by Virgo reclining in the southern sky, Böotes above, and the cross shape of Cygnus the swan in the northern sky.

This evening we printed out the final copy of Richard's dissertation, accompanied by suitably dramatic weather. Around dinnertime, the sky southwest of town grew positively black with massed cumulonimbus clouds. Lightning flicked like snake tongues at the lower slopes of Green Mountain, just above town.

The storm swept closer and closer, until finally it was directly overhead. At first the sky turned a sickly yellow, then deep purple, then velvet black, as if the darkest of nights had already fallen. Lightning flashed and thunder boomed all around. Violent gusts of wind roared out of the southwest. We listened anxiously for tornadoes. The electricity flickered off and on, turning our attention back to the computer and printer. At last came rain, a roar of water. It pelted down, mixed with soft hail, until the streets were running rivers, the parking lot gutters overflowing. The din was chaotic—blinding flashes of lightning cleaved the early darkness, rain pounded the roof, thunder shook the ground. After about forty-five minutes, the rain began to slacken. The storm moved away eastward, taking the show with it. The flashes of light dimmed, the thunder receded to a mutter, and finally the sky cleared.

Tonight's storm is a vivid example of the variety of influences that shape our weather here at the edge of the plains. Our wonderfully Wagnerian local thunderstorms are generated by the rumpled Front Range topography, which produces enough unsettled air to spawn legions of thunderstorms, in concert with the flat, sun-warmed plains surface; a reservoir for the moisture that gives the storms their life. A weather phenomenon peculiar to the northern Front Range gives them extra kick. The Denver cyclone—a lee eddy, a large swirling counterclockwise cyclone of air—is born when southwesterly winds curl around the Palmer Divide between Denver and Colorado Springs. The cyclone swirls upwind of the divide, usually centered north and east of Denver in Adams County (the site of Denver's proposed new airport). From above it looks like a huge, slowly spinning circle, its perimeter extending north towards Fort Collins, south to the Palmer Divide, west to the foothills over Boulder, east past Denver over the plains. Its rotational motion helps spawn thunderstorms, and, especially in spring and summer, tornadoes. Tonight's brief but spectacular storm, drenching Boulder with nearly an inch of rain, was one of a cluster of storms spawned by the cyclone, including four tornadoes that brushed the plains in a north-south line just east of us without incident.

Tomorrow will likely dawn fair, the sky blue and clear again, only to be filled with puffy cumulus clouds and icy veils of cirrocumulus as the sun warms up the soil and evaporates some of this evening's rain. Today's rain supplies moisture to build tomorrow's clouds, which will likely return moisture to the earth. An elegant cycle.

Friday, 16 June ❧ Last night, right after we went to bed, the wild plum thicket outside our bedroom window exploded with tremendous growling and grunting and squealing. Listening carefully, we discerned two animals fighting, then one animal running away, squealing horribly. Although the grunting sounded un-catlike, we assumed it was just the neighborhood cats fighting again. We lay in bed laughing about the sound until a bit of breeze wafted a choking cloud in through the open windows, a horrible smell like burning rubber and musk combined. "Skunk!" We sat up quickly, trying not to breathe. But it was too late to remedy the problem: closing the windows would only have shut off the breeze, trapping a roomful of still, skunky air inside. So we burrowed under the sheets, breathing shallowly, counting on the breeze to eventually blow the stench away.

What happened to cause the horrible noises and odor was a confrontation between one of the many feral cats that haunt the thicket behind our apartment house, and a skunk. This is baby season, a fractious time of year for both local skunk species: small spotted skunks and the larger—about cat size—striped skunks. Baby skunks born last month are growing fast, so females are out hunting aggressively. Unfortunately, so are the feral cats. Cat/skunk conflicts tend to be, as the air in our bedroom testified, explosive.

Still, I like the skunks. They are quite desirable neighbors. They eat mice and rats, help keep insect populations in balance, and unless roused, mind their own business. They only use their noxious spray in their own defense. I can't say as much for the feral cats—they fight and yowl outside our bedroom windows nearly every night. I think that I much prefer the occasional smell of skunk!

On my way to the post office this morning, I took a detour down the Boulder Creek Path. The creek is carrying a load of June thunderstorms and late snowmelt. This morning it looked and sounded like a desert wash after a storm, more mud than water, a high brown rushing flow, craggy with standing waves, busy with rolling rocks and hurrying water. The splashing, cracking, thumping, rushing, and rumbling drowned out all other noises. I walked slowly downstream, watching the roiling flow and listening intently to the tangled threads of sound.

Past the library bridge, in a patch of completely still air flooded with sunlight, it was snowing! Beautiful fluffy white snowflakes drifted slowly towards the rushing water, backlit by the bright sunshine. For a moment, my brain was fooled. Then memory identified the "snowflakes" as cottonwood seeds, descending from catkins above, their fluffy tuft of down allowing them to float just like big crystalline snowflakes. The lawn by the library was adrift in June snow. Everywhere were downy cottonwood seeds, floating in airy white puffs across the grass. Only this snow won't melt.

Sunday, 19 *June* ✿ This last weekend of spring was a long one. In what turned out to be the hottest week of the summer, breaking temperature records across the West and Midwest, we drove to Ames, Iowa, for Richard's interviews at Iowa State University. If these interviews go well, we could be moving to Iowa in September.

We left Boulder on the Diagonal Highway at midafternoon on Friday, headed for Fort Lupton. Thence north and east on Interstate 76 to follow the South Platte River out of Colorado, aiming for its confluence with the main stem of the Platte in Nebraska. From there we would follow the Platte downstream on Interstate 80 until the highway strikes out across the cornfields of eastern Nebraska, headed due east. In just 672 miles we would drop nearly 4,000 feet in elevation and cross the hundredth Meridian, trading the arid, open space of the West for the flat, fertile farm country of the middle of the continent. To me, Iowa epitomizes the Midwest, where the landscape is no longer wild, instead scribed with a rigid east-west/north-south grid of roads and rectangular fields, and crowded with houses and towns.

Up and down we drove over the shimmering surface of the plains, watching as the high peaks gradually grew bluer and less distinct in the Volvo's rearview mirror. Before we joined the South Platte at Fort Morgan the Front Range shrank to an insubstantial smudge under the towering grey thunderclouds. (I craned my neck to watch as we drove farther away: was that smudge the mountains, or just the grey veils of rain trailing from the massed cumulonimbus?) By the time we spotted the green ribbons of cottonwood forest lining the South Platte, the Front Range had disappeared, merged into the weather lining the western horizon. No more mountains. I resolutely turned away to watch the landscape ahead.

As the landscape flattened, the huge expanse of the sky commanded our attention. Enormous thunderheads billowed in the hot afternoon air, bulging so high that their tops spun off icy tendrils, burgeoning outwards to spawn daughter clouds around their periphery, then gradually decaying as the next generation grew and billowed upwards. We watched one cloud through the whole cycle from its birth and its growth into a towering thundercloud, to its eventual dissipation after spawning several daughter storm cells. We spotted it first from Niwot, a robust young cumulus cloud, its top spotlit in a gap between lower clouds a hundred miles or so east of us. From Niwot to Fort Lupton we drove straight towards the burgeoning cloud, marveling as it grew upwards and also increased its girth. And still it kept growing, eventually dominating the sky for miles around, on the threshold of becoming a thunderstorm system.

We drove along its north side in the late afternoon when we turned northeast along the Platte River. By the time we passed Sterling, the cloud was monstrous, a mature cumulonimbus, towering high over the original bubbly cumulus layer in a massive column, spreading outwards at the very top in a filmy layer of shimmering ice where the column met the frigid air of the tropopause. The whole looked like a voluptuous Victorian woman confined to a corset with a hundred-mile waist. And still it grew. By the time we reached North Platte, Nebraska, where the two branches of the Platte River twine together in the wide, shallow green valley, the original massive cumulonimbus was half-hidden by lustily increasing progeny. The semicircle (on the north and east sides of the parent cloud) of cumulus clouds grew and swelled upwards, drawing on the energy in their dwindling mother until they eventually matured into full-fledged, anvil-topped cumulonimbus themselves. As the evening sun slanted low some 300 miles east of where we first spotted it, we watched the mother cloud catch the light for the last time, a filmy pink ghost of its former robust self, now dissipating quickly, overtopped by its vigorous progeny and their own growing circles of offspring.

Despite the relentless heat, the sunset was a splendid one, lighting the immense sky with brilliant colors through the long late-spring evening. As the sun slanted low, it tinted the bottoms of the cumulonimbus to our east and south a lovely rose-pink. Rose-pink burned magenta as the sun slipped below the horizon, then faded to violet and grey-blue. The show wasn't over yet. The cloud bottoms to the east dimmed to obscurity, but the whole western half of the sky glowed brighter and brighter, flaming as if on fire. Brilliant bands of gold, then orange, crimson and scarlet spread from the horizon across the sky. Finally darkness fell, and the brilliant cloud colors in the west too waned, first to rose, then violet and finally dove grey.

Darkness brought little relief from the heat. The air rushing in the open vents was still hot and, as we continued east past the "dry line" of the hundredth meridian, increasingly wet. We sped along on Interstate 80 into the night, following the lush green threads of riparian forest along the Platte River, crossing and recrossing the Platte, the cement ribbons of the interstate never so winding as the channels of that braided prairie river.

Late in the afternoon of the next day, wrung with sweat, we arrived in Ames. We abandoned the Volvo in a shaded parking garage and took refuge in an air-conditioned hotel room overlooking the central quad of the Iowa State University campus. From our fifth floor room I could see miles and miles of gently undulating landscape shimmering in the heat of a midwestern summer evening. Softly rounded patches of rich green woods broke up the rectangular pattern of fields, roads, fields, roads. No mountains in sight. The air lay close over the pastoral landscape, heavy as a wet towel. Dusk brushed the evening sky with broad pastel strokes, pearly with moisture.

I fell asleep that night wondering if this level landscape and hazy, close horizon could become the stuff of home.

Wednesday, 22 *June* ✒ Yesterday was Midsummer's Day, the day after the summer solstice, the beginning of summer and the longest day of the year, when the sun is at the farthest north point in its apparent yearly north-south journey. Since the spring equinox the days have slowly lengthened, maturing into the luxurious days we think of as summer. Now the trend reverses and the days begin to just as slowly grow shorter until the light hours equal the dark hours at the autumnal equinox in September. But for now the nights are still short, the daylight coming early and lingering late in the delicious verdance of summer. How strange in these first days of summer to be far from the Rockies, becalmed in the mid-continent under a sea of hot, shimmering air.

Rain—a rare and wondrous occurrence in this drought summer—woke me at about five o'clock this morning. At first, I lay in bed, groggy still, unsure of what had nudged me from sleep. Slowly I grew conscious of the soft sound of rain on the slate roof overhead. Still I lay in bed, sure that I was dreaming. When I saw a dim flash of lightning, I knew. I scrambled out of bed, drew the curtains, and kneeled on the floor to look out of the window from our fifth-floor vantage point. It was indeed raining. A pastel thunderstorm, the edges of the towering cumulonimbus above tinted gorgeous pearly colors—rose and pink and yellow—by the rising sun. Water rained gently out of a pale violet and pink and yellow-green sky. It was a peculiar thunderstorm, the action set on "gentle

cycle"—no slashing wind, no pounding rain, no sizzling flashes of lightning, no sonorous rolls of thunder. All was hazy,
soft. The thunder never rose above a throaty mutter. Even the
lightning was muted, as if from a dimmed bulb, and strangest
of all, pink. The air, saturated with water, clothed the scene in
diaphanous mist. West of the solitary thunderstorm, the sky
was cloudless, opalescent pale blue. I kneeled on the floor,
face pressed to the window glass, mesmerized by the dreamy
quality of the storm, until the rain stopped.

These past few days, while Richard participated in the obli-
gatory dance of seminars and interviews, presentations and
lunches, I braved hundred-plus-degree heat and stifling hu-
midity and explored.

Iowa is extraordinarily level; its soft, planar land surface is a
gift of continental glaciation. Glaciers the likes of which the
even most ice-carved parts of the Rockies have never seen
blanketed the stable half of the continent at least four times,
beginning 2.5 million years ago. The tons of slowly moving
ice stretched from northern Canada south into Nebraska,
Iowa, Illinois, Indiana, Ohio. In Iowa, the oceans of ice
ground down the relatively soft limestones and sandstones at
the surface of that old landscape, removing the existing topographic relief with the ease of a belt sander oblitering the
raised grain of weathered wood, then retreated northward as
the climate changed, leaving the newly smoothed surface
blanketed with a fifty-or-more-foot thick mantle of rock powdered as fine as cake flour.

In the interval since the glaciers last retreated to the Arctic,
wind sculpted the floury blanket into dune-like hills in western Iowa; and water incised gentle valleys at regular intervals
across the state, carving just enough relief to sparingly mark a
topographic map. The till weathered into rich, fertile soils,
nurturing oceans of head-high tallgrass prairie. Shallow
valleys grew lush deciduous woods. Now a disciplined quilt of

rectangular fields—sprouting either soldier-straight corn rows or curly mounds of soybeans—covers the landscape.

Besides the dreadfully level landscape and the ingredients for world class agricultural soils, the glaciers' repeated grinding had another result: rocks are rare in this part of Iowa, worthy of comment. Occasionally I spied one, sitting out by itself at the corner of a field, usually a grainy black-and-white diorite boulder, crisscrossed with raised white quartz veins, carried here by the ice from hundreds of miles north.

Ames is a small town, quiet at this time of year when the university is not in session. Like Boulder, silver maples, basswoods, and oaks shade the streets and the spreading lawns around the houses. The people I've met display unfailing friendliness; the town atmosphere is refreshingly unpretentious and unhurried. But no mountains interrupt the level line of the horizon, the air is soft and wet, the landscape verdant and bursting with an abundance of life—flowers, grasses, trees, birds, mammals, insects—unknown in arid ecosystems.

We left Ames and headed home to the Rockies late this evening, driving west in the hot, soggy night air. Fireflies flickered like fallen stars in the tall grass of the roadside ditches. Before his last interview this evening, Richard asked me if I could live here. I surprised myself with my reply. "Yes," I said. All the long hot drive back across Iowa, then Nebraska, climbing gently, inexorably up to the exhilarating open spaces of the arid country past the hundredth meridian, then across the high plains, squinting to see the first glimpse of the blue smudge on the horizon; all the long drive back to Boulder, I wondered about my reply.

Saturday, 25 June ❧ Home again. The day promises to be blazingly hot, but at least the air is blessedly dry.

This morning's weather is peculiar: the clouds drift west across the sky. West. Weather nearly always comes from the west here and moves east, but these small cumulus clouds, flat-bottomed with tiny cotton ball-fluff tops, are going the opposite way, pushed by an east wind. Somewhere north of Boulder a high-pressure area generating an enormous clockwise wheel of wind is centered. Above Boulder the winds are coming around the bottom of the wheel, driving the clouds across the sky backwards, from east to west. It is an eerie sight, these moist cumulus clouds drifting west towards the mountains, taking precious moisture from the droughty plains and depositing it on the mountains, reversing the usual flow.

The backwards cloud flow this morning is just another oddity in this, the driest spring the mid-continent has experienced in fifty years. Record high temperatures combined with record low rainfall across the northern Rockies and plains are searing soils, withering crops and rangelands, shrinking lakes and streams. The Mississippi River has dropped to its lowest water levels since 1934. The river that drains over half of the North American continent is carrying so little water that it cannot float barges all the way to the Gulf of Mexico; it is so low that a tongue of salt water has crept up along the bottom of the river almost to New Orleans, threatening to ruin that city's water supply.

Thursday evening, on our drive home, we crossed the Platte River at Grand Island, Nebraska. The flow of all three channels combined looked lower than the evening flow of Boulder Creek. Each channel was mostly dry, with just a silvery, toe-deep film of water threading its way through the maze of sandbars, tree trunks, and irrigation head gates. But when we crossed the South Platte (the smaller tributary) the next morning, 300 miles upstream, it was a real river, with many times more water than that of the whole river downstream. Why? The flow of the South Platte is augmented by water "borrowed" from rivers across the Continental Divide in order to supply the thirsty households and businesses of the Denver metropolitan area. After the South Platte flows through Denver's water and sewer pipes, it flows back to its bed. But that unnaturally generous flow doesn't get far downstream before it is borrowed (and returned much diminished in quality and quantity) by irrigation withdrawals. Between Fort Morgan, Colorado, and Grand Island, Nebraska, the valley of the Platte is carpeted with thousands of acres of irrigated fields; their head gates and pumps draw the South Platte down to a thread before it ever reaches the main stem of the Platte.

In the abstruse world of western water law, water belongs to the users on a first-filed, first-served basis. Historically, until a particular river basin was clearly wrung dry, whoever came along and filed a claim to use water was awarded the right to withdraw that amount of water each year. Those with the oldest claims have the highest priority. Because water rights were approved without regard to geography and with little understanding of groundwater hydrology, water in a particular river basin might be allocated over and over again as the river flowed across the plains. It was years before water engineers understood that water "borrowed" for irrigation returned to the river slowly, if at all. In arid areas, much irrigation water is gulped by the thirsty air. The remainder journeys through the soil, often taking weeks to return to the drainage from whence it came.

The Platte is one of the over-appropriated rivers—in this crazy system, water users have the "right" to withdraw more water than the river carries. In a normal year, junior users (those with newer water rights claims) must bow to the rights of senior users and close their own head gates as flows drop in late summer. But senior users can continue to use water until the riverbed is dry. (Except in states with in-stream flow laws, fish, wildlife, plants, and the rest of the aquatic and riparian ecosystems have no right to water.) This drought spring, water users are already drawing the main body of the river so low that it doesn't look like it is carrying enough water to keep a fish alive. As a matter of fact, in mid-May, normally a time of high water, it clearly wasn't. Six weeks ago, a seventy-five-mile stretch of the Platte in Nebraska dried up completely. Forty thousand carp, channel catfish, and minnows—and billions of algae, insects, and other life—died in the newly created desert of the sandy channel bottom.

Monday, 27 *June* ⚘ Today the clouds are blowing the normal way again—from the mountains, across the plains.

The alley alongside the irrigation ditch was inviting this morning, a cool tunnel of fragrant shade where the sweet smell of honeysuckle blossoms mixed with the chuckling sound of running water. In the tangled vegetation of the ditch bank, I spotted the season's first chrome yellow goldenrod, a real late-summer flower. Goldenrods are tall, rangy plants topped by hundreds of tiny flowers in flat clusters. The flowers are yellow-green when they bloom but turn golden within the first day or so, hence the name, goldenrod. Goldenrods have an undeserved reputation as hayfever irritants since they bloom at the same time as ragweed, late-season grasses, and other plants with light, wind-borne pollen. Goldenrod flowers do not contribute to hayfever sufferers' agonies: their pollen grains are not wind-borne; they are heavy, designed to adhere to bees' and other insects' legs rather than float on the wind into sensitive human nasal passages.

Thursday, 30 *June* ⚘ Today is the last day of June, a day of fittingly confused weather. June began like fall, cool with a dusting of snow in the hills one day; then turned wildly stormy, with intense thunderstorms and rain, even tornadoes; then jumped to late summer drought and record heat. Today is wonderfully cool and cloudy here in Boulder where we are shaded by a solitary island of cloud. But the sun continues to bake the high peaks to the west, the plains to the east, and Palmer Divide to the south.

Last night we watched bats hawk in the pools of light cast by streetlights over a lawn by the old library on campus. They flickered through the air like pudgy, wide-winged swifts. How odd to see "blind" bats using their sonar system to catch insects in the bright light of the sodium vapor lights!

Bats are the only mammals that fly, and although they are not actually blind ("blind as a bat" notwithstanding), their vision is poor, so they depend on a very sophisticated sonar system to navigate and catch insects. Watching them flutter around the walkway lamps, chasing moths attracted to the light, I marveled at their agility. They fly by echo-location, emitting supersonic sounds that bounce off of solid objects and then are picked up by the bats' specialized large ears. They judge the distance to and location of surrounding objects by the speed and quality of the returning sound waves.

Bats' queer, fluttering flight is similar to that of both insects and birds, but their wings are unique. Each wing is a double membrane of bare skin that stretches from their hind legs to the tips of their finger bones, like twin capes extending out from each side of their body. The light skeletal trusses of their framework are modified from finger, hand, and arm bones. If we had wings like bats, they would extend from our outstretched arms to the sides of our bodies and down our legs to our toes! Imagine standing upright, stretching your arms out wide (your arm bones are half as long, with your wrist where your elbow used to be, three very long, narrow fingers extend the rest of the length of your outstretched arm) and flapping your big membranous wings into fluttering flight. Imagine being able to fly in twilight or even complete darkness with impunity, by using your sonar to chart a flight path around trees, lamp posts, buildings, cliffs, and other perils. Not to mention catching insects on the wing.

Bats have been around quite a while: fossils similar to the bats we watched last night have been found in rocks as far back as the Eocene epoch, some 40 *million* years ago. Back

then these Rockies were fairly new but already heavily eroded, and not yet uplifted the final 5,000 feet or so to their present height. The terrace where we stood watching bats was
being built then by an ancient stream pouring cobbles and
sediment out of the mountains, helping shape a region-wide
erosion surface called the summit erosion surface. As the lower mountains were ground down and the adjoining basins
filled up with their debris, the two eventually achieved a common level, hence the erosion surface. Later, the two parted
company again, after renewed Rocky Mountain uplift and several million years of basin erosion. The once-continuous surface is now split—the terrace we stood on one remnant, the
other remnants thrust high to become the congruent ridgetops visible near tree line, below the serrated high peaks.
(Other erosion surfaces developed at different times; our bat-
watching terrace is one of the easiest to identify.)

We stood and watched the bats flutter, making a circuit
round and round the perimeter of the open area between
buildings. Fragments of high-pitched chattering were barely
audible, perhaps low notes in their high-frequency sonar systems, just within the range of human hearing. We walked
away towards home and the end of our day. The bats fluttered
on, as they have for millions of years.

July

Friday, 1 July ᴥ July is beginning hot and dry. Soon after it rose, this morning's blazing sun dispelled the night's coolness. The forecast cold front with predawn clouds and the unfulfilled promise of thunderstorms has drifted east.

On our morning walk we heard a lovely whistling two-note bird call between two houses on Spruce Street. The caller appeared to be a ventriloquist: the call first came from high overhead in the tall old cottonwood trees, then from a smaller green ash behind us. We looked and looked, but couldn't spot the bird. Finally it swooped down from the big cottonwood close over our heads and landed in a birch tree nearby. It was a small bird, about the size of a house finch, but much slimmer, and without the fat finch bill. Its plumage was plain, smooth olive-brown on the back, yellowish on the front. It had a neat crest atop its head, a faint creamy wingbar across the lower part of each olive-brown wing, and a pale ring around each eye. The bird sat on a birch twig, jerking its long slender tail, and calling. In a moment another bird, almost identical, flew out of the ash tree and landed in the birch also. Not a ventriloquist; two birds. The first darted out into the air, caught an insect, then flew back to its perch to eat. That told us what they were—flycatchers, probably cordilleran (formerly western) flycatchers.

The two flycatchers sat in the birch tree for about another minute, jerking their tails and occasionally calling. Suddenly, one flew over to the porch of the big brick house next to us, darted under the beams of the porch, and lit on a small nest, plastered neatly into the corner where a stone window lintel met the porch wall. Ah, hah! The other bird stayed in the tree, jerking its tail, darting out in the air to snatch insects, and calling.

We walked quietly up the alley next to the porch (on the far side from the nest) and watched the bird perched there. Incubating eggs? Or just getting ready to lay eggs?. We couldn't tell. From that distance, we could clearly see the grasses, moss, birch bark, and pale whitish hairs (dog hair?) that comprised the fabric of the cup-like nest. We watched for a few minutes more, then went on our way quietly, so as not to disturb them.

Cordilleran flycatchers are one the most common small fly-catchers in the Front Range foothills. They arrive in late spring, migrating from their winter range in Mexico and Central America, and nest in deciduous woods. They are insect eaters (their family name, flycatchers, commemorates that acrobatic agility at catching insects in flight) consuming mainly ants, bees, and wasps, but they also eat beetles, moths, caterpillars and flies. Ideal residents for any porch!

This afternoon I saw three butterflies, all near the tangle of wild vegetation along the alley and irrigation ditch. First was a golden skipper, sunning itself in the warm dirt of the alley. It held still for long enough for me to get a good look at its wings before it flew away. Skippers look and act like moths— their dark, unobtrusive coloring and largely nocturnal habits make them seem more moth-like than butterfly-like. Golden skippers are folded-wing skippers, distinguished from other skippers (and other butterflies) by the way they hold their wings when sunning themselves or resting. They hold their forewings upright, perpendicular to their outstretched hind-wings, like bright-colored origami-paper creations. This but-terfly was one of the more colorful skippers, with rich golden-amber inner wings outlined by silky dark borders the color of sweet sherry.

Then a cabbage white butterfly fluttered across the alley and downhill through a backyard just below the irrigation ditch, testing the shrubs for flowers. Cabbage whites are easy to spot because they are big—about three inches across— bright white butterflies. Each forewing is marked with two dark spots: one a bulls-eye in the middle, one slightly smaller and greyer, by the lower edge. The tips of the forewings are shadowed with a dusky grey triangle. Cabbage whites are Eurasian natives, introduced in Quebec in 1860 and since distributed widely across the North American continent. They are familiar to most vegetable gardeners, because, as their name suggests, the caterpillar stage feeds on cabbage and other mustard family greens.

Downhill in the same yard, another butterfly, a big yellow and black western tiger swallowtail, searched for nectar in a group of tea roses. It lit on a large pink rose, crawled over the first rank of petals, and stuck its proboscis down in the crack between the petals. Not finding any nectar, it crawled over the next rank of petals, and tried again and again. It fluttered to another rose, and a third, with no more success. Finally, it fluttered over to a tall stalk of blue delphinium flowers nearby and immediately struck nectar in the base of the flower. The gaudy yellow and black butterfly must have drunk the delphinium stalk dry. It crawled slowly from flower to flower, unrolling its long black proboscis to sip deeply at each. Highly bred horticultural varieties with double or triple flowers—like the tea roses—do not provide good butterfly dining. Their multiple sets of floral parts are confusing and usually contain less nectar, since they put more energy into producing tissue. The "wilder" delphinium, with nectar and reproductive parts of a normal flower, was simply a better prospect.

I am surprised to have found so few butterflies on my walks through town. Perhaps our neatly trimmed, weed-free, and pesticided lawns and gardens are sterile habitat. Butterflies' abundance is dependent on the abundance of their host plants—the plant that the adult females lay their eggs on and that the caterpillar eats as it grows. Some butterfly species, like the western black swallowtail, are specific to a single species of host plant—in this case, wild tarragon. Others, like the closely related western tiger swallowtails, are more catholic in their tastes. Western tigers use willows, poplars, aspens, alders, and sycamores as host plants. Butterflies with specific needs serve as highly visible indicators of the health of the ecosystem that grows their host plants. For example, the species of fritillaries, orange butterflies with striking black and silver spots, found along the Front Range, are dependent on native violets. Those of the dry grasslands and foothill shrublands use Nuttall's violet, birdfoot violet, or common white violet. Those of montane and alpine areas of the Front Range depend on mountain blue violet. Almost all of the fritillaries in North America depend on one or more native violet species for their host plant, except the fritillaries that occur exclusively in the arctic-alpine and subalpine meadows (where violets do not occur). If the balance of the plant species in these ecosystems is upset, causing violet populations to dwindle or increase, so too will the vivid fritillaries.

Perhaps butterflies are like miners' canaries—low numbers and lack of species diversity in urban areas may be a warning about the health of our home ecosystems.

Monday, 4 July ❧ Today typifies July weather: last night's low was in the sixties, the morning dawned cloudy but soon cleared, the day's high will be in the nineties with a thirty percent chance of thunderstorms. Of all the months, July's weather is the most monotonous. After the wonderful variety of May and June, it is hard to imagine a whole month of essentially identical days.

Wednesday, 6 July ❧ Earlier this morning, the sky exploded with a positive zoo of clouds—big clouds, little clouds, wispy clouds, solid clouds. All shapes and sizes of puffy little cumulus and bits of wispy cirrus dotted the western sky. A big swirl of stratocumulus (*stratus* = "blanket," *cumulus* = "heap") hung out east over the plains. Now it is overcast, and the zoo has given way to an even grey stratus tent ceiling blanketing the entire sky from the west.

After nearly a year of these daily walks through Boulder, I am delighted to find myself never jaded or bored. Each walk brings some new detail to attention, some small occurrence that stops me, in awe all over again, as if I were discovering for the first time the beauty and richness of the world. These small reminders come as grace notes, transfusions of the innocent sense of wonder that keeps me from growing old.

On our walk together downtown, Richard spotted a huge, strikingly beautiful moth roosting on the plate glass window of a store on the Pearl Street Mall, out in the open for all to see. It was a sphinx moth, a big, heavy-bodied moth with long wings like a hummingbird. It hugged the plate-glass window, its long wings folded over its thumb-sized body. Body, wings, legs, and antennae were all plush as velvet and richly colored, its legs and antennae deep chocolate brown, body and wings marbled a rosy tan color. Large, chocolate brown patches—like parallelograms except for their concave sides—made deep, velvety shadows on either side its head, and on its forewings. Its wings were marbled like picture agate, with wavy dark brown hairlines on a background varying from palest pink to darker saddle tan.

Sphinx moths are nocturnal, usually seen at dusk as they speed from flower to flower, hovering like hummingbirds to unfurl their long proboscis and drink nectar. It must have been just resting there for the day, after flying about feeding on night-blooming flowers. Sphinx moths rely on their tree bark-like coloring to hide them from the sharp eyes of hungry birds and other predators. This one would have been well camoflaged on the trunk of a tree with deeply furrowed bark (the dark chocolate brown patches look like shadows in the furrows, the marbled part like the layers of platy bark) but on the smooth plate glass of the store window it stuck out like the proverbial sore thumb, an invitation to predators.

Thursday, 7 July ❧ Late this afternoon, cumulonimbus clouds began bubbling upwards over the foothills. When I picked Molly up after day camp, they were tall and very grey, pregnant with showers. The air felt sticky and hot, full of blowing dust, ready for rain. Gusts blew and grey-black clouds boiled upwards, but the first scattering of showers held off until evening. Although the rain didn't last long, the cool, wet air was a relief.

Dusk came early, hurried in by a new wave of showers. At about eight o'clock, the sky turned violet-black. Then the rain began full force—gusts lashed the plum branches against the back windows, water poured down, lightning flashed through the darkness, thunder rattled the windowpanes. The first violent shower passed overhead quickly, followed by a brief calm lit by distant stabs of lightning. Then the next storm blew over, loosed its *sturm und drang*, and died. After a pause, it was followed by another, and so on, for the next two hours, as if a special effects crew were rehearsing over Boulder. Bursts of lightning lit Molly's bedroom as I read her bedtime story.

Thundershowers this late in the evening are rare—the average peak of thunderstorm activity above Boulder is late afternoon. By dusk, the thunderstorm wave usually has moved past us out onto the plains, carried along by the prevailing westerlies like pods of whales in ocean currents.

Despite an abundance of bluster, the storms didn't yield much rain for Boulder: the National Weather Service reported only five-hundredths of an inch of rain. And a rain gauge two miles north recorded only a trace. But Niwot, seven miles northeast, reported four times as much rain as Boulder. Such spotty precipitation is characteristic of thunderstorms. Each cumulonimbus is a tower of rising warm, wet air. Once the air cools and consequently is wrung dry, it must sink to the ground again. Hence, each thundercloud is surrounded by a ring of clear, dry air like a reverse doughnut whose the hole is the bubbling mass of thunderstorm.

Farther north and east, Fort Collins was flooded by three-quarters of an inch of rain, mixed with three-quarter-inch hail, in a half-hour storm. Two feet of water ponded on Highway 287 by Ted's Place (up the Poudre from Fort Collins), closing the highway for several hours. Out on the plains east of Loveland, storms dropped three to four inches of rain. And while Denver reported only a trace of rain, Aurora, on Denver's east edge, was directly under an open faucet, receiving two to three inches in only ninety minutes!

Tuesday, 12 July ᴥ River sounds fill the soporifically warm air. I sit with my back resting against a knobby granite boulder on a nearly bare, steep, gravelly slope above the South Fork of the South Platte River, taking a much-needed break. This is the third afternoon of the Institute for River Ecology, my week to cram my brain with information about the ecosystems in and around flowing water. I am already up to my ears. We are sampling geology, botany, aquatic biology, history, water engineering, wildlife, land, and people management. Each day, from after breakfast until dark, overflows with speakers, field trips, data collection, more speakers....

One of this morning's lecturers, a rancher from the Sweetwater Valley in Central Wyoming, asserted that ranching can "improve" riparian areas. She illustrated her talk with comparative pairs of photographs—historic and modern—of the family ranch, homesteaded by her grandfather-in-law in the late 1800s. The early photos, taken by the Hayden Survey in the 1870s, essentially reflect the riparian ecosystem before agricultural impacts, when native ungulates—buffalo, antelope, and deer—dominated. The modern photos show approximately the same location, in the same season, one hundred years later.

The photos show stark contrasts. In the early pictures, the river, low and clear, flows between high, eroded sandy banks in a grassy valley. Bare soil and sandbars dominate. The mod-

215

ern photos show higher water, the river flowing between gently rounded grassy banks, lined by a thread of willows and other shrubs. This last points out a drastic change in the yearly flow regime of the river. Before ranchers began diverting the flow to flood–irrigate river bottom hay meadows, the river typified a healthy scour/drought regime: it ran high in the spring, scouring its channel, flooding out over the adjacent meadows to deposit a yearly accumulation of silt and fertile soil; and by the end of the summer it dropped lower and lower as the mountain snowpacks shrank, nearly drying up before the fall snows. Streambank vegetation was discontinuous because of the wide fluctuation in water flows. Now, irrigation has evened out seasonal flows. Spring floods are no longer a yearly occurrence, and late summer and fall flows no longer shrink to a trickle, because the soil of the irrigated hay meadows acts like a sponge, slowly releasing water to the river throughout the season. Hence, the character of the riparian area has changed. It looks much prettier to our eyes—gone are the wide sandbanks left by spring scouring, the gravelly bars exposed in low flows of late summer; they are replaced by grassy banks lined by willows, quiet meanders where swans float. But is this proof that ranching has benefitted the riparian ecosystem? Is it an improvement to change the river's flow pattern and replace one community adapted to the scour/drought regime with another adapted to a stabilized flow? Is it a "better" or "healthier" ecosystem now because we humans think that it is prettier? It is clearly a *different* ecosystem, that much we can tell. But comparing the two is like comparing apples and oranges.

A dipper flies downstream below me, wings barely clearing the spray of the river. Swallows dart through the air, catching insects over the river, sometimes whipping right past my head. Around me the dry slope is speckled with color: vivid scarlet gilia flowers, pale yellow cinquefoil, creamy dusty miller, pink sticky geranium, violet-blue harebells, golden stonecrop. The already narrow, V-shaped river valley narrows further here as the river to squeezes around an especially resistant bit of granite in its rush down, down, down out of the mountains, headed for the plains. The riverbed is peppered with enormous chunks of granite, rolled from the slopes above as the river cuts its channel deeper. Water fills the air with rushing, roaring, cracking, and splashing sounds. The landscape is alive with movement: roiling water, swooping and darting swallows, fluttering butterflies, zooming hummingbirds, the upstream wind ceaselessly winnowing dry bunchgrasses' seed heads. Dancing, dancing, dancing.

There is the dipper again, flying upstream. It lit atop a boxcar-sized boulder in midstream and hopped down to a ledge near the water that would be an ideal spot for it to enter the river were the water not so high and turbulent. The plump dark bird walked right up to the edge of the creamy, rushing water, halted, bobbed in place for a minute, then took off. Upstream, it landed again by quieter water at the tip of a small, midstream island just above the bend.

This fork of the South Platte is running nearly as high as spring flood stage. The water thunders by at 2,000 cubic feet per second—about ten times the normal July flow of 200 to 300 cubic feet per second. In order to augment the Platte's flow for Denver's thirsty taps and to meet obligations to users with prior water rights downstream on the drought-stricken plains, we borrow water from the Blue River, a drainage that flows into the Colorado on the other side of the Continental Divide, and pour it into this fork of the Platte. The resultant flow is not only higher than normal, but also colder and more turbulent, full of scouring sediment. Later in the season, when irrigators no longer need the extra water downstream, the gates at the other end of the twenty-six-mile-long Roberts Tunnel will slam shut, abruptly decreasing the flow in this river. Suddenly, water temperature, flow, turbidity and the other parameters that define life for the denizens of this aquatic ecosystem will shift dramatically. Residents will either adapt or die. Abrupt changes in flow regimes like this—when whole rivers are turned on and off at human convenience like the flow of a faucet—are anathema to relatively stable aquatic ecosystems.

We tinker with earth's systems as recklessly as children with chemistry sets, disregarding warnings, dismissing long-term consequences, driven by a sense of what—excitement? challenge? Do we think ourselves omniscient, indestructible? Such river basin tinkerings are serious. When experiments of this size go awry, the result is not just a smelly house, a stained carpet, or a burned hand; here, lives are lost, ecosystems mangled, our global home damaged.

Friday, 14 July ✒ Yesterday evening I walked the mile from our last field trip stop to the old stone mercantile quickly, eager to be first in line at the outdoor pay phone. The early evening air was pleasant, full of swallows swooping and diving in their aerial banquets. On my first try, no one was home, but after waiting and letting others in the queue make their calls, I finally got through. The news from home was both wonderful and sad: Richard had passed his dissertation defense. Molly answered the phone and said excitedly, "He's Doctor Dad, now Sus—Doctor Dad!" Our sojourn in the Rockies is coming to a close. A door slammed in my mind at Molly's elated words. The sparkling evening air dimmed. Fini.

After dark, the air stayed warm long after the last light faded from the sky. The group met outside on the terrace of one of the cabins for a lecture/discussion on ethics: the idea of respect for other life, simply because it is. Led by a philosophy professor from Colorado State University, we argued about the wisdom of valuing other life by subjective, human-centered terms, like "prettier" or "better." Prettier according to whom? Better according to whom? The professor maintained that the point of view in which we take our species as absolute and value everything else relative to its utility to ourselves is "morally naive." I would add, "And destructive in the long term."

He posed examples and asked us how we would react. For instance: While cross-country skiing in Yellowstone National Park in the winter, you come across a bull bison that has fallen through the ice in crossing Yellowstone River. It is trapped. If not pulled out, you are sure that it will die. What do you do? Flag down passing snowmobilers, throw a rope around the bison and attempt to use the snow machines to pull it out? Summon a park ranger to shoot the bison and "put it out of its misery?" Leave it to die, or perhaps struggle free, letting the natural system run its own course? If we "rescue" the bison, it will die some other time. We have not "saved" its life, we have only altered the course of events temporarily, leaving one less carcass to nourish the eagles and coyotes and ravens, one less skeleton to provide calcium for the small rodents and minerals for the soil.... The examples provoked lively, often emotional discussion. Over the course of the evening, viewpoints shifted from a majority expressing confidently that we wise humans should always intervene to "save" the poor helpless animals, to more thoughtful, less arrogant responses. At the close of the discussion we trailed off to our dark cabins, heads buzzing, brains tired.

We like to call ourselves "stewards" over all the earth, those charged with taking care of our global home. It is becoming increasingly clear that the earth does not need our management; further, our selfish efforts have more often proved to be harmful. We are progressing from the old paradigm in which species competed tooth and nail for survival, to a new paradigm of cooperation. Survival for humans, and perhaps the whole system, depends on our ability to live within the means of this world, to behave cooperatively, acting with respect for the whole web of life—not just cute animals—from the smallest single-celled bacteria to the most complicated ecosystem. Can we learn to leave a dying bison alone? Will we ever understand that most basic of natural processes—death—as a global recycler, necessary to continue the business of life?

Tuesday, 19 July ᴥ Today we drove to Laramie so that Richard could turn in the official copies of his dissertation and sign the last forms. Last week was his thirty-eighth birthday; next month, we move to Iowa.

The sound of rain sent us to sleep last night; the same gentle splattering accompanied our waking long before dawn. A cold, damp breeze blew in the windows. The raccoons snuffled in the darkness out back under the wild plums. Molly cried out suddenly from her bedroom, caught in a nightmare. After Richard soothed her and came back to bed, I lay awake, unable to recapture sleep, made uneasy by the continual patter of the rain. All-night rains belong in the climate of Puget Sound, not here in the shadow of the Front Range. Rain at night is odd here, strange, out of kilter.

It rained while we took our showers, rained while we ate breakfast, rained as we loaded the car, rained while we dropped Molly off to wait for her day camp bus.

We drove north along the foot of the Front Range in the rain. The cloud ceiling hung grey and pregnant, just above the tops of the trees, concealing even the foothills. The visible world was flat, grey, blurred by the abundant water. Details stood out: a flock of Canada geese grazed in the golden stubble of newly combined wheat stalks, the birds' wet plumage somber as a congregation of Amish farmers; a solitary white pelican wheeled against the leaden sky like an ungainly kite; a kestrel hovered with fluttering wings high above the pale green stubble of a mown hayfield; and, blurring all, the rain, streamers of rain falling on bright green cornfields, black streaks of rain running down furrowed cottonwood trunks....

The rain ceased as we climbed up out of the tight valleys between hogbacks that line the Front Range, past the last ranchettes, up on the rolling granitic surface that is the divide between Colorado and Wyoming. The grey ceiling lifted until only the high peaks were muffled in cotton-wool fog. The landscape stretched out in all directions, a rolling expanse of rangelands punctuated with occasional red sandstone buttes; open country stretching without interruption to the blue-grey wall of the distant mountain ranges.

Up here on the rolling grasslands, we are in Wyoming long before we reach the state boundary. This landscape is the epitome of cowboy country—open, wild, undeveloped. The sky and land seem to stretch away forever together, unfettered. Ranch houses and cabins are widespread, nestling in hollows and in the scattered ponderosa forest; the air is clear, unsullied by densely concentrated exhaust pipes; the fences are few, the soil too thin and dry to be plowed. Even the roads blend in, following the contours of the land's surface. The foreground merges seamlessly into midground into background, the whole wild space stretching away to the swell of the horizon. Such landscapes are the home of my heart. Their most abundant resource—often dismissed as emptiness—is open space, which constrains neither imagination nor spirit.

Tuesday, 26 July ❧ After last week's one rainy day, the weather returned to the monotonous procession of sunny, hot, and rainless July days—late-summer drought weather, come early this year. But this morning dawned cool and cloudy, the sky filled with low, foggy clouds like a Puget Sound morning, except that these didn't fill the whole sky and block out the sun. They flowed outwards from the summit of Green Mountain and the rest of the foothills like slowly spreading lava, leaving the eastern half of the sky cloudless, but hazy blue-green from the smoke of distant forest fires. By midafternoon the cloud blanket had evaporated in the hot sun, leaving the air parched.

Last night the cricket chorus lulled us to sleep again. The insects' two-note "song" has filled the evening air for several weeks, commencing at dusk and continuing into the night until about midnight. The chorus is strikingly rhythmic: hundreds of cricket wings scrape synchronously, a bump on one wing striking a series of ridges on the other like fiddlers sawing one string.

Our choristers are members of the tree cricket subfamily of crickets, which includes crickets that live in tall grass and forbs, and sing only during the day; and crickets that live in shrubs and trees, and sing only at night. Ours are clearly the latter, both from the timing of their chirping, as well as its location—the sounds all come from a zone at about human head height. Since insects are poikilothermic—their body temperature and therefore metabolic rate are tied to the temperature of their external environment—the speed and pitch of their song increases or decreases as the ambient air temperature varies. With our snowy tree crickets, counting the number of chirps in thirteen seconds and adding forty gives the air temperature in degrees Fahrenheit. Cricket-temperature is surprisingly accurate, never varying more than two degrees from our thermometer.

Thursday, 28 *July* These hot summer days have brought two-foot-long, olive-green bean pods to the catalpa branches, lemon-custard-yellow tomatoes to the tomato plants in our tub garden, and the trilling sounds of hummingbirds winging south. The wild grapes are still green, but the chokecherries are now mostly black and ripe, the wild plums the color of mellow claret. Raccoons snuffle and scrabble, foraging for fruit in the thicket behind the apartment building at night. They are fat already, preparing, I suppose, for whatever winter may bring.

Early this morning the patches of sun were already scorching hot, despite the night's coolness. A group of streaky purple finches chattered from the branches of the small box elder tree that hangs over the irrigation ditch in the alley. A bright yellow-and-black tiger swallowtail hung upside-down, wings tightly folded, under a long, curving leaf near the top of the peach-leaved willow.

A cordilleran flycatcher called from a box elder tree downhill. It darted gracefully into the air from its perch, then returned, beak full of its gossamer prey. Could it be one of the pair that were nesting on the porch of the brick house on Spruce Street? That nest is abandoned, whether because the young hatched and are already fledged, or because of the continual disturbance of people coming and going, is impossible to tell.

Two robins fed on chokecherries, crawling ungracefully over the chokecherry bush in their pursuit of ripe berries, bowing the slender branch tips under their weight. The quick, darting flight and precise midair turns of the tiny flycatcher made the robins look bumbling indeed.

Sunday, 31 *July* ❧ Here is peace—what luxury! I sit on a simple wooden bench with my back against a smooth wood deck rail, looking up at the wall of grey peaks from which issue the headwaters of the stream gurgling down this quiet valley. The Never Summer Range, so called because it remains spotted with snow through the summer, is massive, glacier-polished, and now, briefly gilded by the golden evening sun. The deck, attached to a yurt, is poised in midair on tall posts above a sloping, sagebrush-dotted meadow midway up the rolling shale foothills of the Never Summers. The yurt, our home for the next three days, is a round, lattice-walled canvas tent furnished with woodstove, cots, table, and cooking utensils. It sits on a south-facing slope just below a grove of white-barked aspens, just above the thread of stream.

Our yurt and its green fiberglass outhouse are the sole sign of humans as far as I can see (except for the cows resting in the shade of the forest across the tiny valley). No cars, no people, no lawn mowers, no telephones…. The only noises are the rushing of the shallow stream splashing between its narrow bands of willows, the chattering of a couple of wrens from the shrubby willows, a cordilleran flycatcher's single-note "weep" call in the aspens above, and the occasional faint whine of jets flying high overhead.

A broad-tailed hummingbird just buzzed my right ear, then flew across the deck and through the open yurt doorway, hovered in front of the crimson fire extinguisher for a moment, and, finding no nectar source there, flew away. I smell dinner cooking on the stove inside.

Earlier today (an eon ago, it seems now) we settled Molly and a friend at Girl Scout camp near Allenspark for their first-ever week away from home. The weather was not propitious for camping: lightning sizzled in the grey sky overhead, the rattle of thunder echoed from the bare peaks all around, alternate showers of rain and soft hail pounded our faces, and we watched the soft trunk of a high-altitude tornado snuffle delicately over the ridge across the valley. Still, we walked them to their cluster of canvas tents, waved them good-bye, and set off on our own adventure.

We drove a zigzagging course from Allenspark to North Park: west to go up and over Trail Ridge Road in Rocky Mountain National Park as snow swirled in showers on the tundra, south along the Upper Colorado River in the splattering rain, west again briefly, then back north to North Park, still under heavy-bellied clouds leaking rain. The rain ceased as we drove a muddy road across North Park towards the high peaks of the Never Summers. We reached the trailhead in the early evening and hastily crammed food, sleeping bags, clothes, books, and laptop computer into our backpacks for the short hike to the North Fork of the Canadian River and this yurt.

We reached the yurt just as sunset began to color the layers of clouds above the open expanse of North Park. We stood on the deck in the long twilight and watched as the clouds metamorphosed to brilliant, satiny ribbons. Cold night air pouring down the valley finally drove us inside to the woodstove's warmth.

Later, a star pulsing in the luminous night sky beckoned through the circular skylight at the point of the conical yurt roof. Back outside to the deck we went. The evening wind blew softly down valley, hushing even the cows grazing the meadow below the yurt. Wisps of silvery cirrus gleamed pale in the western sky. Star after star winked on, undimmed by glaring urban skyglow. Overhead the Milky Way appeared, freckling the vast black arch of the sky with billions of points of light. The expansive landscape around us went dark. Silence settled over the valley with the night.

August

Tuesday, 2 August ᐤ This morning we woke to predawn quiet, the only sound the hollow plopping of dewdrops
striking the wood floor as they dropped from the canvas skin
of the yurt. The air was chill, almost foggy. We wriggled out
of our warm sleeping bags and quickly built a fire in the
woodstove. After dressing, we took our breakfast out to the
deck. The sun had not risen over the black wall of the Never
Summers, but the sky was clear, promising another hot day.
We could see forever, or so it seemed: above, the jagged grey
peaks loomed close; leafy aspen groves and golden-brown
grasslands cloaked the rumpled foothills around us; to the
west, the level expanse of silvery grey sagelands and emerald
green hay meadows carpeted North Park; farther west the
white-spotted peaks of the Park Range marked the western
edge of the Rockies. As we finished breakfast, the sun poured
over the Never Summers, filling the valley with golden light
and quickly dissipating the cool dawn air. We stuffed much-
reduced loads into our packs, washed dishes, swept the yurt
floor, and heaved on our packs. Outside, we pulled the door
shut, stopped on the deck for one last drink of the heady
view, then hiked down the valley to the car.

By the time we topped Cameron Pass, the sun was high in
the blue sky and the day bid fair to be a classic August scor-
cher. We parked in a picnic area at the pass, a notch cut in the
Never Summers, and searched for late wildflowers. We found
the creamy flowers of marsh marigold blooming in the brown
grass and grainy snowbanks of the wet meadows. Sixty miles
east and 5,000 feet below us, past the mouth of the winding
Cache la Poudre canyon, the farmlands and urban areas of the
Front Range were visible, shimmering in the heat. We
climbed back in the Volvo reluctantly, not yet ready to return.

Poudre Canyon, part of the National Wild and Scenic River
system, lies almost completely within the Arapaho-Roosevelt
National Forest. The Cache la Poudre River has incised a
narrow, steep-walled valley into the crystalline rocks of the

Front Range, following joints and fractures in the hard rock. The upper canyon drops quickly, the river a froth of cascades and falls; the lower canyon loops and twists, sometimes nearly meeting itself as it winds down towards the plains. While most Front Range canyons have erupted with development, Poudre Canyon's steep, rocky slopes and twisting reaches have remained relatively wild, but easily accessible. The river is a favorite of kayakers and anglers both for its wildness and variety: here the clear flow churns and tumbles in spumy, boulder-strewn cascades; here it scribes wide, shallow, riffle-laden curves in a level valley bottom.

Like most Front Range canyons, Poudre Canyon is ripe for a catastrophic wildfire. From about fifteen miles downstream of Cameron Pass to the confluence with the South Fork of the Cache la Poudre, the overstory on the densely forested steep slopes of the north-facing side of the canyon averages about fifty percent standing dead trees, killed by recent bark beetle and spruce budworm epidemics. Combined with heavy fuel accumulations from nearly a century of fire suppression, the result is a ticking time bomb with an indecipherable timer. As with most Front Range canyons, natural fire is not only inevitable here, but an important part of the forest ecosystem, a recycler of nutrients, a thinner of stands, a provider of diversity. Unlike most Front Range canyons, development in Poudre Canyon is restricted to the canyon bottom, the easiest place to protect from wildfire; further, most of the land along this stretch of the canyon is managed by one land manager, the U.S. Forest Service, greatly simplifying the administrative problems of fire management. The wild reaches of Poudre Canyon provide a unique opportunity for natural fire management.

What would happen if natural fires were allowed to burn in Poudre Canyon—with extensive monitoring and management? Most fires would remain small, ignited by lightning strikes near the top of the ridges where fuels are least dense.

The few fires that grew past the typical quarter-acre-creeping-around-in-the-duff stage could move downslope and finger into the dense, partly dead forest, but would still be restricted by the many natural fuel breaks. Fires with the potential to cause problems could be suppressed. Controlled burns could be used to reduce fuel levels and burn firebreaks in potentially catastrophic fuel accumulations. Areas swept by fire would be opened up, regenerating as grassland, shrubland, or even forest, depending on the site environment and strength of the fire. The resultant diversity of vegetation communities would allow niches for a greater diversity of life, from bighorn sheep and mountain bluebirds to butterflies and aspen trees. Forests thinned by fire would be healthier, less susceptible to epidemic outbreaks of wood-boring insects. The natural firebreaks produced would reduce the probability of unmanageable, catastrophic fire. The Forest Service (and therefore, we the taxpayers) would save money in both the short and long term. Current dollars spent in fire suppression would be dramatically reduced; future costs of continuing fuel accumulations, ever-increasing fire danger, lost diversity, and lower forest health and fertility would be minimized.

Imagine a fire interpretation and monitoring team responding to natural fires in Poudre Canyon, instead of fire fighting crews. Teams would study and monitor the progress of each fire, deciding to spend the money and resources to suppress fires only if necessary, instead of automatically throwing the agency at each fire. Fire ecologists and interpreters would arrive to set up temporary exhibits along the highway near the fire and attend local gatherings; talk about the progress of each fire, explain the place of natural fires in Front Range ecosystems. Imagine active management of natural fires instead of reactive management; healthier and more diverse forest and grassland ecosystems; a public better educated about natural fire's place in the ecosystems where we live....

We sped around the last curve and the canyon walls dropped away. The river slid, silvery and rippling, over its cobbled bottom, headed towards the shimmering sunlight on the plains.

Thursday, 4 August ⤢ Another chill, wet dawn

briefly relieving these months of hot and dry weather. Last night we fell asleep to the splattering of rain and rushing of gusty winds. This morning we woke to stillness, rain continuing to trickle from the pendulous sky. Foggy clouds drifted in, smothering the ridges in a grey, cottony blanket.

By midmorning, the fluffy cloud cover cracked. Wherever the sun shone through, it was searing. The rain ceased, but water hung in the air, palpable, sticky. Still, by the time I huffed up the steep hill in the dusty alley to the irrigation ditch, I was thirsty. Along the ditch, the humid air was mercifully cool. Even the sound of running water feels cool in this searing heat.

The dog days of August—still, muggy, hot. Today's weather forecast predicts afternoon highs near 100 degrees, and a thirty percent chance of thunderstorms. And tomorrow likely the same, the day after that too…. Oh, for the biting cold of a winter morning or the blasting vigor of a chinook!

Wednesday, 10 August ⤢ This morning I woke be-

fore four o'clock, too excited to sleep. Today I fly home to Wyoming for a week's visit.

Dawn came as Richard drove Molly and me downtown to catch the 5:40 a.m. airport bus. The eastern sky glowed pale blue, washing away the stars, except for three bright planets along the ecliptic: Venus, the brightest, about five fists above the eastern horizon; Jupiter ahead of it several fingers farther west; and Mars, a faintly reddish planet beginning the long descending curve towards the western horizon. The thinnest possible crescent moon shone in the now pale yellow eastern sky. A closer look revealed the whole orb, one edge a bright silvery crescent lit by the sun, the remainder a shadowy white wraith, pocked with darker dry "seas."

The sun rose as the bus traversed the plains towards Denver. First, an orange glow spread above the dark line of the plains. The glow focused like a spotlight, then in a moment, the first third of the burning orange globe slid above the black rim of the plains, too bright to watch. The sun seemed to rise again more than once, sinking back below the dark horizon as the bus dropped down into a valley, sliding above the rim of the earth again as the bus topped a mesa. By the time we reached the nearly deserted lanes of Interstate 25, the sun had freed itself from the horizon. The tall buildings downtown and the peaks in the west were aglow with soft pink light.

By the time I saw Molly off and boarded my plane, a twin-engine, fifteen-passenger affair, the morning was well under-way. As I bent over to squeeze into the tiny cabin, the hip-hopping, three-hour flight to Cody loomed long. But soon we were bumping slowly along the taxiway, a gnat among dragonflies. Our turn came and we were away up the runway, both propellers accelerating to a grey blur. The little plane jumped from the cement into the air, bobbing in the cross draft from the big jets. We quickly rose, and Denver and the plains spread out below as we flew northwest. The mountains grew from just a line on the western horizon to fill the whole view. Over my shoulder, a layer of pea-green smog lay like a foul veil along the horizon above the plains—the plume from the exhaust pipes of the Front Range. Ugh.

No matter, I am going home. Home to see Heart Mountain rising, a lumpy monolith, from the sere floor of the Big Horn Basin; to scan the ragged Absarokas lining the horizon, each dark ridgeline distinct in the clear air; to walk the folds and creases of the sedimentary layers of the basin itself, rumpled long ago into domes and arches as the earth's crust was slowly compressed. Home to smell the dry sagebrush, the acrid tang of dust blowing on the wind; home to feel the clean, dry air, the shivery cold wind pouring out of the mountains at dawn. Home where the world is etched by the clear light. I want to distill the essence of that landscape and take it carefully away with me like a precious liquor to be opened and savored later, when I am far away.

Thursday, 11 August ✒ I woke long before dawn on this my first morning at home, my sleep disturbed by the soft feel of ash and dry smell of smoke. In a moment I was wide awake, alarmed, until I remembered the forest fires. This smoke is from distant fires burning in and around Yellowstone National Park. The cool night winds blow it down valley to pool in the basin. I fell back into a fitful sleep, troubled by dreams of crackling orange flames and choking grey smoke.

When I finally roused myself and looked out the window, the visible world had shrunk, muffled in the peculiar dry and dusty fog of smoke, sucking moisture out of every membrane it touched, depositing on every surface a pale layer of fine ash. The downvalley westerlies had ceased and the east wind was busily piling smoke up against the Absarokas, shrouding the Cody side of the basin in this queer fog. I could barely discern the camel-humped summit of Heart Mountain, just a few miles north.

After a quick breakfast, I left Cody in a borrowed car with Emmy Lou Harris crooning from the tape deck, bound for Jackson. I planned a circuitous route in order to view as much of my home as roads touch: north up the basin over Skull Creek Pass on the west flank of Heart Mountain, then up and over the rounded incline of Dead Indian Hill, through the North Absarokas along the Clarks Fork of the Yellowstone River, entering Yellowstone at the northeast corner. From there I would follow the wide valleys of the Lamar River drainage across the north part of the park, down the Yellowstone River to Mammoth Hot Springs. From Mammoth I would climb up past the Gallatin Range, drive south through the park, traverse the central plateaus, run along the undulating shore of Yellowstone Lake, follow the Snake River out the south edge of the park, then climb up the last forested ridge before cruising downhill into Jackson Hole.

As I drove north over Skull Creek Pass to the road that would take me up into the Absarokas, the familiar landscape shimmied in the smokey haze. Atop Dead Indian Hill, filmy grey smoke flowed over the waves of Absaroka ridges, blurring their knife-sharp edges. And everywhere, on each breath I took, the sharp, pungent smell of forest fires.

The smoke is controversial, inciting passions hotter even, it seems, than the flames that produce it. For those who would like to see natural fire play their role in Rocky Mountain ecosystems, the smoke is exciting. This bids fair to be the year that we have a chance to study fires bigger and more varied than any in recent times, real *wild*fires, beyond our limited control. These are fires of historic size, giving us the opportunity to observe their effect on the ecosystems: to watch the mosaic of unburned, partially burned, and wholly burned vegetation respond after the fires pass; to see how animal and insect distribution patterns change; to monitor streamflow and sedimentation. But in those reared on Smokey the Bear, especially those living downwind in the towns and smoke-filled basins, the smoke plucks chords of fear and anger. We fear that the fires will flare up into a giant firestorm and blaze through the mountains to torch our towns. We fear that our beloved Yellowstone will never be the same, the scenery that grips our hearts and rings our cash registers will be left a scorched wasteland. Editorial pages of local papers, local radio talk shows, conversations in cafes and bars ring with anger—righteous anger that park and forest managers are allowing fires to "destroy" Yellowstone Park and the surrounding wilderness.

Although natural fires have been allowed to burn (with close monitoring) in Yellowstone National Park and the surrounding wilderness areas for over a decade, previous fires have not inspired such a flood of controversy. Because never before have the fires been truly wildfires, too big to be controlled by fire fighting technology. How did Yellowstone's most controversial summer begin? Lightning from the usual thunderstorms ignited fires in May and June, before the summer rains. These were allowed to burn on the assumption that the normal summer rains would slow them down and eventually put them out. Over half of the lightning-caused fires burned themselves out before mid-June, behaving as managers predicted. But after an unusually wet spring came a historic drought, the driest summer in 112 years of weather records. First the late June and early July afternoon thunderstorms—a fixture of Yellowstone Plateau summers—did not materialize. By mid-July, when fire suppression began, a never-before-experienced combination of weather factors had seared forests and grasslands like a giant oven, reducing moisture levels of small fuels (grasses, forbs, and small branches) to below that of kiln-dried lumber. The Yellowstone area was literally tinder-dry. And still the rains held off. In late July came the last straw: a series of dry fronts, pushed by high winds, blasted across the area from the southwest, week after week, pushing fires ahead of them. The surviving lightning-caused fires, plus one human-caused fire, began to merge, growing into firestorms—generating their own weather, charting their own course, unaffected by every fire fighting technology thrown at them. As of this morning, fires in the park area have touched somewhere around 200,000 acres. Hence the fog of smoke drifting downwind to cast its ashy pall night after night over ridge and valley, basin and town.

I drove into Yellowstone at the quiet northeast entrance. The lodgepole forests were green and peaceful, Soda Creek ran clear and cold, shimmering over the rounded cobbles that line its bed. Baronette and Abiathar peaks sat like dark sphinxes atop the ridges of umber-colored volcanic layers. Hazy smoke blurred the air. The nightly television news stories and daily newspaper headlines led me to expect perhaps a wall of towering orange flames, singed wildlife squealing as it fled the ravaging fires, and the acrid odor of burning flesh and feathers. I met only the quiet rushing of the stream and the rustling of the breeze, smelled the pungent odor of sun-warmed pine sap and the ever-present smoke.

I drove down Soda Creek and into the wide sagebrush-filled valley of the Lamar River, idly watching the dark humps of bison grazing in the meadows I passed. I crossed the Yellowstone River on a high steel arch and drove up across the northern edge of the volcanic plateaus, through patches of Douglas fir forest in the rolling sagebrush grasslands. Bluebirds and Steller's jays flew across the road, Barrow's goldeneyes swam in a small pond. A small herd of elk grazing near the narrow highway jammed traffic. The sun went behind a towering cloud of grey smoke, casting eerie orange twilight over the landscape. But still no devastation.

We have come so far as a species, but understand so little of natural processes. Fires in these forests and rangelands are recyclers, taking the nutrients stored in dead and downed branches, twigs, and grasses and returning them to the soil in a form that plants can use. Low- and moderate-intensity fires act as fertilizers in arid ecosystems where decomposition is extremely slow—fire gets the job done quickly, nourishing the soil for new life. Without periodic fire, the ecosystems lose vigor, unable to use nutrients locked up in dead plant tissue. And without periodic fire, the forest/grassland mosaic closes in, evolving into dense forest with fewer niches. Suppressing fires has thrown a spanner in the works of these systems, ensuring that the inevitable rebalancing will involve wide oscillations, and perhaps the loss of some species. A few species—spotted owls, for one—appear to survive only in large expanses of mature timber. The habitat of these species has been decimated by overharvesting—logging mature forests faster than they can replace themselves. Although fires of this summer's magnitude will create new habitat for these species by starting large areas of new even-aged stands, a hundred years or more will pass before the stands mature into good spotted owl habitat. Hence, because of previous short-sighted forest management practices and one extraordinarily dry year, the spotted owls' balance is precarious.

Late in the afternoon, I drove south towards the fires around Old Faithful and in the southern part of the park, watching an increasingly spectacular sky. A brown smudge of smoke rose over the Gallatins from the Fern fire in the northwest corner of the park. Ahead, a pearly column of smoke billowed from the advancing front of the North Fork fire west of Old Faithful. Farther south and west, the Lewis fire spewed a rolling grey fog. Under the smoke, sunset began early, in late afternoon. The sky stained dramatic orange as the light slanted through the billowing smoke. I drove through miles of green forest, past golden-brown meadows, and vari-colored geyser basins. Elk grazed in the meadows near Norris geyser basin, undisturbed by rolling billows of smoke in a fiery sky.

Late that evening, the sun set as I coasted down the long hill into Jackson Hole. Here, the air was crystal clear. The Tetons rose like a writhing dragon from the flat valley floor, their bare heights etched by magnificent purple shadows.

Saturday, 13 *August* ✍ Yesterday began melancholy, the dawn weighed down by the lid of thick grey rain clouds that compressed the world to just the level surface of Jackson Hole. A Scotch mist: grey, chill, wet, not-quite-fog, filled the air. Bad weather for forest fires. I woke early and dressed quietly in the predawn dimness, crept upstairs and stepped outside into the exhilarating chill. I stood still for a moment, overwhelmed by the smell of wet sage, then climbed the hill to a log cabin half-hidden in the aspen grove at the foot of the ridge. There I sat, on the edge of the porch with its view out over Jackson Hole, desperately homesick. I huddled chin-to-knees against the cold, watching the clouds scud by in the pale morning light, and cried. Salty tears mixed with sweet rain. Aspen leaves whispered softly, given voice by the falling rain; the wet air sang with a heady mixture of sage, drying grasses, and elk dung. Streets and houses cluttered the imme-diate view, ending abruptly in the golden grasslands and sil-very sagelands that flow over the level surface of Jackson Hole like a tapestry, bending up at the edges to merge with the low grey ceiling of clouds. The spiny heights of the Tetons and the other dragons that guard the sky around Jackson Hole were hidden in thick cloud pudding.

By midmorning, big blue sucker holes rent the cloud blan-ket, enticing my host and me out on a field trip up the Gros Ventre River into the mountains bounding the east side of Jackson Hole. My host is a geologist by profession, and the Jackson Hole country is the home of his heart. He knows this landscape as a lover would—knows its history, its secret places, where the hot springs rise steaming in the cool morn-ing sun, where the antelope and elk come to lick salt and other minerals from its slopes, knows its quirks and its charms. It is a big landscape, not subtle, formed by massive earth movements—whole mountain ranges folded, thrust over each other like mating tortoises, faulted, and let loose to slide away; then were sculpted by water and wind and ice into dramatic forms. Even the colors of the rocks are beyond the common: vermillion, red, mauve, pale cream, golden tan, faded moss green; striped and marbled, brilliant and subtle. A landscape equally generous with visions and dreams, loneli-ness and nightmares.

We ate lunch atop a ridge with a view over all northwest Wyoming: from waves of pinnacled Absaroka ridges punching the sky in the northeast, to the long swell of the Wind River

Range forming the southeast horizon; from the nearby peaks of the Gros Ventre Range riding rounded shale hills like ships on swells, to the distant dark forested plateaus of Yellowstone. And, directly west, the improbable rise of bare rock that is the Tetons. Everywhere we turned, my host had a story to tell. His words revealed the secrets of the landscape with the wave of a magician's wand. But I could not record his stories, or even take notes, my hands remained still, my brain, like Gulliver in Lilliput, meshed in a silvery web of emotion.

By the time we retraced our winding route back to the Hole, I was exhausted. The sapphire sky was congested with huge cumulonimbus clouds, their grey bottoms snagging on the peaks of the Tetons and smearing the view with falling rain. I ended the day back at my vantage point on the porch of the little cabin, Jackson Hole lined with bands of white foggy clouds along the steep lower slopes, chill rain dripping from the grey sky. A ray of watery yellow sun slanted for a moment across the Hole, then dusk slowly gathered in the day, throwing a cloak of ever-darker grey over the wet landscape. Rain splattered my face with the smell of sagebrush as I walked slowly down the hill.

Today I sit in the warm sun on a smooth-as-satin weathered lodgepole pine trunk washed up as winter flotsam on the shore of Yellowstone Lake. The lake stretches for miles, filling a collapsed volcanic dome like a piece of fallen sky, at this moment deep blue and ruffled like wrinkled velvet. The air, scrubbed clean by yesterday's rain, reveals a landscape etched with memories. Here I grew into an adult, pursued my field ecology career, lived the years of my first marriage. It is home to me still. Each valley, each undulating or craggy ridgeline, each meadow, each bit of pattern in the dark forest cover is familiar. I know not only their names, I have touched their secrets, studying their recesses on foot, horseback, by Jeep, from the air.

How could I ever have been so naive as to think that this trip home would make leaving the landscape of the Rockies easier? Surrounded by the landscapes of home, I am gripped by a nearly suffocating urge to simply plant my feet and stay. I ache at the thought of leaving again, knowing that the going will rip a part of me out, the me that is rooted in these huge, arid, boundless landscapes. I hug my arms around myself, anticipating the parting, trying to hold myself intact. It is futile. I must go; I want so badly to stay.

Hail mixed with rain splatters the keyboard of my laptop computer, falling from a small cumulus cloud overhead. Sand flies bite my ankles. The air is sticky, unpleasantly hot. Cobwebby masses of willowherb seeds trail by on the breeze. Long swells wash rhythmically up on the shore—splash, splash, splash.

Once I get up from this log and walk back to my car, I begin the leaving. The road away runs east along the lake shore across Pelican Valley, then up through the forests, past the sulphur yellow and ashy white earth of steaming hot springs, winding up and up to the gap in the Absaroka ridge that is Sylvan Pass, then down and down and down the twisting North Fork of the Shoshone River, finally emerging in the Big Horn Basin at Cody. From there by plane to Denver, bus to Boulder, and thence, gathering my family and possessions around me, by rented truck to the cornfields of central Iowa. Once I leave this log, there is no looking back.

Wednesday, 17 *August* ❧ The irrigation ditch wasn't flowing today. This hot, dry weather has shrunk the creek so low that it fails to fill our ditch. Without flowing water, the alley is no longer a cool, shady refuge, bubbling with melodious, life-giving water. It is just another dusty alley, silent but for the ghosts of breezes rustling drying leaves. Even the finches and robins have deserted it. The life has gone out of that piece of my walk.

Friday, 19 August ⚹ This evening we climbed Mount Sanitas for a picnic, to share one of our favorite walks with our visiting friend Blanche. Touring town with her, I have seen Boulder's magnificent landscape anew through her eyes, a poignant experience now that we are leaving in two weeks.

After loading sandwiches, fruit, and rhubarb wine into Richard's knapsack, the three of us walked slowly up the hill on Maxwell Street in the warm, languid evening air. The sun slid far west towards the ridges, pouring beams of golden light through the canopy of silver maple leaves. Long shadows stretched across the ground. We talked as we walked, pointing out our favorite Victorian houses and gardens, discussing architecture and garden design and life. All was unusually quiet. No cars passed, no children ran shouting through yards, no doors slammed. Time seemed stilled in the slanting golden light and warm air.

Past the end of Maxwell Street, we turned uphill on Sunshine Canyon Road, passed under the big cottonwoods that edge the tiny stream, then left the road for the sunny grassland of Sanitas Valley and hiked up the steep trail that climbs the end of Mount Sanitas.

The grasslands that seemed so green and lush on Mother's Day were a ragged carpet, crackling dry, tinted ephemeral gold by the evening sunlight. Clumps of amber little bluestem towered over the bleached leaves of needle-and-thread grass, junegrass, and blue grama. Even the late summer wildflowers were dried and stiff. Delicate brown heads of coneflower, completely bald without their ragged fringe of petals, stuck up tall. Tiny stickseed pods clung with hooked, burr-like claws to our socks when we brushed them in passing. Bug-eyed grasshoppers jumped like rattling noisemakers from the dry stalks. Uphill below the end of the ridge, a few faded purple asters still bloomed in the shade of a twisted Douglas fir.

We clambered up the steep trail around the cliffs, then followed the humpy ridge top until it rose high enough to

242

provide a panoramic view. Eastward, the level plains flowed out to the curving rim of the earth; westward, waves of forested ridges rose higher and higher to the bare, gap-toothed skyline. We mounted a tabletop-like rock on the ridge crest, spread out our picnic, and poured our wine in time to toast the fading day.

Cool breezes flowed over the ridgetop from the mountains above, warm late sunlight streamed over us. The rim of the earth edged upwards slowly to snag the sun, finally drawing itself over the brilliant golden disk a centimeter at a time. For a moment earth and sun were one, caught on the horizon, then the sun disappeared, loosing twilight and earth simultaneously. We ate our dinner as the shadow of the Front Range crept out in a rippling slate blue tide across the plains. The cloudless western sky slowly faded from gold to aquamarine to pale blue-violet. Each peak stood out black as velvet against that translucent backdrop. Lights flickered on, first below us in town, then eastward, following the wave of darkness as it washed over the plains. We walked down the trail in the last pale twilight, descending into the darkness of orange streetlights.

Tuesday, 23 August ☙ It is hot today, the air still and prickly humid. The sky, tarnished by haze from distant forest fires, is cloudless. So different from the crisply clear, sparkling cerulean blue sky after a thunderstorm.

The year is cycling back around again. The sun has moved about two of my fists south of where it rose at the summer solstice, closer to the wall of the neighboring condominiums. Soon the morning light will not shine in our east bedroom window, and the shadow of the foothills will creep over town earlier each evening. The catalpa pods are beginning to shrivel and split open, the wild grapes dangling from the vine across the ditch are like dusky purple marbles, the clusters of chokecherries, long since ripe, have been eaten. The irrigation ditch runs intermittently—some days the alley is a chuckling water garden, some days just a dusty tangle. Fringes of red algae line the banks of Boulder Creek where the water is low below the diversion dam at Broadway. The cottonwood leaves are edged with gold.

Up Ninth Street, a foundation hole gouged in a sloping backyard exposes the top ten feet of the skeleton of Mapleton Hill. Where a weathered white clapboard garage once stood and a sweet tangle of old lilac bushes bloomed, now is a generous window into the earth, cut by toothed jaws.

At the bottom of the hole, ochre layers of interbedded shale and sandstone extend down out of sight, dipping steeply down to the east, bent out of horizontal by the rise of the Rockies. Upwards, the angled ochre layers are truncated by a horizontal layer of rounded cobbles and gravel. The contact between the two layers is an undulating line suggesting an old erosion surface, including the concave bit of old stream channel. A whitish layer of caliche (salts left when groundwater evaporates) dribbles like thin toothpaste from the zone of contact. Here is a discontinuity—the cobbley layer is more or less parallel to the current surface, but the bedrock tilts at about forty-five degrees.

The shale and sandstone bedrock, deposited in a shallow sea that lapped an ancient shore, was originally level, parallel to the earth's surface. Millions of years after the layers were deposited, crustal compression slowly heaved the Rockies up under this thick blanket of horizontal sediments. The sediments bulged, buckled, and broke at the edge of the uplift, eroding backwards to the level of the plains. Eastward, the intact portion of the sediment blanket tilts gently downward under the Great Plains.

The layer of cobbles and gravel, level above, undulating below, is an old stream deposit, debris eroded from the rising mountains and rounded as the stream tumbled it down. The

244

stream decelerated sharply when it reached this gently sloping surface, and dropped much of its load. Its channels migrated across the surface of the terrace, rerouting its course as debris accumulated, until a combination of uplift and changing climate caused the stream to desert Mapleton Hill.

Above the cobbly layer is a thin smear of chestnut-colored soil, an uneven crayon line punctuating the contact between stream deposits and nearly three feet of modern soil. Upwards of the chestnut smear is pale yellow-ochre subsoil streaked with shiny, ribbon-like trails where the teeth of the dozer blade compacted the clay particles. The profile is palest at the bottom, grading progressively darker to rich sienna-color in a thin layer at the surface. It is this top dark layer, a mere six inches deep, that is the fertile skin of this arid country soil, home to the host of micro- and macroorganisms that turn death into life. Here in this fragile skin, the cycle turns.

Friday, 26 *August* ❧ Yesterday the winds aloft blew out of the northwest, and the air filled with hazy amber smoke. The sun rose like a floodlight; dawn blazed orange. In the late evening, when the moon rose over the rim of the planet, it emerged slowly, huge and dull bronze and nearly round. We stopped to watch it rise, silenced, as if we'd never seen the moon before.

Monday, 29 *August* ❧ Tomorrow we leave. The clacking of my keyboard echoes in the living room, bare but for this computer, balanced precariously atop its own packing box. The big yellow truck, packed tight with our furniture and belongings, shows out the window where we first saw the raccoons marching up the stairs.

This morning we walked around town for the last time, touching our favorite places. Memories streamed up like bubbles rising to the surface of a fertile pond. We walked first uphill on Maxwell past small Victorian houses—stopping to peer through the open gate of the one whose austere board fence hides a lush sunken garden—to Sixth Street, where we turned north across Mapleton Hill. We ran our hands over ripples etched by ancient winds in the salmon-colored sandstone pavers. The stones' edges are blackened with lichen, their flat surfaces tilted at odd angles by bulging silver maple roots. One chill, early spring morning, Richard and I walked this way, holding hands. Silver maple leaf buds were still clenched tight, the shaggy grey branches bare; clumps of violet flowers dotted pale spring green lawns; mating starlings screeched and whistled overhead. A pair of magpies chased each other, courting, through the dark spruces by the stone house at the corner of Sixth and Highland. The sky glimmered like polished turquoise, and the red slabs of the Flatirons leaned close.

This morning's air was already hot, except in the shade of the leafy canopy thrown by arching silver maple limbs. The starlings were silent, the magpies nowhere to be seen. The violet flowers were long gone, their tightly nested, heart-shaped leaves dark patches in pale, dusty lawns.

We sat on the bench in the pocket park at the edge of Mapleton Hill, watching the shifting breeze dart here and there, listening to the soft sounds of the shallow ribbon of water sliding down the irrigation ditch. A fine veil of forest fire smoke filtered the sunlight, casting orange highlights like sodium vapor streetlights. Muffled traffic noises sounded from Canyon Boulevard, close below, a world away. Down the hill a tall cottonwood full of rustling summer leaves screened both noise and view. Here, we discovered one evening last September that if we sat on this bench, we could dabble our feet in the invisible stream of cool air flowing down the valley. That evening the cottonwood was nearly bare, the few dry leaves still clinging to its branches rattled like a ghostly snake. The spare bones of Flagstaff Mountain showed through the tree branches, the sumac leaves along the irrigation ditch bank glowed crimson in the dusk. Pale golden light lingered in the western sky, silhouetting the dark jagged line of the ridges above.

This morning, we stirred ourselves and walked down the steps toward Canyon Avenue and the Boulder Creek green-belt, joining the creek path at the west end of the kids' fishing pond. Late this winter, Richard and I walked this way on a warm afternoon that promised spring. The shallow pond was still frozen over with opaque, milky spring ice, the surface snow-cone slushy. The branches of the cottonwoods were bare against the intensely blue sky. The creek ran high and noisy between banks frosted with soft layers of grey ice.

This morning the pond was shallow and pea-soup green, the water fogged with a fine veil of algae. The cottonwood and elm leaves hung limp in the hot sun, brittle and dry. The creek ran low, a quiet murmur just discernible over the noise of passing traffic.

Downstream under the library bridge, a puddle of cool shade lay under the cement span. We stopped and sat on the bench, listening to the water. Early this summer, I happened on a blizzard here, the air white with cottonwood seeds. Each silky pod of down floated its seed slowly earthward in the hazy sunlight, drifting over the library lawns in clumps of downy fluff.

At the footbridge east of the library, we turned aside to cross the creek. The clear water slid past quietly over a sal-mon-colored sand bed. The green tunnel of riparian shrubs and trees was a tattered and worn awning, faded by the sum-mer sun and wind. No trout swam in view, and the creek mur-mured softly of late summer heat, shrunken snowbanks, high mountain meadows drying golden-brown. A wisp of down-stream breeze brought the pungent odor of warm pine sap.

We walked up University Hill and through the maze of red-tiled roofs and sandstone-faced buildings of the campus in the now-hot and sultry air. We stood at the edge of the hill, looking north across Boulder, along the hazy waves of the foothills. Then we turned zig, zag, down the path into the cool, quiet shade of the greenbelt again. We crossed the creek and continued upstream in the shade to downtown and the Pearl Street Mall.

From there we walked slowly, savoring the final repetition of our daily walk—towards the mountains on the Mall, up the alley that cuts between Pine and Spruce streets, along the irrigation ditch, and over the crest of the hill. Always slow, I trailed even farther behind Richard and Molly. At the top of the hill I stopped and turned a slow full circle, looking intently east over the sea of plains, south across the valley along the face of Boulder Mountain, west up Mapleton Street at the ridge of Mount Sanitas, north along the range, then overhead at the hazy blue sky. I squeezed my eyes tight shut, the panorama reversed, light on dark, on my eyelids. I opened my eyes and swiveled slowly once more. The foothills rose unchanged in a great hazy wave above town. The sun still hung in place in the pale sky. The atomic clock ticked another tick. I walked slowly on over the hill to where Richard and Molly waited next to the big yellow truck.

Time to go.

❧

This book was designed by Clifford Burke, and
typeset from a Macintosh computer. The text is
Weiss, the decorative embellishments Zapf Dingbats;
the display type Weiss Italic. Linotronic output by
Image Systems, Boulder, Colorado.

❧